10/25 $2

Think Proactive:
new insights into decision-making

Often, the decisions we face in our business and personal lives have threats and opportunities which are not self-evident. The need for sharing genuine experience and applying decision methods with prudence has never been so crucial. Unfortunately, a large body of literature about decision-making has been derived from the perception of management as a neat linear process starting from planning and organizing and proceeding to implementation and control. While partly accurate, this conventional wisdom is too simplistic for use in analyzing contemporary problems and issues. Think Proactive constitutes a substantial departure from these orthodox methods which have too frequently led us to fragile and short-lived right or wrong decisions.

This book contains numerous real-life examples and practical methods to improve the quality of decision-making in a dynamic world. It is written for managers, executive secretaries, advisory personnel, entrepreneurs and individuals who merely wish to gain new insights into decision-making. In it, the author reports on the issues facing North American and European decision-makers with whom he works frequently. It is also a byproduct of his ten years' experience as Chief Executive Officer of the Professional Development Institute, a small Canadian organization with a worldwide reputation.

Think Proactive offers new insights into management. It helps to set and validate objectives and priorities, plan strategically, gather intelligence data, assess threats and opportunities and manage risk, conflict, perceptions and values. Without being categorical, the writer introduces the concept of authentic leadership and suggests some characteristics of effective leaders regardless of the organization setting—large or small, private or public. Power, authority, rewards and penalties are treated as means to get the work done with due regard to integrity and human dignity.

Think Proactive thoroughly discusses useful instruments to manage personal time, detect early warning signals of work slippage and assign responsibility and accountability clearly. It emphasizes the need for coaching aspiring counterparts and making allies and even opponents act as useful resources. It suggests schemes to build and structure teams and organizations, avoid the trap of unfinished business and evaluate individual and group performance.

The book is structured to serve as a lasting reference long after it has been read. The comprehensive figures and graphs demonstrate the intricate and potent relationships between the concepts, functions and ideas of Proactive Decision-Making. Actual case histories and examples were selected to support the concepts and make the content lively and even entertaining. The writing style shifts deliberately from the abstract to the familiar. A special effort has been made to confine the vocabulary to the day-to-day language repertoire, except where the quality of the message would suffer.

Think Proactive

New insights
into decision-making

A.P. Martin

Canadian Cataloguing in Publication Data

Martin, A.P. (Alain Paul), 1945-
  Think proactive

Includes index.
ISBN 0-86502-000-0

1. Decision-making. 2. Planning. 3. Management.
I. Professional Development Institute. II. Title.

HD30.23.M37   658.4'03   C83-090016-0

U.S. Library of Congress
Catalogue No.: 83-670054

All rights reserved world-wide under International and Pan-American copyright agreements. No part of this document can be reproduced, stored in a retrieval system, or transmitted in any form or by any means, electronic, mechanical, photocopying, recording or otherwise without the prior written permission of the author.

Copying or photocopying is a violation of the copyright law. Orders for this book are filled promptly by:

The Professional Development Institute
P.O. Box 1181, Station B, Ottawa, Canada K1P 5R2.
Phone: (613) 523-3333, Telex: 053-3159

© Copyright, A.P. Martin, 1983   ISBN 0 86502 000 0   Printed in Canada

To Hélène and Cécile

Acknowledgement

I am grateful to friends and clients who have in many ways helped to make this book possible. In particular, I wish to thank James L. Hayes, President, the American Management Association; Patrick Rich, President of Aluminium Company of Canada; Tom Gentles, Saskatchewan's Deputy Minister of Transport; Olivier Giscard D'Estaing, Chairperson of INSEAD, Paris; Dr. Herbert Shepard, Chairperson of the Gestalt Institute of Cleveland and Honorary President of The Professional Development Institute; Dr. Ralph Katz, Professor at the Sloan School of Management (M.I.T.); Dr. Eleanor Schwartz, Dean of the Graduate Business School University of Missouri; William O'Keefe, Vice-President of the American Petroleum Institute; Robert Long, Director of Advanced Studies at the U.S. Bank Administration Institute; Elizabeth Zechel, Program Administrator at the Federal Treasury Board; Dr. J.E. McGowan, Assistant Deputy Minister, Canada Department of Agriculture; Dr. Hans Wirdenius, professor at the Royal Institute of Technology in Stockholm and research associate at the Swedish Personnel Administration Council; Dr. Robert J. Jackson, Chairperson of the Department of Political Science at Carleton University and last but not least my research assistant Joanne Mitchell and the dedicated PDI staff: Louise Brooks, Dawn Francis, Alice Laframboise, Suzanne Laplante, Jacob Moerman, Marie-Pascale Parmentier and Robert Valin.

I have been influenced by scholars and executives, many of whom are cited in the chapters that follow. I am particularly indebted to the pioneering work of Richard Beckhard (M.I.T.), Peter Drucker, Bertrand de Jouvenel (Paris), Herman Kahn (the Hudson Institute), Dr. Herbert Shepard and the late Marcia Guttentag of Harvard. I would also like to acknowledge my indebtedness to the exceptional people I encountered at seminars from whom I learned a great deal.

A.P. Martin
Ottawa, Ontario
Canada

Table of Contents

Part One 15

The foundations of Proactive Decision-Making

Chapter 1

The practice of Proactive Decision-Making

1.1	The management of contemporary issues	17
1.2	The evolution of Proactive Decision-Making	19
1.3	Present definition of Proactive Decision-Making	19
1.4	Prerequisites	20
1.5	Proactive Management philosophy	21
1.6	Who needs it?	23
1.7	Conclusion	25

Chapter 2

The proactive options

2.1	Introduction	29
2.2	The inactive stance	29
2.3	The compliance stance	30
2.4	The active stance	31
2.5	The proactive option	31
2.6	The non-option	34
2.7	Differentiation is in!	35
2.8	Conclusion	36

Part Two 39

Proactive Decision-Making The on-going functions

Chapter 3

Authentic leadership

3.1	The on-going functions of Proactive Decision-Making	41
3.2	Definition and characteristics of authentic leadership	42
3.3	Interpersonal skills	42
3.4	Management skills	43
3.5	Attitudes	44
3.6	Desirable attitudes	45
3.7	Conclusion	45

Chapter 4
Synergy, team-building and coaching

4.1	Synergy	49
4.2	Example	50
4.3	Team-building	50
4.4	Characteristics of high performing teams	51
4.5	Conditions requiring teamwork	52
4.6	When is it unnecessary or detrimental?	52
4.7	Coaching	54
4.8	Conclusion	55

Chapter 5
Power

5.1	Definition and characteristics	57
5.2	Forms of power	58
5.3	Business illustration	61
5.4	Two government illustrations	63
5.5	Sources of power	65
5.6	Conclusion	67

Chapter 6
Authority and rewards (And other means of influence and control)

6.1	Means of influence and control	69
6.2	Rewards	70
6.3	Authority	70
6.4	How much authority is necessary?	71
6.5	Conclusion	75

Chapter 7
Conflict management

7.1	Essence of conflict	79
7.2	Productive conflict	79
7.3	When is conflict personal?	80
7.4	Need for accurate diagnosis	80
7.5	How to diagnose conflict	81
7.6	Conflict management	85

Chapter 8
Perception and value management

8.1	The need for perception management	95
8.2	Perception management is in!	95
8.3	Walt Disney production	96
8.4	Misperception of technical excellence	96
8.5	The case of a North American airline company	97
8.6	The bank story	99
8.7	Management of values	100
8.8	Conclusion	101

Chapter 9
Time management

9.1	Introduction	103
9.2	Daily time management	103
9.3	Meeting management	104
9.4	Issue management meetings	104
9.5	Importance of slack time	109
9.6	Conclusion	109
	Appendix: The Proactive Passport	111

Chapter 10
The scanning function

10.1	Definition	117
10.2	Some applications	117
10.3	Scanning resources and organization	119
10.4	Sources of scanning information	120
10.5	Scanning tips	127
10.6	The scanning process	127
10.7	Screening techniques	128
10.8	Conclusion	130

Part Three 133

Proactive Decision-Making
Sequential iterative functions

Chapter 11
Sequential iterative functions

11.1	Introduction	135
11.2	How much time should it take?	136
11.3	Who should participate?	136
11.4	Some caveats	137

Chapter 12
The preplanning phase

12.1	Introduction	141
12.2	Mission-setting or review	141
12.3	Mission-setting process	145
12.4	Interface planning	146
12.5	Objective-setting and validation	154
12.6	Differentiation and integration step	157
12.7	Outcomes of the preplanning phase	157
12.8	Illustration: CWG Inc.	159
12.9	Conclusion	162

Chapter 13
Strategic planning phase
Work definition instruments

13.1	Strategic planning instruments	165
13.2	The charter	167
13.3	The critical success factors	167
13.4	Assumptions	171
13.5	Assumptions management	172
13.6	Summary	172
13.7	Risk analysis	174
13.8	Value analysis of the plan	175
13.9	Evalution scheme	176
13.10	Interdependence grids	176
13.11	Prework strategy	177

Chapter 14
Strategic planning phase
Organization design instruments

14.1	Responsibility chart	185
14.2	Role differentiation	189
14.3	Role integration	193
14.4	Emerging applications of responsibility charting	194
14.5	Authority structure	195
14.6	Abortion, succession and termination planning	199
14.7	Conclusion	202

Chapter 15
Operational planning

15.1	Scheduling	205
15.2	Resource allocation and budgeting	205
15.3	Management Information System (MIS)	206
15.4	Conclusion	206

Chapter 16
Implementation

16.1	Implementation case	209
16.2	Summary	212

Chapter 17
Impact and process evaluation

17.1	Evaluation wisdom	215
17.2	Strategic and behavioral issues in evaluation	216
17.3	Evaluation timing	217
17.4	Data validity	217
17.5	Summative evaluation	217
17.6	Process evaluation	218
17.7	Metaevaluation	219

Chapter 18
Concluding remarks   221

Index   223

List of Figures

Chapter	Figure	Title	
3	3.1	Proactive Management functions	38
3	3.2	Proactive Decision-Making model	40
5	5.1	Management of change—"Dopers" formula	64
6	6.1	How effective is authority as a means of influence and control?	72
6	6.2	Authority and dependence—an overview	73
6	6.3	Management styles and preferences	76
7	7.1	Observation grid—conflict diagnosis	82
7	7.2	Diagnosis of conflict boundaries—the population parameter	86
7	7.3	Sources of conflict	87
7	7.4	Conflict diagnosis grid	88
7	7.5	Potential interventions in conflict management	90
7	7.6	The process of conflict diagnosis and intervention	92
9	9.1	The Proactive Passport: two year objective section	105
9	9.2	The Proactive Passport: monthly objective section	106
9	9.3	The Proactive Passport: weekly planning section	107
10	10.1	First example of Daily News Bulletin	122
10	10.2	Second example of Daily News Bulletin	123
10	10.3	The most important job characteristics	126
10	10.4	First draft future wheel on standard videodiscs	129
11	11.1	Proactive Decision-Making model	134
11	11.2	Detailed Proactive Decision-Making chart	138
12	12.1	Hypothetical statements of working missions and published missions	143
12	12.2	Hypothetical demand system for Activair airline	148
12	12.3	Hypothetical interface plan for a single demand	149
12	12.4	Priority assignment	155
12	12.5	Hidden versus stated objectives	156
13	13.1	The program charter	166
13	13.2	Critical success factors—business case	168
13	13.3	Critical success factors—government case	169
13	13.4	The process of assumption management	173
13	13.5	Cross relevance grid	178
13	13.6	Cross-supporting grid	179
13	13.7	Strategic model for management of change	183
14	14.1	Responsibility chart	186
14	14.2	Basic responsibility chart for building a garage	187
14	14.3	Responsibility chart: U.S. President's trip	188
14	14.4	Organization structures	196
14	14.5	How task complexity affects subordinate/boss ratio	200
14	14.6	Trans Alaska pipeline—organizational changes	201
16	16.1	Expected time and resistance to institutional or technological change for different levels of intervention	212
16	16.2	Alternative interventions for change and related time/report	213

Part One

The foundations of Proactive Decision-Making*

Part one consists of two chapters outlining the issues and the background which led to the establishment of the framework which expands the number of options available to decision-makers. The philosophy of Proactive Management and its potential users are also briefly discussed.

---

*For the purpose of this book, Proactive Decision-Making is assumed synonymous to Proactive Management.

Chapter one

The practice of Proactive Decision-Making

1.1 The management of contemporary issues

The main theme of this book is that Proactive Management can provide a framework for diagnosing current problems and issues and improving both strategic planning and management of change beyond the myopia of immediate financial returns. In this context, an *issue* is defined as a potential opportunity, a demand, a misperception, an emerging threat, a plausible constraint or an obstacle to achieving an end.

Issue management is the process of building up an awareness of corporate strengths and weaknesses and matching them with the relevant environment's opportunities and threats. Whenever feasible, it attempts to convert threats into opportunities. It provides strategies to shelter the organization against residual threats. It starts by assuming that organizations do not have fundamental weaknesses—that is, a weakness is only a strength deployed in the wrong direction!

Decision-makers are now facing a host of interdependent and often conflicting issues, all of which are characterized by a high degree of uncertainty. This state of affairs is gradually becoming a way of life in organization management. In the future, it will have an increasingly profound effect on the conduct of business and on our daily lives.

Issues include surprise events (Tylenol, DC10, Three Mile Island, Iran), recessions, political instability, supply uncertainties, stringent regulations, advocacy, rampant crime, organized external hostility and regionalism combined with unprecedented high costs of labor, a sharp rise in the price of energy and scarcity of money and critical resources. In an effort to deal with these issues, political intervention armed with insufficient know-how and short run imperatives led to abrupt changes and further difficulties. "The monetary system deteriorated. The patterns of exchange rates shifted widely. The return on capital declined. Structural unemployment emerged in new forms not explained by cyclical phenomena. Inflation remained high in the absence of full utilization of productive capacity. Value-added between the primary factors of production (labor and capital) suffered major distortions."[1]

The combined effects of these forces make it nearly impossible to "manage by objectives" and maintain a reasonable performance, not only because risks and uncertainty are hidden but also because the situation is dynamic and will continue to change at an alarming rate.

The actual losses which occur in organizations due to non-productive management of these issues are enormous. For business corporations and government agencies already suffering severe setbacks, there is no relief in sight from the productivity and issue management challenge. Far from it, individual and organization problems seem to get worse. Nowhere is the situation more visible than in the automotive, energy-dependent sectors and public institutions, where we must quickly learn and initiate new ways to "do more with less" as a means of survival.

Notwithstanding these difficulties, personal disagreements among planners and policy makers emerge over the importance and urgency of objectives, often resulting in open interpersonal warfare, underground subversive networks and enormous drains on resources and managerial time. Apart from different perceptions and values, for all but a few decision-makers, the stakes are too high to achieve a dispassionate interest in tight budget reviews, personnel cutbacks, reorganizations, acquisitions, mergers, product phase-outs and related *forces majeures*.[2]

Paradoxically, the common instruments to scan, identify and diagnose these complex problems and explore alternative solutions have been deceptive to say the least. With reactive and even active strategies, personnel discontent and hostility continue. In order to prevent these adverse transition effects, classical management techniques such as Management by Objectives (MBO), job enrichment, Zero-base Budgeting and Evaluability Assessment (EA) applied in isolation are clearly inadequate because they were conceived to fit the less dynamic world of the pre-eighties.[3] As an example, EA and other studies of government programs have often left managers "far worse off than they would have been had they never existed".[4]

In the best case, these approaches would at most help management to do the minimum to get by. In the worst case, lacking the cooperation and the combined efforts of the relevant veto powers, the process becomes a futile exercise and may result in dismal failure.

1.2 The evolution of Proactive Decision-Making

The need to understand executives' requirements under these conditions emerged in the sixties and gathered momentum during the First International Future Congress held in Oslo. A sociotechnical model was applied by the author at a General Dynamics' subsidiary to rationalize strategic planning and positively reinforce work simplification in 1968. Then, at Du Pont, components of the approach brought new insights to systems analysis, salary administration and marketing decisions.

The original aim was to design a relatively simple issue management method that was flexible enough to enable sound comparisons between alternative management strategies both at a high level of aggregation and at the working level. The model evolved rapidly from planning to reflect the state-of-the-art of *organization development* and qualitative evaluation theory. It was also tested in government milieux and other corporations throughout the seventies where additional benefits were achieved.

In addition to the earlier requirements, there was a need to differentiate sharply between issue scanning, description and analysis, on the one hand, and interpretation and evaluation, on the other, bringing the model to its present form now at the heart of Proactive Management philosophy. For the latter to remain in line with corporate and sociotechnical developments, there will undoubtedly be further changes in the future. In fact, very few practical methodologies survive without any change.

1.3 Present definition of Proactive Decision-Making

Proactive Decision-Making is a dynamic process through which organizational policy, technological and institutional change can be governed, directed and managed effectively. It helps the user to come to grips with future considerations and contingencies. It is not an extrapolation process (which is what most models are). Specifically, Proactive Decision-Making is a sociotechnical process to identify new opportunities, understand perceptions, diagnose controversial issues and manage individual, group and corporate behavior.

For all organizations, it is an on-going *personal* and *collective* effort to fully articulate and refine the core mission and actively influence its environment to sustain a continuous optimum sociotechnical success and sound economic performance.

With respect to profit-making companies, Proactive Decision-Making reflects a concern for more than a single bottom line. As E. J. McCormack of Rockefeller Associates and Board Member of General

Foods said, "If the corporation is to prosper, it should recognize its responsibility for the well-being of the society of which it is a part." In other words, economic viability is a necessary but not a sufficient prerequisite. Earned legitimacy (social acceptance) is also imperative for long term survival.

1.4 Prerequisites

Effective application of Proactive Decision-Making requires several prerequisites, some of which are introduced in this section.

1. It requires a constant awareness of current perceptions, emerging values and institutional norms governing society in a period of major transitions.

2. It assumes a conscious struggle to reduce uncertainty by sharply examining assumptions and explicitly probing perceptions, attitudes and feelings in order to shape environmental contingencies adequately.

3. It ought to include a strategic management of change based on innovation and positive reinforcement with a genuine use of power as an alternative to authority whenever appropriate. Here, *power* is defined as the ability to influence the system as perceived by the system, while *authority* is the exercise of the legitimate right to enforce decisions.

   The Californian l978 anti-smoking proposal can be contrasted with the Canadian Participaction program to illustrate the difference in impact. In the aftermath of Proposition 13, a group of Californian citizens attempted to petition the government to use its authority to incorporate anti-smoking rights in the Constitution, but in vain. An adversary force, the Citizen of Common Sense, managed to neutralize the anti-smokers' efforts within a few weeks.

   In Canada, the Bureau of Health Promotion has opted for *positive reinforcement* through the Participaction program which promotes good health and fitness in lieu of anti-smoking legislative action (authority) that would have had little, if any, significant impact.

4. It necessitates a readiness to reexamine the myopic overemphasis on efficiency in every aspect of corporate life and individual behavior as illustrated in the following paragraphs.

   Managers from industry and financial institutions spend time and effort to secure adequate returns on equipment, loans and technical capital. Paradoxically, far less energy is spent on individual growth, professional development and coaching which are critical factors for the return on investment in human capital. Moreover, the reward system is also skewed toward the former.

   This dilemma can be illustrated by the short tenure of MBA

graduates with their first employer and the indifference with which large organizations accept staff resignations. Yet, the cost of attracting and recruiting replacements of MBA graduates is overwhelming in many of these firms. A proactive organization, American Express, went a long way to correct the discrepancy with its fast-track executive development program and a system for multiple career options.[5]

A more recent example came from RCA's board of directors which fired 59 year old chairman Edgar Griffiths "despite his devotion to the bottom line...Under Griffiths RCA's revenues and earnings have more than tripled in five years. But his accomplishments eventually counted for little when weighed against his shortcomings as manager of people. Instead of grooming his successor, a task that any corporate head must unavoidably confront as retirement approaches, Griffiths permitted the matter to languish unresolved."[6]

Likewise, in the public sector, an investment of personal effort and public funds in the care of senior citizens at the poverty line may neither be as efficient nor as effective as job creation for youth but just as, if not more, equitable.

5. Depending upon the complexity and the magnitude of the issue at hand, several tasks may require an interactive team approach, grouping the pertinent information sources not only to facilitate informed decision-making, but also to ensure the commitment of the relevant power groups prior to implementation. The process reduces dysfunctional conflicts, promotes open confrontation where appropriate, and prevents the exercise of subsequent veto powers, a major source of delay for many projects and decisions.

External support can be sought. But even then, the active participation and the total commitment of the client are required, irrespective of the organizational setting. Management retains both the ownership of the process and the power to veto its direction throughout the duration of the exercise, regardless of the background of the professional support resources.

1.5 Proactive Management philosophy

Traditional scholars view influence as bad or unethical. They seem to forget that, "except when we are asleep, influencing goes on all the time. Employees modify the behavior of their bosses, bosses modify the behavior of subordinates, government leaders and competitors modify our behavior and vice versa."[7] In the corporate world, excessive reliance on spontaneous and open interaction is not only naive but could result in an uncalculated risk, particularly when dealing with subtle adversity. In our time, suspicion is almost sufficient to ruin careers as dramatized by the case of Bendix Chairperson Bill Agee and Vice-President Mary

Cunningham[8] summarized later in the chapter about authentic leadership. Influencing is a complex form of behavior. It requires attention, effort, skills and experience to be done well.

With respect to ethics, Proactive Management is neutral. Like most instruments of change, it can be misused. Our hope is that executives have a clear idea about their own standard of ethics and a sincere appreciation for the values of others. However, even when the practitioner's behavior and attitudes are governed by some widely shared norms regarding freedom, self-determination, democracy, equity, privacy and justice, ethical dilemmas are inevitable.

Experienced decision-makers consider naiveté itself to be unethical. They know that ethical action does not follow from good intentions alone. Existing technologies such as MBO used in isolation seldom equip them to deal with creative adversity on an equal footing. Unless ethical dilemmas are managed explicitly, suboptimization or bad compromises, concessions or losses could occur.

Proactive Decision-Making views being a constructive influence as an integral part of the manager's job, often by necessity rather than by desire. It presupposes a code of conduct where political leaders and corporate executives fully consider the inequities which their decisions (or indecisions) may inflict on others. Its philosophy helps to anticipate and deal effectively with complex demands and strategies. While not wishing to employ too many aphorisms, the following ideas can be offered to illustrate the point.

1. **Pay due attention to changing ethics and conflicting values.**
2. **Never ignore the critical mass: if you ignore it, it won't ignore you.**
   In this book, the *critical mass* is defined as the minimum number of people or groups whose commitment is necessary to unfreeze the existing resistance, facilitate the readiness for change or prevent the exercise of veto. Commitment can be active, subtle or tacit (i.e. on a non-objection basis).
3. **Start where the system is.**
   Always probe the level of dissatisfaction with the *status quo* prior to embarking on a change effort whether the change is technological, political, structural or institutional.
4. **Validate relentlessly.**
   In management and in politics, validity is double-edged: the perceived validity is as important, if not more so, than the objective validity. Validate relentlessly. Test for semantic clarity, genuine misperceptions, paradigm traps, hidden agendas, value congruence and perceptions.

5. **Locate the decision points as close as possible to the information sources.**
   With technological progress, information can be processed faster. However, it is becoming highly perishable because intelligent and powerful players are responding with even greater speed to 'beat the system'. A short decision-making cycle increases the chance of working with fresh information. That is why it is desirable to locate the decision points as close as possible to information sources.
6. **Everything must come to an end.**
   Plan as early as possible the termination and the succession to let go before the Pareto trap.[9]
7. **Abort wisely.**
   Abandon ship when necessary. Abortion scenarios should be continually validated and fully integrated with every strategic plan.
8. **Seek support and constituents.**
   Do not act alone. Learn to use the leverage of family and friends to assist, advocate, endorse, challenge and implement your plans. Attempt to turn foreigners and foes into allies (i.e. family and friends), when feasible.
9. **Expand your notion of capability.**
   Most decision-makers have self-inflicted boundaries with respect to resource allocation. Their concept of capability is limited to their own resources such as people, capital and technology. In proactive terms, these are considered conventional resources and are increasingly scarce. In real life, we usually have access to a vast reservoir of strategic resources. The latter include the resources owned by others but which can be available to achieve our aim. Strategic resources can be used overtly (everyone knows), covertly (only the owner knows) or in a *blind* manner (the resource owner acts for you without knowing it). The allocation process should consider the strategic resources owned by fools, foes, foreigners, friends and family (in that order).

1.6 Who needs it?

The effectiveness of Proactive Decision-Making has been demonstrated in situations which could not be readily solved by technical ingenuity alone. Since the seventies, proactive experiments have quietly revolutionized the decision-making climate. Based on current experience, the methodology applies to four levels of social systems: namely, the individual, the group, the organization and the community.

1.6.1 Application to individuals

At the individual level, the process can be used for life planning. In the past, it has been applied to career assessment, pre-retirement planning, situation analysis and management of personal change. More recently, MIT's Professor Ralph Katz found it helpful to study job longevity issues. Throughout the USA, some clients found their career planning horizons broadened beyond the incremental thinking scenarios provided by existing methods.

As an example, participants in the author's workshop on the subject brought up the issue of individual compensation. Appropriate rewards should be related to both knowledge and work. Many middle managers felt that there is little opportunity for rewards for what they do. For instance, many of them spend a great deal of effort to groom newcomers to the job. They perceive that the discrepancy between university graduates' expectations and reality causes traumatic frustrations and work hard to correct the problem. However, only lip service is paid to the effort, and the contribution is rarely valued adequately by employers. To this end, personal strategies were developed.

The appropriate rewards, as perceived by each participant in the current life stage, were the basis for the process. The corporate policy standards and authority constraints perceived by many turned out to be self-inflicted boundaries. The concepts of power and influence led to possibilities that had never been used nor even explored in the past. Within a few months, several participants reported some progress in managing the change of their personal compensation schemes.

1.6.2 Application to groups

At the group level, Proactive Decision-Making helps to clarify mission(s) and common objectives, and plan work and interface strategies with the surrounding environment. It is also a valuable tool to diagnose interpersonal issues. The group can be a family unit, a corporate task force, a local or an international project team.

With some caveats, intimate systems can also benefit from the process. Pilot experiments with spouses, couples and work-related dyads or triads particularly in Montreal and Vancouver have yielded encouraging results. Thus, Proactive Decision-Making would be considered to analyze the issues of dependence, reciprocity, choice, polarities, compatibility, team-building and the phenomenon of finishing or letting go.

1.6.3 Application to organizations

At the organization level, the framework applies to either an organizational unit such as a branch, a service department or to the whole corporation. With caution, the process is adaptable to planning, problem-solving and decision-making in a wide range of intra and interorganizational issues. As demonstrated by examples throughout this book, Proactive Decision-Making has made a contribution to increase the viability and improve the legitimacy of modern organizations here in North America and to a lesser extent in Western Europe.

1.6.4 Application to society

At the community level, Proactive Management can help to set objectives and explore strategic options to deal with social demands and threats. From equal opportunity issues to election platforms, health care, social services integration, urban planning, energy conservation and waste management, modest benefits can be derived from a careful application of Proactive Decision-Making.

Considering the nature of this book, the focus will be on organizational applications.

1.7 Conclusion

This chapter has introduced the issues facing corporate management and government leaders, the historic roots, the philosophy and potential users of Proactive Decision-Making.

In summary, the framework offers neither a recipe nor a magic formula which would single-handedly lead to better performance. It has been developed in response to the need to deal with human and corporate issues, proceeding from perceptions, information and values to interpretation and experiments, from options to consequences, from decisions to prework, action, termination and impact evaluation.

The next chapter will outline the choices facing decision-makers in dealing with an issue regardless of its sponsors or advocates. The second part of the book will be devoted to the on-going functions of Proactive Decision-Making. The third part, the main body of the book, provides a step by step description of the sequential iterative functions of Proactive Decision-Making. The last chapter provides provocative concluding remarks and some further caveats to avoid pseudo-application of Proactive Management.

References and notes

1. E.V. Lehnep: Facing the Future, OECD, Paris, 1979
2. W.Warner Burke: Current Issues and Strategies in Organization Development, Human Sciences Press, New York, 1977.
3. A. P. Martin: MBO Middle Age Crisis, The Professional Development Institute, Ottawa, 1979.
4. Arnold Barnett: Threats to Evaluation, notes prepared for PDI quarterly seminar on the topic. Full length stories about Dr. Barnett's applied research in this field appeared in the Wall Street Journal, the Washington Star, the Los Angeles Tribune, the Boston Globe, Le Monde, Der Spiegel and Scientific American.
5. Notes from a working session with Dr. Samuel Abramson, Vice-President, American Express, July 1980.
6. Time Magazine: February 9th, 1981, page 48.
7. Adapted from a presentation made by B. F. Skinner at the opening session of the Behavior Modification Conference held in Los Angeles in February 1980.
8. Peter W. Bernstein: Upheaval at Bendix, Fortune, November 3, 1980.
9. The Pareto trap refers to the maldistribution of effort toward results. There is a widely held belief that 80% of the effort leads to only 20% of the results, particularly during the completion phase of an undertaking.

The on-going functions

- Leadership
- Synergy
- Team building & coaching
- Power
- Authority
- Scanning
- Management of values
- Conflict management
- Perception management
- Time management

The sequential iterative functions

- Preplanning
- Strategic planning
- Operational planning
- Implementation & control
- Termination/succession/abortion
- Impact evaluation

The options

- Wait and see
- Compliance
- Active
- Proactive

Proactive management functions

Chapter two

The proactive options

2.1 Introduction

Corporate decisions are made based on implicit assumptions. The failure to explicitly probe the boundaries of these assumptions often leads to a limited range of options. Even in legal issues, executives tend to perceive the situation in terms of black and white, i.e. actively cooperate with the current system or break the law and suffer the consequences. There are cases, however, where neither of these two alternatives is appropriate, particularly in transnational affairs. A third option, to do as little as possible to get by, may perhaps be the only viable strategy.

That is why Proactive Decision-Making assumes that regardless of the potency of external demands, including statutory compliance, the manager always has at least four choices as defined below.

2.2 The inactive stance

The first option is to stay put, i.e. remain *inactive* or adopt a *wait and see* attitude. A hypothetical humorous story can be used to illustrate the point:

During a meeting with a separated couple interested in temporarily renewing their relationship, a marital counsellor asked: "What happens if you get pregnant?" Without hesitation, the couple responded: "We will cross that bridge when we get to it!"

Such an attitude is not uncommon in decision-making and policy formulation. There are, however, situations where its rationale could be totally justified. In particular, the wait and see stance is often temporarily adopted when available information is much too inadequate to project the decision outcome such as in buying a new untested machine or process. It is an essential option when precipitate action can lead to prolonged adverse consequences.

Likewise, the option is generally effective when the level of dissatisfaction with the status quo is insufficient to facilitate immediate change. It can also be the prudent alternative when the surprise effect could fuel a strong negative reaction.

In the above cases, the inactive stance is often wise as an interim strategy. However, staying put is unfortunately frequently overlooked as a viable alternative to deal with an issue particularly in international politics. Sweden and Switzerland throughout the postwar years have learned to keep their options open by "staying put" while other nations have paid the price of early alignment.

2.3 The compliance stance

The compliance stance is to do only what is necessary to get by or put colloquially: *stay out of jail.* This alternative is often retained in instances where the effort can neither contribute to an increase in revenue or service or a decrease in costs nor improve the corporate posture over the foreseeable future. Decisions related to external audit, security, safety, back up, alarm systems, insurance and government compliance often fall in this category. There are instances, however, where the proactive option is preferable vis a vis government, as illustrated in sections 2.5 and 2.7 below.

The compliance stance can also be a temporary strategy to deal with a sudden crisis, such as nominating an acting caretaker to fill in an unexpected vacancy, or to undermine the potential lead of a competitor venturing into an unknown market. The IBM move toward Data Base Management Systems started with the provision of DL1 as the first step to whet the customer appetite for IMS, announced in 1968, but which became operational only several years later. DL1 was the minimum investment for the company to get by and maintain its edge on competition at the time. Subsequent IBM strategies in Data Base Systems were clearly proactive.

2.4 The active stance

The active stance is to do what is *normally* expected. Practitioners of MBO usually see this as the only choice, thus overlooking the other options. While an active stance may indeed be the only feasible alternative, the decision-maker ought to explore the full range of avenues.

Doing what is expected may not be enough as experienced by IBM in the late sixties and Bell Telephone in 1980. Throughout the USA, IBM suffered a middle management drain even though its staff were treated as well if not better than other middle managers in the computer industry. Competitors like Control Data, Honeywell and Digital Equipment Corporation gained immensely at IBM's expense. Newcomers like Wang, Amdahl and Cincom Systems flourished overnight. Finally, a sweeping reorganization took place.

As for Bell, it could not foresee its technicians and operators moving toward radical unionization. The company had a competitive reward structure. It was actively doing what is normally expected in the utility sector. Bell knew it. The employees did not. *Advocacy advertizing* was overlooked. With the highest supervisor/operator ratio ever, Bell is now working uphill to regain its employees' trust.

An active stance is, however, *perceived* as fair in public service staff relations. The demands for parity are moves to force the government's treasury to do what is "normally" expected to maintain compensation schemes in line with the private sector.

2.5 The proactive option

The proactive option is to see the situation as an *opportunity* regardless of how threatening or how bad it looks and to influence the system constructively instead of reacting to it.

During the 1974 postal strike, the longest in Canadian history, the Professional Development Institute, faced with a temporary loss in the direct mail business, saw the situation as an opportunity to offer Post Office executives (among others) a unique seminar titled "Managing in a turbulent environment". The program went on successfully at the peak of the conflict while the competitors were still complaining about the mail strike! A similar scenario was repeated in 1981 when the July strike was seen as an opportunity to help managers understand new responsibility charting instruments to facilitate the transition toward the creation of the new Post Office Corporation.

The proactive option considers the contribution each stakeholder can make to help deal with the issue facing the organization. A *stakeholder* is defined as anyone with a vested interest in the issue. Interest can range from survival to mere intellectual curiosity! Stakeholders include both allies and opponents.

Even in instances where the issue does not affect the organization *per se,* the proactive option assesses the means to help the company or the government ride on it and benefit from its existence by achieving other goals. This process of acting in the shadow of another issue is called *hitch hiking*. It has been said that Israel has made use of the process on countless issues.

Unlike premature decisions which are difficult to reverse later, the proactive option is often a gradual shift built on consolidation of incremental strength. It should also permit the flexibility to retreat temporarily or strategically if and when necessary, particularly when the validity of information about the opponent behavior becomes suspect. The third part of this book provides a sequential iterative process to help keep multiple options open and facilitate such strategic moves.

Xerox phased planning and Matsushita multiple baseline approach combine compliance and proactive options in new product development. Their moves are characterized by covert pilot experiments, surprise introduction, concentration on early adopters, moderate incentives for trade-offs and consolidation of new territory with overwhelming resources and relentless dedication to service.

Proactive decisions usually go on unobtrusively. In 1976, the 50 million dollar Olympics broadcasting system went on schedule, within budget and well beyond the quality expectations of all viewers and parties with a vested interest in broadcasting. The project was a remarkable success despite the unprecedented constraints created by the mismanaged billion dollar site construction program. Highlights of the proactive planning approach follow.

Approximately five years prior to the project deadline, the Director of Planning, Mr. P.M. Gagnon, conducted a detailed analysis and assessment of different sources of uncertainty and risks such as the power of labor to strike, material shortages and security. A projected correlation was established between the degree of risk and the project visibility over the program life-cycle.

Strategic timing of activities was essential. A low profile pace of management was judiciously chosen until all essential activities were completed. Contingency time was built into the project schedule taking

The proactive options

into account the potential work stoppages and expected delays inherent in seeking "back to work" court orders or injunctions. Back up, restart and recovery systems and budget reserves were tightly managed to balance risk with costs and benefits. While the press headlines and government scrutiny have focused on the mediocrity of management of the construction sites, the excellent TV and radio coverage went almost unnoticed.

In the public sector, a close look at the achievements of federal strategists in the management of terrorism, Pehr Gyllenhammar at Volvo, Bob MacNamara at the World Bank and Henry Kissinger's tenure with the U.S. Administration reveals series of proactive decisions. Apart from the snapshot decision to use authority and invoke the War Measures Act, the subsequent strategies with which Canadian terrorism was proactively neutralized could be said to have saved Canada from the kind of upheavals facing governments elsewhere throughout the seventies such as airplane pirating, kidnappings and racial violence. Moreover, by 1980, virtually all terrorists had voluntarily returned home from exile, preferring to face the Canadian justice system instead of "living in style" in Cuba or even Paris. This record is unprecedented in modern politics. Even Robert Charlebois, who in 1970 was an influential voice in the antifederalist youth movement, now considers his former opponents, the Prime Minister and Mr. Paul Desmarais, the President of Power Corporation, as his best friends.

As for Kissinger, historians in the future are likely to reveal the role he played in building a critical mass around the former President of Egypt, Mr. Anwar Sadat, and jointly setting the climate and the scenario for Sadat's journey to Jerusalem. The trip was perhaps anything but as spontaneous as announced by the press.

Among the most daring proactive contributions known to the author, the performance of Volvo's president, Pehr Gyllenhammar, is unique. He struggled to find innovative solutions to make the work place both human and more productive. As he wrote in his book *I Believe in Sweden*: "...humanization of work and efficiency can be compatible. Indeed, I believe that, in today's society, they are inseparable." As a matter of fact, the novel design concepts successfully implemented in Skovde, Kalmar and other plants are living proof of his beliefs.

The proactive stance can uncover opportunities which might otherwise be overlooked. In the following case, the proactive approach helped to reduce polarization between the company and its regulators. It led to a creative response carefully planned to shift the nuclear energy debate from immediate to long term benefits. As a result, the parties' positions evolved from adversary to collaborative postures.

Prior to the proactive intervention, news headlines reflected the views of the anti-nuclear movement and local politicians who claimed that nuclear reactors were wasteful, costly, inefficient, unsafe and conducive to nuclear proliferation. The company reacted by indicating that nuclear energy was safe, secure, cost-effective and needed. Its response was largely ignored until the proactive strategy was set in motion. The latter took advantage of the untapped resources of the employee network which included their spouses, families, neighbors, friends, schools, professional associations, social clubs, elected representatives and suppliers.

The new posture did not attack the movement's claims but provided some facts about non-nuclear energy costs to the poor including the projected heating and transportation bills, the cost of manufactured goods, the cost to home owners. It also stressed job creation, impact on foreign policy, decreased dependence on OPEC oil, portability, flexibility and upward compatibility of the facilities with the most efficient energy system on the horizon (fission from breeder reactors). It recognized that waste disposal can be harmful if unregulated although experience has proved nuclear waste to be more manageable than acid rain and carbon dioxide which have already inflicted severe damage on the ecosystem (lakes and atmosphere). Spouses joined hands to create issue groups.

The proactive approach led to the formation of a corporate constituency which paid off within the first year during a state-wide referendum. While its adversaries were portrayed as selfish, the company was perceived as helpful.

2.6 The non-option

There is also a fifth choice, namely "go to jail", which is clearly dysfunctional in a business environment although it may generate support in either a labor leadership race or a political struggle against a nondemocratic system. The return to power of Indira Ghandi in India and the reelection of Jean-Claude Parrot at the head of the postal union movement are two examples. As for business decisions, lacking foresight, a surprising number of executives have fallen into this trap as illustrated in the next paragraph.

In this context, an insurance company prematurely opted for a head-on confrontation with the Government of Quebec on the language legislation issue. The move was done with little, if any, consideration for the adverse effects and risks. As a result, the company lost a sizeable portion of its market share in Quebec.

2.7 Differentiation is in!

This section outlines how various organizations responded in different ways to the language issue. While the insurance company was moving out of Quebec, other leading companies adopted different approaches with remarkable success.

Rather than suffer the consequences, an advanced technology manufacturer decided to do as little as possible to get by. The manufacturer found that the legislation applied to every corporation with headquarters' staff of fifty or more. It reduced its Montreal work force to forty-nine and quietly moved the balance elsewhere.

As for British Petroleum, it adopted a wait-and-see attitude while the language topic was in the headlines. In the meantime, perceived in isolation, the provincial income tax scheme further contributed to the top management drain throughout Quebec. British Petroleum found it increasingly difficult to attract English-speaking high salary earners, a fact that led to the relocation announcement early in 1980 while the press was occupied with federal election news. The strategic use of *hitch hiking* was timely.

On the other hand, a medium-sized bank went for the active stance. It did what is normally expected, i.e. the policy of leading financial institutions such as the Royal Bank and the Imperial Bank of Commerce. It also relied on attrition, job visibility, positions with high turnover rate and new staffing policies to achieve its target. Advanced technology and strategic units were gradually relocated. Reflecting on the success of the strategy, a senior executive said, "How could anyone blame us for such a decision? As far as the language issue is concerned, our bank is no exception. We are part of the financial community."

As for Alcan, a world leader in aluminium smelting and processing, it decided to see the new situation as an opportunity, and called on Patrick Rich, who has gracefully faced similar issues in Latin America particularly in Brazil. As the president of Aluminium Company of Canada, Mr. Rich has played a proactive role with unions, the government, academia and the social elite in Quebec where Alcan is now offered as a model corporate citizen. Not only the Quebec Minister of Finance, but Indian bands and even the union leader publicly praised Mr. Rich personally, creating a remarkable precedent in healthy labor management relations. The recent decision to move Alcan international headquarters from the financial district to a more historic site in downtown Montreal further reflects the company's desire to identify with the community. The announcement of that decision reminded the author of Alcan Latin American headquarters in the quiet district of Ipanema, away from the financial business heart of Rio (Botafogo) or Sao Paolo.

2.8 Conclusion

In *The Future Executive*, Harlan Cleveland provided an outstanding definition of the core problem of the decision-maker in a complex organization. "It is to make the best *choices* around whom to bring together, in which organizations, to make what happen, in whose interpretation of the public interest."[1]

Within a range of possible futures, Proactive Decision-Making lends recognition to the existence of multiple choices regardless of the issue. The socioeconomic opportunities and the adverse consequences (risks, costs) of each of these choices should be weighed before deciding which way to go. Although the final decision may ultimately be a personal preference in all but a few instances, the decision-maker ought to consider an array of factors and make assumptions, risks and contingencies explicit. The process improves our ability to adapt to the unpredictable. In order to select the best choice (or a series of choices over multiple time horizons), imagination, insight and creativity combined with the on-going functions of management described in the next part of this book can be extremely useful.

References and notes

1. Harlan Cleveland: The Future Executive, Harper & Row, New York, 1972.

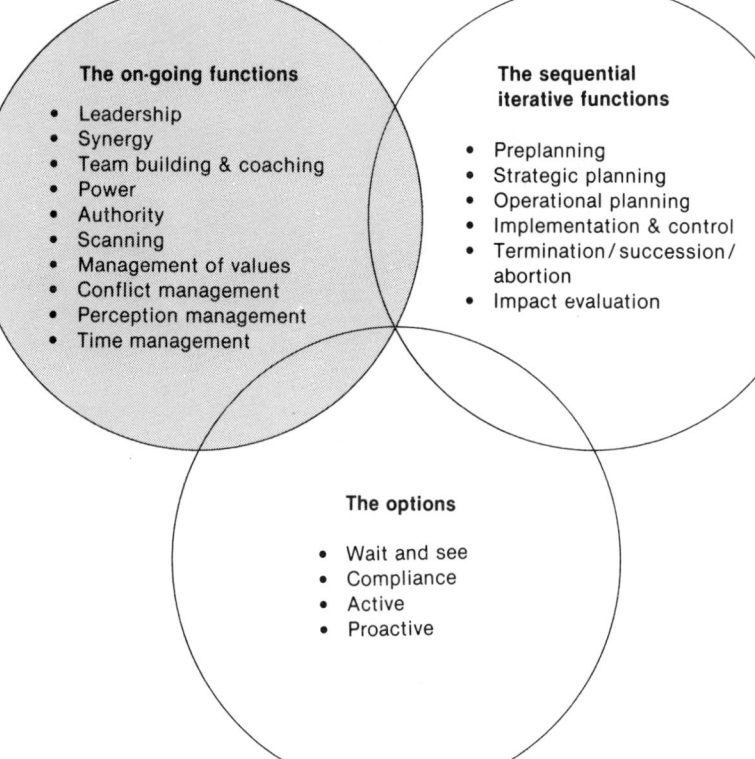

Figure 3.1: Proactive management functions

Part Two

Proactive Decision-Making: The ongoing functions

By the end of 1982, nearly one thousand decision-makers will have applied the Proactive Decision-Making framework which evolved over a twelve year period. The current version contains all modifications based on up-to-date experience. It is graphically illustrated in two figures. Figure 3.1 is a summary of the detailed version to be found later in Figure 11.2.

Two classes of decision functions are identified in the model. The first class consists of the ongoing functions of Proactive Management and will be the focus of the second part of this book. The sequential iterative functions constitute the second class which is organized in three phases. Flexibility to loop within a phase or back to a previous stage as unexpected events emerge is thoroughly discussed. The application of this class of functions will be examined in the last part of the book. As for the options listed in the model, they have been defined in the previous chapter.

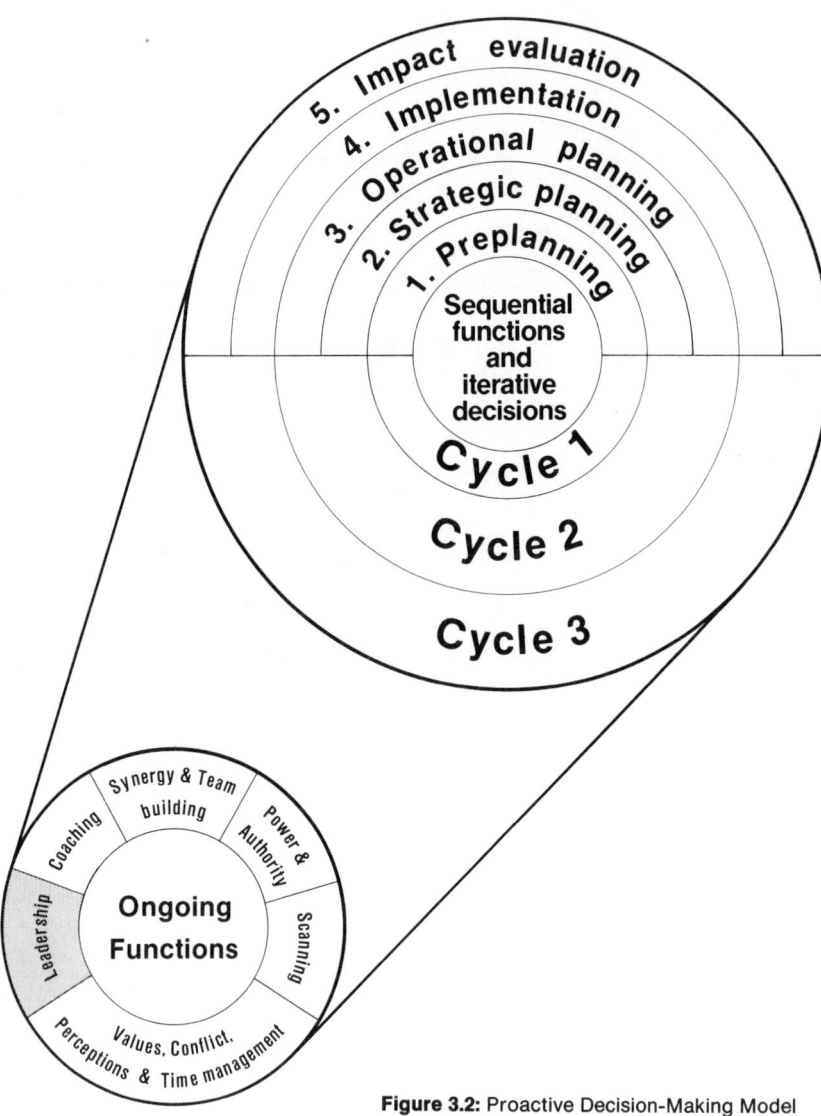

Figure 3.2: Proactive Decision-Making Model

Chapter three

Authentic leadership

3.1 The on-going functions of Proactive Decision-Making

The linear theory of management and its derivatives date back to the Taylor and Fayol eras. While partly accurate, these models are too simplistic for examination of contemporary issues. Decision-making is far too complex to be reduced to a single activity path.

Proactive Management has contributed to the practice of leadership and decision-making in many ways. It has improved the application of the classical sequential functions by providing a comprehensive framework and new analytic instruments. The result is more flexibility in planning. It also permits the thorough assessment of the merits of phased incrementation when it is desirable to keep multiple options open. Incrementation prevents premature transition and commitment to full implementation. Under conditions of high uncertainty, it becomes a viable route to move cautiously from issue identification to stakeholder analysis and from objective-setting to strategic planning, implementation, termination and evaluation.

In addition to the sequential iterative functions discussed above, Proactive Management focuses on other important activities which have been overlooked by theorists. These activities are called on-going functions because they indeed require continuous attention in every stage of Fayol's sequential model, be it planning, organization, implementation or evaluation.

On-going functions include intelligence-gathering (scanning), authentic leadership, synergy, team-building, coaching, the use of power, rewards and authority and the management of values, conflicts, perceptions and personal time. This class of functions requires a substantial amount of the decision-maker's time and effort. In borrowing from the theory of kinetics, these functions can be called the driving force of Proactive Decision-Making. That is why they are represented graphically by a small wheel in the Think Proactive model (Figure 3.2).

The on-going functions will be described separately for presentation purposes only. The fact is, leadership encompasses all the other elements. None is independent. Except where necessary, remarks will not be repeated. This chapter covers authentic leadership. The remaining chapters of Part two are devoted to synergy, coaching and team-building, power and authority, scanning and management of perceptions, values, conflict and time.

3.2 Definition and characteristics of authentic leadership

Authentic leadership is the ability to effectively and constructively influence individuals or groups on a given issue. It also assumes a genuine openness to influence from others. The characteristics of effective leaders are not universal. On the contrary, leadership is relative, situational, territorial, transitional and distributive rather than monolithic.

Notwithstanding the above, there are some fundamental attributes that seem to contribute to the growth of corporate and political leaders in both large and small organizations. Apart from self-awareness, perhaps the most potent of these is power, the subject of another chapter. Next is a blend of interpersonal skills, attitudes, problem-solving abilities, management skills and to a lesser extent task knowledge. All of these are interdependent.

3.3 Interpersonal skills

Interpersonal skills include effective *listening, supporting* and *differing*. *Empathy* is a significant factor in effective listening. As for *supporting*, the practice of giving people recognition and credit even for a partial contribution is essential. *Differing* is the ability to express clearly the difference and articulate the concern in a constructive and unthreatening manner to avoid a defensive response. The presence of these behaviors enhances leadership skills.

Compatibility is another arena of interpersonal activity which requires on-going attention. The pattern of interpersonal behavior can change dramatically from a normal state of affairs to a situation of crisis and high stress depending upon awareness, motives, norms, perceived needs and anticipated consequences. Lee Iacocca, the president accountable for the success of Ford's Mustang car, was fired by the company's chairperson because their "chemistry was different". The compatibility deficit became clear after a surprise event, namely the mid-seventies energy crisis.

Interpersonal compatibility includes socializing, directing and intimacy. *Socializing* is the degree to which the person takes the initiative to invite participation in what he/she does, attempts to be included in what others do and also accepts invitations from others. By the same token, *directing* is the degree of assertiveness and initiative undertaken to influence others and also the extent to which the individual is open to influence. *Intimacy* is the level of effort mobilized to initiate a close and personal relationship with others and the level of response to initiatives from others.

Both the presence and absence of these behaviors can be strengths provided they are deployed in the right direction. Executives and political leaders should be clearly aware of their strengths and related *boundaries.* They should deploy the strengths in situations where they tend to do well. They should build an entourage to make up for compatibility deficits and act through others in situations where they do poorly or which could result in incompatibility.

3.4 Management skills

In this context, a skill is defined as practiced know-how or applied knowledge.

Newcomers to managerial jobs are expected to turn into effective leaders overnight. Unlike pilots, physicians and lawyers, they are denied the time for apprenticeship. Even business school graduates are not adequately prepared to make policies and assume decision-making responsibility without active guidance. Most MBA case studies "monitor the wrong variables, generate statistical illusions" and train students to deal with problems from the perspective of no one other than the president, a position which few if any reach in their life-time! To face real-life challenge, education is necessary but not sufficient. On-the-job *coaching* is proving to be of key importance in developing the skills required for effective leadership. These skills include:

1. the ability to identify, *coach,* inspire and counsel aspiring leaders;
2. the skills to *understand people,* achieve synergy, promote creativity, build teams, be assertive and collaborative, influence constructively, reach consensus, manage values and conflicts, behave politically and see the strategies behind the traumas and dramas of news headlines;

3. the skills to develop viable *concession strategies* and constructively exploit the dynamics of ephemeral coalitions without vanishing under the strengths of their tidal waves;
4. the *flexibility to keep multiple options strategically open and move prudently* as long as both the conditions of high uncertainty/risk and low commitment prevail, so that no major opportunity is missed;
5. *scanning and analytical skills* to work with imperfect information, ambiguous and complex networks, collect, analyze and digest large amounts of soft information, assess uncertainty, manage risks and hostility and convert problems into opportunities;
6. *planning skills* to set and thoroughly validate the mission and objectives, define work, explore strategies, allocate roles, identify information requirements, design structures, control progress, evaluate impact and adequately *plan succession* continuously;
7. skills to constructively *terminate unproductive relationships* and *abort ineffective ventures* in time;
8. skills to *manage time* as a scarce resource and to evaluate regularly the contribution of work and leisure time to personal growth;
9. skills to maintain a high degree of *self-awareness* and to know one's own style and personal tendencies.

3.5 Attitudes

Attitudes are deeply held beliefs. They are the attributes of the personal value system. As such, they cannot be observed directly. They are mostly inferred from our behavior. Attitudes are relative and somewhat culturally bound. Each group or society has a set of norms. Traditionally, conformity is rewarded and usually expected. Unless earned by status, originality is discouraged and can be reprimanded, particularly at the top.

The case of Bendix Chairperson Bill Agee and Vice-President Mary Cunningham exemplifies the inclination of both Wall Street and the press establishment to penalize nonconformism even when accompanied by outstanding achievements. Instead of accolades, Bill and Mary were unfairly subjected to scrutiny. Even Fortune Magazine[1] joined the bandwagon of the gossipy news syndicates by running a cover story with subtle antagonistic remarks. The sad and troubling fact is that "investigative" journalism failed to draw attention to the difficult policy and strategic planning issues that Mary Cunningham fought to successful conclusions during her short tenure with Bendix Corporation. Had Agee and Cunningham considered the four proactive options, perhaps the issue could have been managed quite differently by explicitly dealing with attitudes and perceptions.

Authentic leadership

The attitudes which may be conducive to leadership are subjective. Nevertheless, there are some basic attitudes in the western culture which foster effective leadership.

3.6 Desirable attitudes

A set of desirable attitudes can be drawn from observing executives at work. The following is a basic list which has been derived primarily from North American leaders with an effective track record in policy and decision-making.

1. Effective leaders have a proactive sense of **responsibility.** They set high standards for themselves. They are deeply *committed* to excellence, fairness, equity and integrity.
2. They compromise easily on matters considered inconsequential but are strongly mission-driven on essential issues.
3. Their perception of the world is broad and realistic. They are flexible when dealing with collaboration, competition and hostility. They are not vengeful.
4. They have a low need to dominate others. While they value and accept public approbation, they have a low appetite for it. They are more motivated by inner desire to get results. Actually, government leaders and multinational executives who expect public approbation are probably in the wrong place! Perhaps they ought to explore independent practice or a career in marketing cosmetics, performing arts and advocacy associations.
5. Proactive leaders have high regard for individual dignity, privacy, rights and integrity.
6. They have a remarkable tolerance for ambiguity and complexity combined with a bias toward optimism. They actively promote and support initiative, value risk and are prepared to live with the consequences.
7. They do not try deliberately to cover mistakes, inadvertent errors or bad judgement.
8. Their awareness is not confined to the immediate environment. They have a clear idea about social norms, family value shifts and can respond to the various demands of life methodically.

3.7 Conclusion

This chapter introduced the concept of authentic leadership. It defined the characteristics and outlined the desirable skills and attitudes for proactive leaders. The remaining chapters of Part two will further elaborate on the concept.

References and notes

1. Mary Cunningham is a Phi Beta Kappa graduate of Wellesley College and an honors graduate of the Harvard School of Business. Before joining Bendix, she was a well respected financial analyst with Salomon Brothers and also the youngest woman to reach the level of Assistant Treasurer for the Chase Manhattan Bank. Ms Cunningham left Bendix to become Vice-President Strategic Planning with Seagram & Sons and more recently Executive Vice-President of Planning for Seagram Wine Co.. The media were far more interested in Agee's and Cunningham's personal affairs than in their performance at work. In the November 1980 issue, Fortune questionned whether a young 29 year old woman, no matter how smart, is qualified to aspire to the position of Vice-President Strategic Planning of a multibillion-dollar corporation. About one month later, the magazine adopted a totally different posture in a subsequent cover story featuring a younger man!

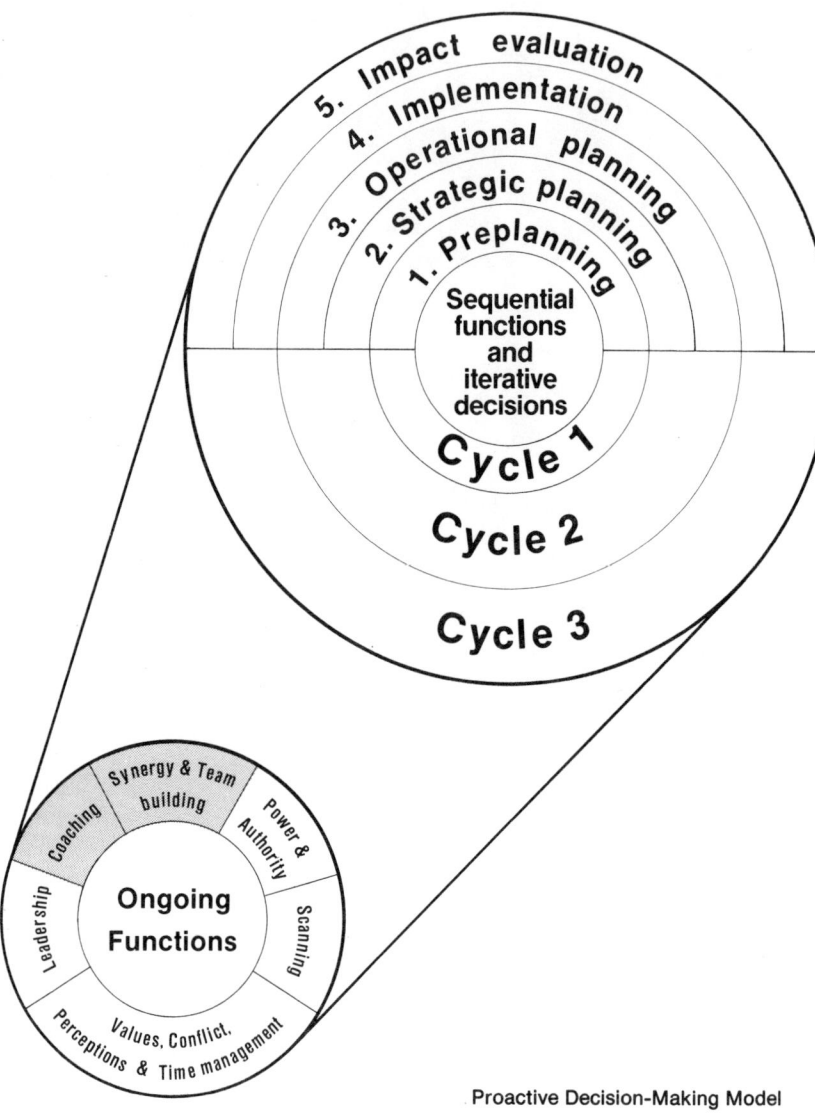

Proactive Decision-Making Model

Chapter four

Synergy, team-building and coaching

4.1 Synergy

Synergy is a process for problem-solving and issue management in a group mode. By working as a team, the value of the solution generally exceeds the sum of its individual parts. As R. Buckminster Fuller said, "Synergy is to energy as integration is to differentiation". It is the opposite of entropy.

Synergy can be immensely beneficial in problem situations, particularly when the conditions listed below are met.

1. All participants expect to potentially win from entering the group problem-solving process.
2. The objectives are shared by the members.
3. Limited information exists.
4. There is neither open nor latent hostility.
5. Group members have individually made an effort to formulate the problem and explore alternative solutions beforehand.
6. Sufficient time can be allocated to permit each individual to air concerns, express support and challenge other suggestions constructively.
7. Leadership is distributed based on the situation and available skills, rather than always confined to one individual.

8. Inappropriate competition between group members is discouraged. Instead, collaboration is highly rewarded.
9. Group size is adequate, ideally from three to six people. Larger groups should be divided into multiple parallel work teams.
10. Members understand the process of working in a team. It can be acquired either through past experience or a formal coaching and team-building process.

Group problem-solving may not result in a synergistic solution if any of the above prerequisites are deficient. Finally, synergy is a team-building exercise in itself. It is a valuable instrument for leadership.

4.2 Example

This illustration from a large petrochemical company helps in understanding how an acute problem can be diagnosed and resolved in a synergistic mode.

For over twenty years, absenteeism, stress and high turnover were endemic among the truck drivers assigned to the Montreal-Toronto freight corridor. Union leaders complained about working conditions and cited the abnormal rate of family separations among the drivers. They pressured the company to expand annual leave, to grant shorter work weeks and to fully refund the expenses for long distance calls incurred on nights spent away from home.

Negotiations were lengthy but resulted in a deadlock. The company was not prepared to create a precedent for other workers and assigned an analyst to document the real cost of union demands. The analyst decided to go to the sources of information to collect the data and validate the objectives. He accompanied a senior trucker on several trips, a move that was reluctantly approved by management. Fortunately, the analyst's empathic ear and genuine concern led the driver to come up with a novel win-win solution for both the company and his peers. Instead of driving all the way to Montreal and staying in motels overnight, the Toronto truckers could meet their Montreal counterparts halfway, exchange their vehicles and head back home the same day. The solution, so humane and financially attractive, was featured in the company annual report.

4.3 Team-building

The traditional hypothesis is that teamwork is desirable because participation leads to satisfaction which, in turn, leads to a greater productivity. This hypothesis is frequently false. Under certain conditions, teamwork may be unnecessary, detrimental or both. Under other conditions, teamwork is productive and therefore necessary. The next sections outline these two classes of conditions and provide the characteristics of high performing teams. *Team-building* is defined as the ability to deal with the issue of people compatibility and create the climate for synergistic teamwork on a regular basis.

4.4 Characteristics of high performing teams

In his pioneering work with Esso and TRW, Herbert Shepard observed executives and professional groups at work. He found striking analogies among highly successful teams in a wide spectrum of work settings ranging from performing arts, airline crews and sports to executive suites.

First, members have a *unity of purpose* and are genuinely committed to each other's objectives. Second, *no one lets the other fail*. Third, *process skills and behavior* are required to some degree. Ed Schein[1] categorized these team-building processes into *group-maintenance* and *task* skills.

Group-maintenance skills are necessary for the team to maintain an "action research" mode. They serve to build, test and maintain a high degree of harmony in interpersonal relations among its members. They include the ability to compromise, encourage participation, keep the door open for new ideas, harmonize relationships, set the standards of communications and the decision-making mode, test the standard and diagnose communication patterns. The effort devoted to group maintenance should be in balance with expected results, rather than seen as an end in itself.

Task skills are aptitudes to process work. People who possess these skills tend to initiate discussions about objectives, work planning and action. They frequently seek opinion and share information, express the need for clarifying and summarizing a point of view, and at some point, test for consensus to prevent unending debates. Both formal and informal feedback sessions can be significant in further developments of task skills and ultimately in performance improvement.

As the team grows and acquires distinctive capabilities to face peculiar situations, these skills will be practiced by a number of members, even if originally initiated by a single leader. That is the essence of distributive leadership.

4.5 Conditions requiring teamwork

Teamwork is desirable in several situations:

1. Perhaps the most common are issues where *limited information* exists. The objective is to produce better results through synergy. Considering the uncertainty involved in making policy and governing, team-building becomes a prerequisite for proactive leadership.
2. Teamwork may be required for *safety or survival* reasons. It can be physical safety such as in the case of night police patrols teaming up against assailants. The reason may be psychological such as that of school teens camping in the dark, small plane bush pilots or the famous British miners case.[2] Last but not least would be a socio-technical reason such as the commercial airline pilots. Most passengers would be reluctant to be flown by a single pilot. Apart from the social resistance, there are obvious technical reasons which make business sense (survival).
3. Team-building could be a *precondition for the critical mass formation* to either gain collaborative or catalytic power prior to embarking on a sensitive change effort.
4. Finally, there are instances where team-building is sought for *cushioning or contingencies.* By closely working as a team and generously sharing information, dependence on any single person is reduced and contingency or slack resources are created. Slack resources are a form of insurance against attrition and other risks which may impair the continuity of work.

4.6 When is it unnecessary or detrimental?

The insufficient number of qualified group trainers has made sensitivity training sessions a sort of free-for-all. It has led novices to naively promote teamwork as a form of magic to cure corporate ills and interpersonal problems. After the early euphoria, a wide disenchantment with sensitivity training followed. As a result, a pioneering U.S. institution, NTL (National Training Labs) unjustly fell on hard times for several years during the mid-seventies.

These events have led the author to research the conditions under which teamwork is either unnecessary, detrimental or should be postponed. These conditions have been derived from a variety of work climates ranging from correctional institutions, airport labor disputes, inadequate cooperation in international development projects, and diagnosis of corporate crises to small business performance evaluation. Some of these conditions detrimental to teamwork are summarized below.

Synergy, team-building and coaching

1. Hostility exists. It can be either latent or open, creative, subtle or direct. Hidden agendas are frequent.
2. Inappropriate competition is encouraged.
3. Interpersonal and process leadership skills are absent or deficient.
4. Poor work planning is encountered.
5. Unhealthy past experience is remembered.
6. Unfair rewards/penalties exist.
7. Godfather support is absent. For instance, in an international project, the godfather is a senior executive in the remote headquarters of the corporation who is personally interested in team's achievement. The resident project team leader can look to the godfather for protection, access to distant powers and support but not direct control.
8. Either abundant information is available to all, making it unnecessary to tie up the whole team, or, alternatively, information is distorted or not disseminated adequately.
9. Inappropriate membership is forced to resolve problems without the participation of "culprits" or the capability to use power as a means of influence and control.
10. Objectives are either unclear, not shared or perceived as not relevant.
11. Work is either boring or requiring an unattainable level of performance resulting in a continuous fear or withdrawal problems.
12. Deadlock issues are getting excessive attention. Leaders are suffering from the handicap of priority myopia and are unable to take interim action on chronic issues. Such overemphasis on problems interferes with important opportunities and denies the team members time to think.
13. Efforts to get consensus are undermined by premature closures, formal voting and frequent authority-centered decisions.
14. Commitments are consistently not honored.
15. The knowledge gained from formal training is transferred to field work without regard for the idiosyncrasies of the real world. Process skills were developed in a social climate different from the work milieu or the training is fragmented and not consistently followed by action research and sessions to update skills.

In order to make teams effective, a series of nonthreatening and cognitive interventions designed to deal with both process and learning deficits associated with some of the above conditions should be considered as a prework phase.

4.7 Coaching

Coaching aspiring leaders and professionals is an on-going function for management. It is perhaps the best contribution senior executives can make to the future of the organization. It requires steady, frequent and methodical work. The objective is to help associates extend their present capabilities.

To this end, the exemplary performance of great coaches and their contribution to the success of athletes, performing artists, missionaries, medical professionals and Japanese industrialists are well worthy of consideration by managers and political leaders. Movies such as *Chariots of Fire* and documentaries featuring Peter Drucker or Vincent Lombardi exemplify the art of coaching. They provide ample material for initiative and action.

Coaching is a demanding task. Great coaches are more than private tutors. They possess what Herbert Shepard calls resonance: "a relationship with other beings which is empathic, responsive, mutually stimulating and expansive for all those involved".[3] They strive to help increase the degrees of freedom and the choices available to the associate. They care and are trusted. They often act as a sounding board in life planning. Their alertness to the law of diminishing returns is essential to prevent the associate from draining all available energy on professional matters. This role is superbly demonstrated in *Chariots of Fire*. While his two athletes were still highly energized to win the Olympics, the coach was already concerned about the aftermath of success. He wisely supported the transition to other valued and more lasting goals: family for one and missionary dedication for the other. This role is also well understood by strategists in two small and potent contemporary air forces.

In order to help others go beyond their self-inflicted boundaries, coaches should discourage obedience, loyalty, dependence and conformity. They should be patient, tolerant, altruistic and dedicated to excellence. They should be eager to invest prime time to study the talent, motives, the capacity for learning and the risk avoidance style of the associate being coached.

Unlike training, which can be fruitful in a group setting, coaching is perhaps best when done in dyadic encounters. Both the coach and the associate should set aside sufficient uninterrupted blocks of time for adequate pre-planning (ex-ante) and debriefing (ex-post) to share perceptions and maintain continuous feedback.

The coach should be skilled in synergy, team-building and interpersonal compatibility issues. Some catalytic power is an asset.

Coaching complements formal training and should not be construed as a substitute for it. Moreover, the associate should be *eager* to invest the time and effort required for career growth. Finally, coaching leads to lasting friendships and can be a rewarding experience.

4.8 Conclusion

Proactive leadership cannot exist without synergy, coaching and team-building skills. This chapter provided an executive overview of what these skills are all about. The next chapter will examine another function of proactive leadership: power.

References and notes

1. Ed Schein: Process Consultations, Addison-Wesley, O.D. Series, Reading, Massachusetts.
2. The arrival of automated mining machines led employers to reduce crews to a single person per vehicle. Within months, British miners suffered emotionally as a result of stress and loneliness in the pit. For more information about the British miners case, refer to: F.E. Emery, & E.L. Trist: Sociotechnical Systems edited by C.W. Churchman & M. Verhulst, Management Science: Models and Techniques, New York, Pergamon Press, 1960.

    E.L. Trist, G.W. Higgin, H. Murray & A.B. Pollock: Organizational Choice, London: Tavistock Publications, 1963.
3. Herbert A. Shepard: Life Planning, a paper presented at 1974 Seminar "Managing in a Turbulent Environment" and sponsored by The Professional Development Institute.

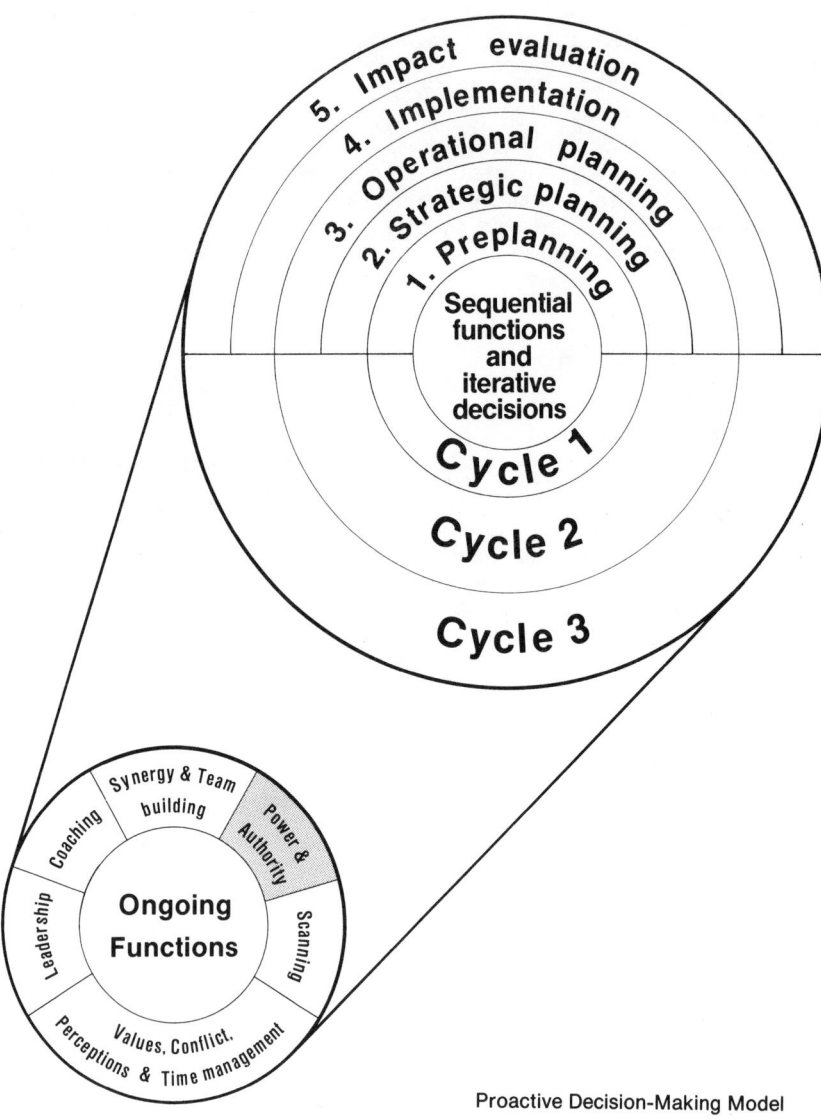

Proactive Decision-Making Model

Chapter five

Power

5.1 Definition and characteristics

Power is the ability to influence the system as *perceived* by it. It is also the ability to give or withhold rewards or punishments as perceived by others. It has several characteristics.

It is *relative* and subject to the balance of power held by subordinates or others. Power is *temporal and transitional.* It is often in a fragile equilibrium. The latter results from the on-going interactions with continually changing forces, demands, stringent regulations, constraints and values from employees, peers, bosses, customers, competitors and change advocates. When cautiously used, power can be subject to the law of positive returns. As Peter Newman wrote in the first volume of *The Canadian Establishment,* "Power tends to connect. Absolute power tends to connect absolutely."

Often society tends to view power as bad. This normative tendency is not necessary. In fact, power is *neutral.* It can serve a good or a bad purpose, depending upon the intentions of those who exercise it, the perceptions of the observer and the consequences for the people who have to put up with it.

Power is *perceptual.* The Chinese derive much of their power from what the rest of the world *sees and thinks* about China. Finally, power is also *territorial.* The territory could be a science, an ethnic group, a correctional institution, a professional society, an exclusive club, a religious cult, a race, a gender, a social class or a combination of these. It is important to define the boundaries of the territory along many relevant dimensions. In short, power is *situational.*

5.2 Forms of power

When considering alternatives to authority as a means of influence and control, the executive should assess the relative merits of three forms of power. Using both the British and American terminologies, these forms are described below.

5.2.1 Coercive-competitive power

Political elections and other leadership races are still fought and won largely by this form of power. It promotes inappropriate competition between individuals or groups. It views the problem as a zero-sum game that should result in a winner and a loser. In several board meetings which the author or his associates has had the privilege to attend, there have been instances where a participant would try to use coercive power against a fellow director. The attacker would simply state, "Joe, I don't think the majority would share your concern!" and then ask the board, "Do you agree with Joe?"

This is an attempt to discredit Joe in advance and rally the majority behind his opponent. Workshop and conference leaders tend also to use coercive power against outspoken participants, particularly when they hit a deadlock, by asking the audience, "How many would share Joan's opinion?" Since the typical executive is rather reserved, only a few, if any, would raise their hands, a situation that leads the speaker to conclude, "Joan, I think you are clearly in a minority position."

It is said that coercive power was instrumental in ousting a score of heavy weight liberal Democrats from Congress in 1980. It may have led to the defeat of Jimmy Carter who consistently undermined its role in the competitive election race. Reagan's victory was aided by the coercive campaign strategies of the so-called "moral majority", among others.

We often use coercive power far more discreetly, in order to win at the others' expense. While this behavior can be cognitive at the beginning, we may be unaware of the process when it develops into a skill. Leading organizational behavior scientists, such as Herbert Shepard and Jane Mouton, have hinted that such behavior may be linked to our prewar competitive mentality, which promoted competition not only in marketing, sports and economics where it is clearly legitimate but also brought it into the working place where adversary behavior may sometimes be dysfunctional and inappropriate to the attainment of corporate goals.

The use of coercive power in trade unions and professional associations is a common practice. During the annual dinner party, the outgoing president of the professional society presents a handpicked candidate and then asks for other suggestions from the floor! The majority of associations have a nominating committee. As John Kenneth Galbraith wrote in *A Life of Our Times,* "Nomination within the AEA[1] is equivalent to election".

Union leaders usually ask for open votes when they wish the members to support the call for a strike. However, secret ballots are called for to increase the chance for a "yes" vote before ratifying a collective agreement with management. Unlike open votes, secret ballots minimize the impact of radical members on the large majority.

Since coercive power is subject to the law of diminishing returns, it should be applied by necessity rather than by desire. Even then, caution and wisdom are required to bring its influence to bear on the issues.

With an assertive group of social scientists, the use of coercive power to discredit an individual and rally the majority behind his/her opponent can be very risky indeed. Almost everyone would spot the manipulative move and vote against it. Instead of asking, "How many agree with Joan?", the alternative is to seek assistance and to ask, "Could anyone help Joan to understand us?" or alternatively to suggest, "I am sure there is at least one person who can understand Joan", and then ask whoever responds, "Could you see Joan after the meeting and get back to us tomorrow if you can't deal with her concern?". This option appeals to collaborative power of the respondent, the topic of the next paragraph.

5.2.2 Collaborative-synergistic power

This form is based on a positive sum game. It views the issue from a win-win perspective. As an illustration: suppose a conflict exists between a couple about the choice of a vacation resort. The man wishes to go to the mountains and the woman to the sea. Viewed from a personal win-lose angle, each partner would try to impose his/her preference at the expense of the other.

The outcome may be a stalemate, i.e. to go nowhere. It could be a bad compromise (go half way between the sea and the mountains), or a good compromise (one week on each side). Perhaps each should go to a different place, as the humorists in seminars often say! However, if they want to travel together, there is a need to find a better solution. Use of a collaborative-synergistic style will point to a vacation resort which is blessed with both the mountains and the sea. Norwegians would call it a submarine mountain! Humor aside, our couple might consider Southern California, Vancouver, Puerto Vallarta, Rio de Janeiro and other famous places.

The exponential growth of the computer time-sharing industry is the testimony of the collaborative power style of Dr. Edson de Decastro who also led the remarkable rise of Data General Corporation. The President of Cincom Systems, Tom Nies, who earned a reputation for his synergistic power skills while at IBM, rapidly created his own international empire (by software industry standards).

Bradford Morse, the Deputy Secretary of the United Nations, broke through the barriers of interagency rivalry, regional coalitions and factions to improve substantially the international emergency relief programs and, in turn, the faith of drought and flood striken victims. His strong commitment to collaborative power and close association with synergy-driven achievers created a rare cross-cultural political consensus and led to the massive involvement of donors immediately after the 1974 World Food Conference. Likewise, Bob MacNamara cultivated collaborative power among World Bank executives and mastered a fair OPEC commitment to tripartite cooperation in major capital projects. The responsible exercise of collaborative power is the hallmark of the top executives of the Canadian banking system such as Rowlie Frazee and Michel Bélanger.

5.2.3 Catalytic-charismatic power

This form of power is the elegant and lazy leader's choice for influencing subordinates. The word lazy is not used in a negative sense. Coercive power uses the maximum psychic investment. It loses momentum in the friction resulting from the effort to achieve equilibrium. By contrast, catalytic power uses the minimum human energy to get results.

In India, the British, in many instances, effectively used the catalytic power of Mahatma Ghandi to achieve better results with the old man's words than could have been produced via the military and the sophisticated weaponry. Mao Tse Tung's red book had for some time catalytic power over 900 million Chinese.

In the early sixties, John Kenneth Galbraith exerted sufficient charisma on both President Kennedy and Prime Minister Lester B. Pearson to be appointed as the only person to the "two man" Joint Commission to resolve the conflict between Canadian and U.S. airlines.

Closer to home, every organization has a few individuals who hold catalytic power over groups for a given set of issues. These individuals are often not members of the hierarchical line of command, sometimes even existing outside the institution. As an example, Dr. Wells, a veterinarian who achieved national prominence in the early fifties as a

Power

result of a surprise event and his personal struggle against the outbreak of foot and mouth epidemics, remained a catalytic power in the Department of Agriculture even long after he retired.

In veterinary medicine, the opinion of Dr. Wells was well respected by government, politicians and even throughout the world. In several instances, it made the difference between the success and failure of agricultural project proposals made to Parliament.

Industrialist Konosuke Matsushita, entrepreneur Paul Desmarais, Cabinet Secretary Michael Pitfield, broadcasters Barbara Walters and Walter Cronkite, Air Canada founder C.D. Howe, U.S. consumerist Carol Foreman, Henry Kissinger and Arthur Schlessinger have also gained catalytic power in the government and public affairs. Establishment institutions such as The Brookings, the Council on Foreign Relations, the Ford Foundation, the Business Round Table, the Trilateral Commission, Harvard, MIT, and The New York Times have traditionally been fertile ground for a great number of influential Americans.

After the 1974 boxing match in Zaire, Mohammed Ali became a catalytic power in equatorial Africa. In an attempt to win support for the boycott of Moscow Olympics, former President Carter asked Ali to visit African heads of states. Thus Carter used the power of Ali instead of the authority of the Secretary of State. He won a great deal of support in that region.

In political leadership, catalytic power is in! Even in the Eastern block, leaders are flirting with it. It was interesting to note how, after coercive threats, the Polish Government appealed to the catalytic power of the Catholic Church to influence the striking workers in Gdansk shipyards in 1980. Had Poland faced the issue sooner, authority would have been used. Here the repeated attempts to use catalytic power as an alternative to authority is a welcome civilized development. It undoubtedly saved many lives in 1980. It does not mean that force is now ruled out. It is still a contingency. One hopes the Polish Government will not use it, even as a last resort.[2]

5.3 Business illustration

This case illustrates the use of catalytic power in a consulting environment.

Recently, the director of management services of a major North American broadcasting network, acting on behalf of the president, contracted a respected consultant to reorganize its structure along matrix lines. In the process of defining the work requirements, the consultant concluded that matrix was not necessary. The director agreed, but felt the conclusions were outside the terms of reference of the project and could not imagine going back to the president with negative findings. Thus, the consultant was asked to seriously consider matrix or some sort of a compromise. He felt that "compromises are all very well in politics, but not in management science!", so he stuck to his findings and forwarded the report directly to the president.

Faced with the dilemma, the director reluctantly tried to support the consultant's findings, but in vain. The president terminated the outside consultant's assignment, shelved the report and mandated another study, this time underlining the need for matrix. After all, he had attended a seminar on the topic! He thought the dual command structure ought to work in his own corporation.

A new consultant was hired. She quickly reviewed the situation, analysed the previous study and reached identical conclusions. However, before formulating anything in writing, she decided to identify the critical mass for the change. She discovered that the president had a great deal of respect for his former professor in the graduate business school. In proactive terms, the catalytic power of the professor might be the critical mass. So far, the diagnosis of the dynamics of power has been done. That is half of the battle. In order to win the other half, she developed a plan to get access to the professor and to commit him to support her findings. Subcontracted for a couple of days, the professor reviewed the report and, to her delight, reached a similar conclusion. In exchange for a fee, he was asked to file a one page memorandum expressing his observations.

Without changing the substance, the new consultant cosmetically modified the format of the old report. She made the content less offensive and focused instead on the advantages of staying put (opportunities for not going matrix). The professor's memo was inserted at the beginning of the report. It certified that the professor had read it and that he concurred with the findings.

The "new" report was presented to the president who congratulated the consultant for the excellent job. A week later, she was offered a new contract to assess the content supervision of the news and public affairs division.

That is the art of using catalytic power. Notwithstanding the importance of the technical know-how, the difference between an effective and an ineffective expert is how much they know about behavior modification through unobtrusive exercise of power.

5.4 Two government illustrations

The first example is the Fishery Treaty which was tentatively signed by President Carter but failed to win the U.S. Congress support. The Government of Canada relied almost totally on the authority and goodwill of the U.S. President and underestimated the power of Congress to veto the deal. The second example illustrates the opposite situation. This is a case where multiple forms of power have been used.

For over a century, Canadian leaders could not reach an agreement to patriate the Canadian Constitution from Great Britain. They focused on the objectives and the process of repatriation but failed to gain domestic support. The conceptual formula of Figure 5.1 can be applied to this issue to define the stalemate. As indicated, the benefits of the change will not be greater than its economic, political and social costs unless a few preconditions are satisfied. The level of dissatisfaction with the current system is sufficiently high. The objectives are clearly defined. The processes toward the objectives are acceptable. The necessary know-how and resources can be mobilized. The stakes and rewards are perceived to be relevant and fair by the relevant stakeholders, which include the 5F's: the family, the friends, the foreigners, the foes and the "fools". In this context, a *stakeholder* is a person or a group who has a vested interest in the issue. Interest can vary from survival to mere intellectual curiosity. The family includes people who sees the change or the organization as essential to their survival. The friends consider it important but not essential. The foreigners are neutral, neither for nor against the change, but may express their opinion about it. The foes' vested interest is annihilation. The "fools" are usually lunatics with fluid or conflicting loyalties. In Proactive Decision-Making, stakeholders are considered potential resources and are strategically used to permit the organization to benefit from issues at large.

Early in 1980, federal strategists diagnosed the stalemate, then orchestrated a skilful master plan to manage the issue. First, the level of dissatisfaction with the status quo was addressed. Originally insufficient to permit the change, it was boosted through awareness and readiness management strategies, contrasting multiple issues such as fish and energy with basic human rights. In addition, the Quebec 1980 Referendum was used as an opportunity (i.e. a proactive approach) to speed up the process.

Secondly, the most desirable plan and several contingency plans were formulated. The most desirable plan was a highly publicized crash project. It was the last attempt to get unanimity through provincial collaboration during summer 1980 conferences. Capitalizing on the failure of the crash project, the contingency plan was already en route.

Think Proactive: New insights into decision-making

This formula was developed by the author to assist clients study the need and readiness for institutional, technological and environmental change.

$$\text{Change} = f\left(\frac{\text{benefits}}{\text{costs}}\right) = f(D, O, P, E, R, S)$$

The benefits of the change will be greater than its costs (economic, political, technological, environmental and institutional) if and only if each variable in the formula is above a threshold value, that is:

D: The level of **dissatisfaction** with the status quo is at the **necessary and sufficient** level

O: The **objectives** are well defined, validated and shared by the critical mass

P: The **processes** (tasks and steps) toward the objectives are clearly understood and are acceptable to the critical mass

E: The **expertise** (know-how and skills) can be acquired

R: The **resources** can be mobilized

S: The **stakes** and rewards are perceived to be relevant and fair

Figure 5.1: Management of change — The "Dopers" Formula

© Copyright, A.P. Martin, 1983   ISBN 0 86502 000 0

The public module of the plan was phased in with a series of scenarios, carefully played simultaneously in Britain and Canada. Advocacy advertizing was instrumental in reinforcing the new directions as early as possible.

The pace of change made it difficult for the Opposition to catch up in the process. The critical mass for gaining support for the massive constitutional change consisted of two people: Bill Davis of Ontario and Ed Broadbent of the New Democratic Party. The first had an influence on the conservative grass roots and enjoyed far more respect than the Opposition Leader. The second could rally democrats across the land but particularly in British Columbia to minimize Western alienation. The price for Davis' and Broadbent's commitment was empowering, a process to be discussed in section 5.5.

Finally, using tactical action-reaction strategies, the Prime Minister spoke publicly against referring the Bill to the Supreme Court (the authority) only to trap the Opposition into loudly advocating legality. However, when the Opposition staged a filibuster to compel the Government to go to court, the P.M. reversed his prior stand and got credit for being more accommodating! The concession strategy was built on the form (secondary objective) not the substance (core objective).

By default, the Government enlisted the virtual support of the media on a non-objection basis early in 1980. In general, the press was somewhat reactive and surprised about the unfolding of these events. But it should not have been. Unfortunately for the public, the press is a long way from building investigative skills in proactive reporting. It has a billion dollar space age technology, but only a shoestring budget for coaching and training news and public affairs professionals.

It is worthwhile to note that this illustration is an analytic account of the political processes, not a normative content evaluation of Cabinet action. It does not judge the merits of the objectives and the ethical dilemmas involved. For political leaders and corporate executives, this is another illustration of how different forms of power can be strategically used before going the authority route. It assumes clear objectives and resolution of value dilemmas.

5.5 Sources of power

Power not only affects the process of organization planning and design, but our day-to-day life and business operations, often in a very subtle way. These examples demonstrate the importance of the use of power as a critical factor in policy analysis and decision-making. Political leaders and corporate executives should seriously consider the costs/benefits of each of these forms of power as an alternative to authority for the purpose of influence and control.

The balance sheet should not be restricted to the monetary items, but also to the psychic and sociotechnical costs and rewards. Overreliance on the formal hierarchy at the expense of power and critical mass considerations can be fatal in policy formulation and decision-making. What are the factors that can bring more power to a manager? The answer lies in the sources of power. These can be *infinite.* Among them:

1. Achievement, success, popularity
2. Access to other power(s), association, referral
3. Perceived knowledge, education (Bacon said, "Knowledge is power.")
4. Access to information, insight
5. Occupational competence, skills, proficiency, experience
6. Legal or social status, rank or position
7. Authority position, sometimes called the honeymoon power, usually gained as a result of a new appointment—some leaders lose it as soon as they open their mouths!
8. Physical appearance, strength, well-being
9. Quasi-control or ownership of resources
10. Wealth, both real and assumed
11. Moral integrity, rectitude including preoccupation with ethics and religion
12. Affection, love, friendship, sex, intimacy
13. Political affiliation
14. Swapping other powers, reciprocity
15. Sheer luck
16. Multiple memberships in committees, task forces, councils, professional associations, boards, clubs and inner circles
17. Anonymity (remember Peter Sellers in the movie *Being There*)
18. Empowering
19. Skilful use of surprise events
20. Exceptional sacrifice

The process of empowering is to confer power through delegation, coaching, close association, shared knowledge, compliments or personal support. Generally, the act of empowering accrues to the initiator even more power through synergy. That is why power is not a zero-sum game, notwithstanding its relative and territorial nature. Many successful politicians and top government executives particularly in Germany and France rely greatly on the process of empowering to grow further.

However, we do not need to study world leaders to see the process of empowering at work. A brief look at our own organization's backyard would reveal managers at all levels who benefit immensely from empowering their own secretaries or executive assistants. Contrast these people with individuals who take little interest in their support staff. A significant difference in performance would not be surprising.

Executives can empower their junior staff simply by visibility, e.g. taking them to a board meeting. By the same token, political leaders can empower a newcomer to the party by being seen together at a press conference or a formal occasion. Here, the cost of empowering is marginal compared to its benefits.

When done proactively, the use of a recognized consultant can effectively empower the client and vice versa. It results in an exchange of "locked" energy which stimulates both and depletes neither, a sort of win-win spiritual encounter.

Each power base is a tangible asset which can develop, depreciate or be traded for another base. A good diagnosis of the perceptions of the dominant coalition and the potency of external forces helps to understand where the delicate balance of power lies.

5.6 Conclusion

The genuine use of power is the secret to effective leadership. However, its potential remains largely untapped by executives. Neglect of power or overreliance on it is a reason for managerial failures in endless situations. Power is a reality of our time that cannot be ignored.

In the absence of power, the decision-maker has several options. The first would be to cultivate it. But the process can be in vain when working against inelastic deadlines. The second would be to reach individuals with catalytic power. The third option is to explore other means of influence and control, the theme of the next chapter.

References and notes

1. A.E.A.: American Economic Association.
2. These notes on Poland date back to the first half of 1981.

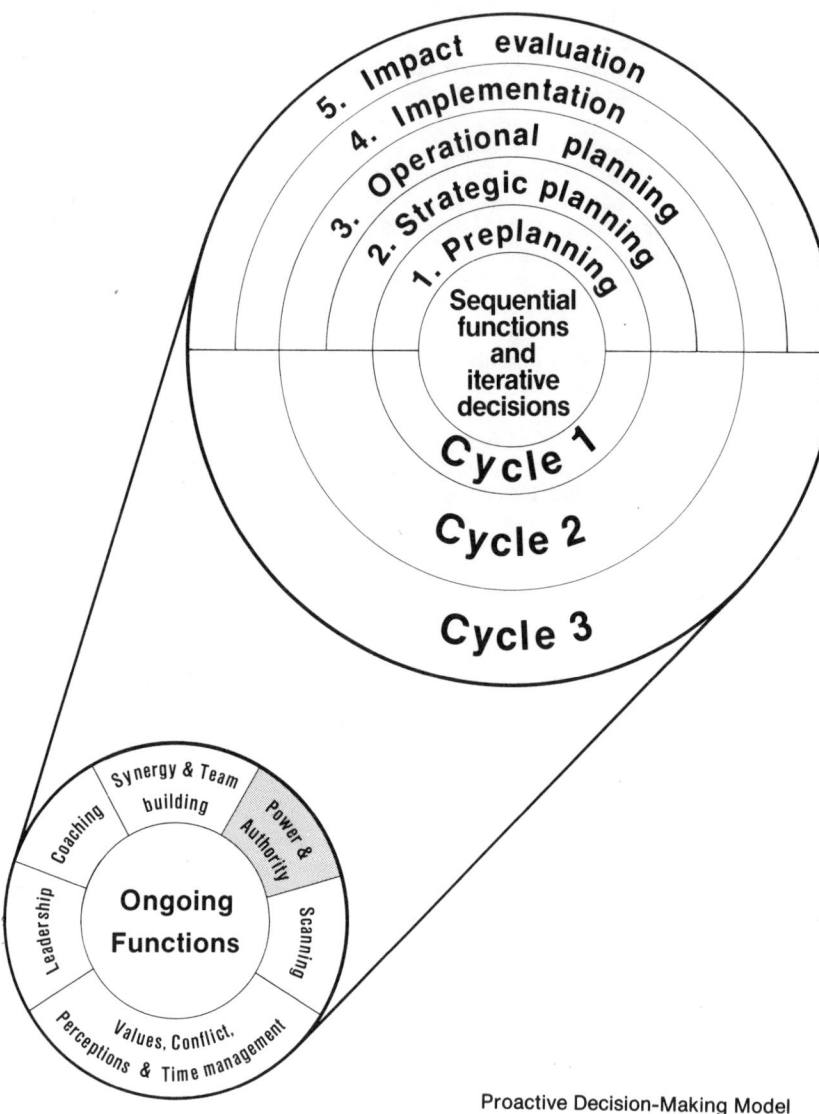

Proactive Decision-Making Model

Chapter six

Authority and rewards
(And other means of influence and control)

6.1 Means of influence and control

Control is the set of practices by which management attempts to ensure that policies and decisions are made and implemented. The process of control should strive to locate not only the data collection but also the interpretation mechanisms and evaluation systems as close as possible to the sources of information to minimize the traps of data reduction and the biases associated with converting descriptive data into inductive information. Both government and corporate auditors fail miserably when they underestimate the adverse consequences of deficient controls on people's behavior.

Control requires the careful understanding of behavior and a thorough diagnosis of the motivational state of the people to be controlled. To this end, several psychologists have spearheaded contemporary efforts to formulate the determinants of behavior. Among these, B.F. Skinner, Douglas McGregor, Abraham Maslow, Carl Rogers and Frederick Pearls have laid the foundations for current theories. Their contribution has been of inestimable help to political leaders and corporate strategists.

Judging from the discussions at recent Behavior Modification conferences and Gestalt symposia, control is a complex process. Practitioners differentiate between inner and outer determinants of behavior, which include the possibility of fulfillment of needs, cultural norms, environmental setting, perceptions of new opportunities and associated risks as well as the degree of self-awareness. What follows is a rather limited outline of alternative means of influence and control. More about the topic can be found in the chapter about Impact and Process Evaluation.

In the absence of power, organizations have sought and applied a great diversity of substitutes. They have used rewards, authority, education, socialization, information dissemination, data collection, measurements, feedback, isolation, self control and boundary management as mechanisms for motivation and influence. None is perfect. Some may be costly, others are difficult to live with in the long run.

6.2 Rewards

Management is responsible for designing adequate mechanisms to motivate and influence people and reward performance. Effective rewards have several characteristics. They should:

1. be perceived as relevant
2. be valued by the recipient
3. be based on merit where not only results, effort, work, risk, commitment, and knowledge are considered but also genuine collaboration with peers
4. be immediate or at least follow an effective schedule of reinforcement with variable rather than fixed intervals and ratios
5. be indexed to overcome the law of diminishing returns
6. be perceived as equitable and fair by others
7. foster a learning climate and collaboration
8. promote initiative and risk management (rather than risk avoidance)
9. deter inappropriate competition by using a fair penalty scheme

Management prerogative to differentiate rewards based on the above is being challenged by labor, equal opportunity advocates, personnel competition policies, collective agreements and compliance legislation. In many instances, the pressure was justified and corporate response has been commendable. However, other organizations facing unprecedented restrictions, are not merely responding to correct endemic inequities, they have surrendered their responsibility to enterprising consultants. Capitalizing on the issue, suppliers have packaged standard reward services. Originally, these limited distributive justice systems only attracted a few Fortune 500 companies. Now even governments are joining the bandwagon.

6.3 Authority

Authority is defined as the legitimate right to make policy and enforce decisions. A widely held misconception relates to the confusion between authority and power. Unaware of the dynamics of power, managers demand and receive more authority in the belief that a corresponding work improvement would result. This hypothesis is rarely upheld. In fact, sometimes the reverse is true.

The distinction between power and authority should be clearly understood to appreciate the magnitude of the problem. Authority is the "legal" right granted by the board of directors to manage an organizational unit. It is reflected in either the organization chart or the legislation. For instance, society gives parents authority over their children. In turn, the children "give" the parents the power. At the age of two, authority and power are compatible. The boundaries overlap. The parents are effective because they seem powerful. At the age of twelve, the young people may take away the power from the parents, making it difficult if not impossible to govern via authority alone.

Apart from legitimacy issues, political leaders and executives should establish the viability of authority before sanctioning a new structure or a management position. The question is: how much authority is necessary?

6.4 How much authority is necessary?

As conceptually indicated by Figures 6.1 and 6.2, the effectiveness of authority is inversely proportional to the degree of autonomy enjoyed by subordinates. Several examples will make it clear.

6.4.1 Where is total authority effective?

In a total dependence milieu like slavery, the master can effectively invoke authority and obtain full results. Historically, servicemen during war time have been in near-dependence situations. For instance, weekly leaves and honorable discharges are not rights, but privileges. The boundaries of individual privacy are severely limited. Obedience is expected. Survival requires discipline. With such virtual dependence on the goodwill of the hierarchy, authority is an appropriate means of control.

Likewise, in some remote regions of Canada, the lower mobility of staff and the limited opportunities account for the greater effectiveness of management authority. Remote cities depending almost totally on a single major employer have traditionally suffered the most, particularly when the employer is also a "benevolent" landlord offering a wide variety of social services.

Similarly in Japan, the employer's presence in the employee's day-to-day life outside the work place is significant. It includes provision of housing,

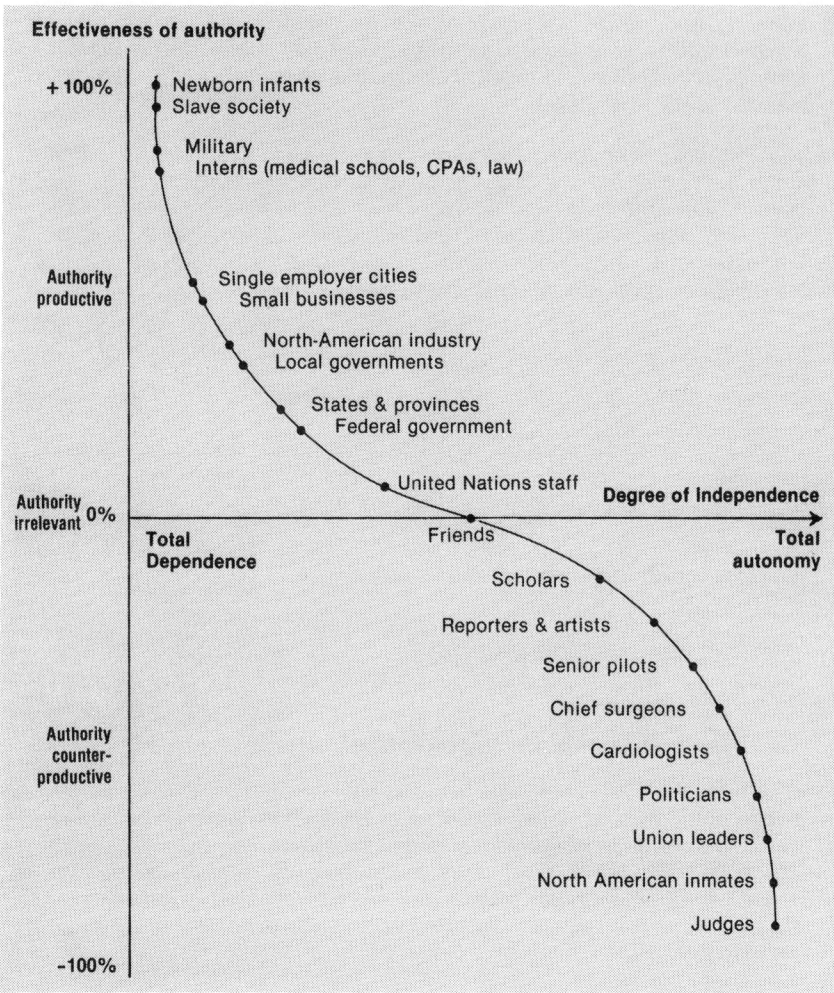

Figure 6.1: How effective is authority as a means of influence and control?

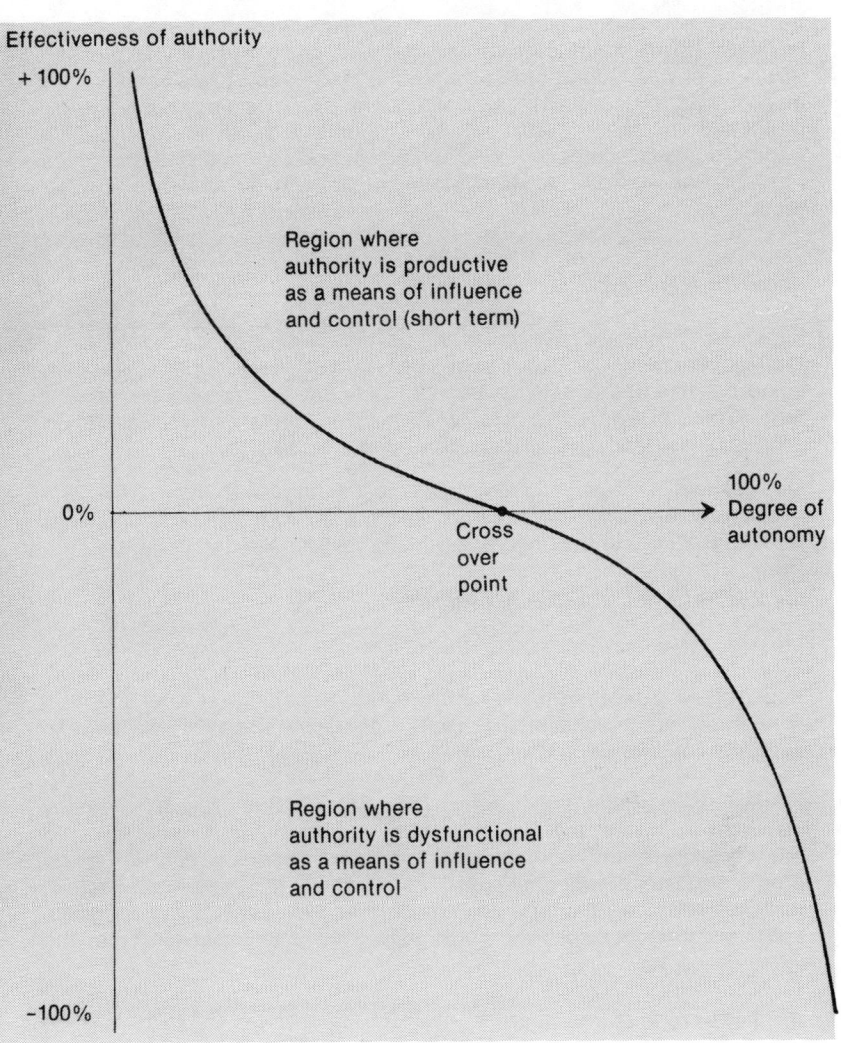

Figure 6.2: Authority and dependence — an overview

transportation, family health care, children's education, fitness, leisure facilities, travel, long term career planning and non-portable pension plans, all of which contribute to a greater dependence. Resignations are discouraged and are virtually nonexistent. Prospective employers are prohibited (by their federation) from offering incentives or attractive wages to promote mobility. Yet, as later indicated, Japanese managers rarely invoke authority in day-to-day decisions, even though it may be productive.

The exercise of authority can therefore be effective in an environment where the employee is completely dependent on the employer.

Paradoxically, we are now witnessing new forms of dependence, vis-à-vis local governments or even labor. Unions are now offering their own fringe benefits and pension plans. The rank and file members of United Auto Workers are buying into UAW pension plans and life insurance policies, a fact leading to greater control of membership.

Medical school interns, nurses, public accountants in training (CPA) and fresh graduates from law schools also put up with authority and near "starving" wages in the hope of getting professional recognition.

6.4.2 Where is it relatively effective?

Moving along the curve from the military to industry, we notice that authority is effective in fewer cases as means of influence and control. However, employees in the industrial sector are still more dependent on their employers than elsewhere. Tenure is not guaranteed. A challenge to authority could result in dismissal.

Further down, government employees enjoy more security. In many instances, the worst that can happen to a subordinate is not to be fired but transferred to another department and perhaps end up being promoted faster six months later! That is why authority is less effective, particularly among national governments and United Nations agencies. Local governments such as municipalities are somewhat closer to the industrial sector.

6.4.3 Where is it irrelevant?

Full university professors and artists are perhaps the least affected by the exercise of authority. Scholars keep doing their own things regardless of the mood of the administration. Chief executives like University of Cincinnati President Warren Bennis had to learn quickly to face this reality in order to excel.

As for married couples, women started on the top of the curve and are gradually moving down to the right despite the spouses' resistance!

What many men do not realize is that we are moving in the direction of full interdependence where authority is neither effective nor dysfunctional. That is precisely the position of close friends. We cannot use authority to influence friends. Any such attempt would not be taken seriously and would be laughed at. In fact, managers who are newly appointed over their peers often threaten their power base in seeking to assert their authority.

6.4.4 Where is it counterproductive?

The lower right quadrant depicts the area where authority is clearly dysfunctional. Any drive by a company president to use authority against union leadership could be counter-productive and may be strongly repelled. The same model applies to all classes of independent social systems including relations between nations.

6.5 Conclusion

The North American economy is rapidly shifting in the direction where subordinates are becoming increasingly independent from present bosses or indeed current jobs. This fact, however, does not imply that the use of authority is inadequate but, rather, that it should be preserved for situations where both the alternative means of influence and control would be inefficient, and the likelihood of obtaining results via authority is greater, i.e. when the *personal* needs of the subordinate are clearly linked to the issues at stake. The degree of authority vested in a manager should therefore not only be based on these needs but also on the appropriateness of authority in relation to other means such as power (Figure 6.3).

In summary, leaders wishing to use authority should look closely at means to increase dependence. However, authority is subject to the law of diminishing returns. As such, it is a scarce resource, to be used only when necessary. Its application is becoming progressively more difficult in educated and affluent societies. Even elsewhere, it should be the tool of last resort.

Fortunately there are alternatives, as seen earlier. The Japanese experience is enlightening. Despite the high degree of dependence between boss and subordinates, managers rarely, if ever, use authority. They strive to gain the respect of their staff and rely greatly on catalytic power and when necessary they can count on the "wise men" within the groups. The wise man is the Japanese equivalent of the European "Uncle", the North American "Godfather" or the devout *fan seng* (bonze) in China.

Think Proactive: New insights into decision-making

In exploring different means of influence and control, executives should look at the benefits, costs, time and other adverse consequences of each option and in the following sequence:

1 – Laissez-faire

2 – Share the facts (hard evidence, data)

3 – Unanimity

4 – Consensus

5 – Catalytic power

6 – Collaborative power

7 – Secret ballots

8 – Open votes

9 – Coercive power

10 – Authority (the immediate boss)

11 – Hierarchy (senior management)

12 – Arbitration

13 – Withdrawal (acceptance of loss)

14 – Forward-type ultimatum (combines conditional pardon with avoiding creation of precedent, e.g. Don't trespass again)

15 – Backward-type ultimatum (calls for withdrawal and compensation and provides a short grace period before the use of force)

16 – War!

Figure 6.3: Management styles and preferences

© Copyright, A.P. Martin, 1983   ISBN 0 86502 000 0

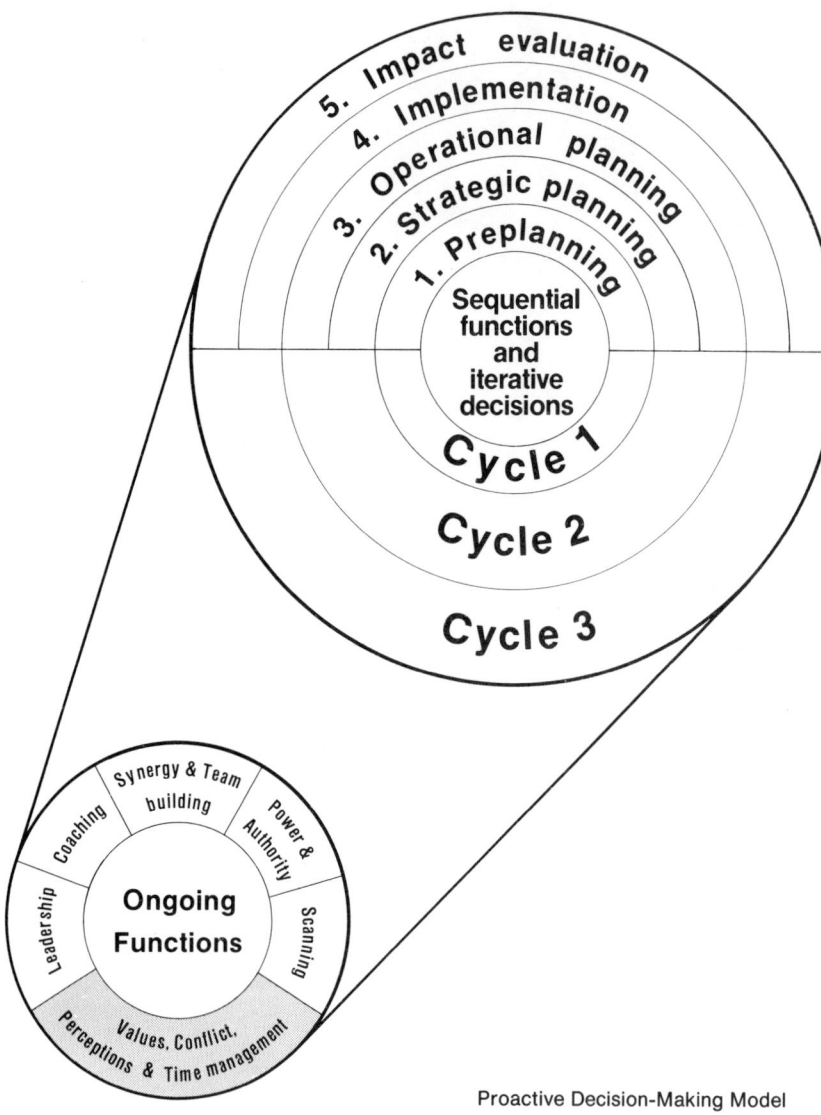

Proactive Decision-Making Model

Chapter seven

Conflict management

7.1 Essence of conflict

The traditional notion views conflict as bad, meaning its presence is undesirable. In modern organizations, conflicts are bound to emerge for several reasons. First, improved education and experience lead to a better appreciation and awareness of issue complexity. Education means choice. It brings to light a host of different ideas and options to deal with the same issue. Second, the greater the tolerance in moral and social values, the more likely that people will readily express differences openly. Third, the scarcity of resources prohibits organizations from adequately testing each promising option or responding simultaneously to all issues. For instance, the focus on maximum profits today means less capital investment for tomorrow. Fourth, the perceived need to respond promptly means that many decisions are based on imperfect knowledge. For all these reasons, conflicts are inevitable.

7.2 Productive conflict

Absence of conflict can lead to slavery. *Conflict can be viewed as energy.* Negative energy is potentially better than none. Energizing behavior can be real if conversion from negative to constructive energy is successful. Energy is commitment to results. It is required to move from the present to the future, i.e. to manage change.

Thus, the objective is to manage conflict instead of suppressing it. Being an organism in its own right, the organization requires antibodies to protect the integrity of its boundaries. To this end, there is a level of conflict that is necessary and sufficient to get results. That is the productive conflict.

The degree of desirable conflict is relative. Traditionally, both the level and intensity of conflict are very low at the beginning of a major assignment and increase gradually only as the implementation process takes place. This is an indication of poor planning. Ideally, management should promote productive conflicts early while the program is still in the planning stage. If the conflict is generated before the decision to implement, it can prevent heavy costs afterwards, particularly in high technology and capital construction investments where the so-called "project surgery" is a common practice.

7.3 When is conflict personal?

Rarely does a conflict start at the interpersonal level. However, poorly managed conflicts almost always end up being personal. What is viewed as a personal conflict between two decision-makers today may be a role conflict. In fact, new people in the same jobs will perhaps be in conflict six months later. Unless the role conflict is diagnosed and managed adequately, an intervention at the personal conflict level only masks the problem for a while until it resurfaces at a new plateau.

In either case, political leaders and corporate managers are ill-equipped to deal with personal conflicts. Not even psychologists agree on the best means of intervention. Gestaltists, psychoanalysts and behaviorists often use different models and prescriptions. The evidence of the real benefits of most interpersonal interventions is marginal at best. Our objective, therefore, is to get at the source of conflict. Luckily, our experience shows that the source is rarely interpersonal, even when perceived as such.

7.4 Need for accurate diagnosis

Not every conflict can be completely managed. There are situations which can only be addressed by deferring action or resigning oneself to the inevitable fact that nothing can be done about them. In either case, the mere *awareness* of the real characteristics and boundaries of the conflict can be a blessed relief in itself. It can spare leaders from endless futile work. Hence, it is imperative to devote sufficient attention to producing an accurate diagnosis. In complex issues, a problem well defined is half solved.

The case of a senior U.S. diplomat at the Vietnam peace negotiations in Paris exemplifies this. The American dignitary suffered a severe stomach pain and feared appendicitis, but when the doctor's diagnosis indicated it was indigestion, he was relieved and rushed to lunch in a three star

Parisian restaurant without even bothering with the prescription! With the diagnosis, the pain suddenly became manageable.

Unfortunately, the diagnosis phase is far too often overlooked. The author has faced countless situations where interventions were rushed in prematurely. The experiences often resulted in high opportunity costs.

7.5 How to diagnose conflict

Conflict diagnosis is complex. The mere act of proceeding with it can in itself create interpersonal problems for the unwary. Systemic methods can be useful, although it is doubtful that such technical approaches could thoroughly deal with social, behavioral and geopolitical issues.

The diagnosis starts with the formulation of perceptions from which the boundaries and the source(s) of conflict can be drawn.

7.5.1 Definition of the boundaries of perceptions

It is important to define how the conflict is perceived by the stakeholders and by third parties, if any. These include the 5F's defined previously, i.e. the family, the friends, the foreigners, the foes and the fools. To this end, separate observation grids can be drafted as a guide (Figure 7.1). The objective is to portray the perceptions of the conflict from multiple vantage points.

Vertically, the grid differentiates between the current and expected levels of each symptom. Within the current level, the perceived boundaries are formulated both when the problem exists and when it does not.

Horizontally, the grid categorizes each perceived dimension or symptom as illustrated below. The questions enunciated here are for general reference and should not be construed as either exhaustive or as essential in dealing with each conflict situation.

(a) The population

Describe the people involved in the issue when the problem exists and when it does not. Is the population homogeneous in its characteristics? What are the people's motivation, affiliation(s), power, authority, skills, culture, trust, previous functions? Who sits where? Who is missing? Who seems to be unwelcome? If a skill deficit exists, how is it perceived? What information is held by each party in conflict? What is their past experience? Who is perceived to be family, friend, foreigner, foe and fool? What should these perceptions be?

Think Proactive: New insights into decision-making

Problem characteristics & boundaries	Actual level when problem is		acceptable level
	present	absent	
Population Participants & stakeholders (Family, friends, foreigners, foes, fools)			
Location Space, motion, vectors, etc.			
Time Duration, frequency, order, time, urgency			
Communications Verbal, non verbal			
Agenda Published & hidden agenda, priorities, options, sequence			
Environment Degree of change, surprise events, change agents			
Stakes Rewards, penalties, risks, perceptions			
Dissatisfaction Degree of resistance, choice			

Figure 7.1: Observation grid — conflict diagnosis

© Copyright, A.P. Martin, 1983

ISBN 0 86502 000 0

(b) The place

In what location, climate and general environment does the problem occur? Where does it seem *not* to occur? What other factors are involved (music, movement, noise, etc.)? What is the shape and structure of the furniture and equipment used for meetings? What informal meeting places contribute to the perceived conflict? What is the architecture of the office space?

(c) The time

When does the conflict seem to occur and *not* to occur? Specify the duration of the symptom, the frequency, the time period (regular hours, night shift, Monday 9 a.m., Friday 4 p.m., pay days, performance review days, contract cancellation days, etc.). Indicate the longevity of the conflict, the frequency of contact, the perceived urgency and the response time.

Is the time itself perceived to be an issue in the conflict? Since when? What changes have taken place in the population, the location, the agenda, the stakes or the dissemination of information recently? Break the new time-cycle into discrete subsets and compare with the pre-change equivalent or similar situations elsewhere (e.g. competitors, other regions). Is the conflict over a deadline, a schedule, a waiting period? If so, what are the priorities and available resources?

The misperception of time is an abundant source of dysfunctional conflict throughout the western world, particularly in North America. The fast pace of living and the knowledge of what technology can do impose rigid and sometimes unrealistic demands on business and service providers.

How far is the work along its life-cycle and how early was the conflict perceived as dysfunctional?

(d) The communications network

What verbal and non-verbal information is exchanged? What efforts are mobilized to give and seek information, opinion, advice and feedback? What is the degree of participation? What decision-making mode is used when the problem is present? Is absent? How much conformism exists and how much is expected? What is the level of inappropriate competition? What is the degree of hostility? Is it cognitive? How is the conflict discussed, if at all? When? What response was originally formulated? What subsequent reaction was observed?

(e) The agenda

Which agenda seems to bring conflict? Which does not? What is the difference between the actual and the expected agenda? How are priorities set? What sequencing of events or topics facilitates or worsens matters? As an example, when performance review and objective setting are discussed during the same meeting, the poor performer tends to spend so much energy on challenging the negative feedback that he or she pays little if any attention to the objective setting exercise.

(f) The work environment

Has a surprise event taken place recently? Who is reacting? Is work characterized by constant and rapid change? What is the frequency of change? What is the legitimacy of the change? Define the source of change. Are the changes essential, important, desirable or merely nice to have? Are they urgent? Who approves the changes? How far are the decision-makers from the performers?

(g) The stakes

What are the perceived and actual risks when the problem occurs and when it does not? Did management stage a seminar, a demonstration or a pilot project to remove the misperception of risk? Who stands to lose or gain the most? Is the loss or gain related to self-image? How is the present behavior reinforced or discouraged?

What are the valued rewards and the actual compensations? Are the rewards and penalties perceived to be equitable, fair or excessive? How is collaboration rewarded?

(h) The level of resistance or dissatisfaction

The perceived dissatisfaction or severity of the conflict should be assessed. Severity can be inferred from the degree of *resistance*. Resistance is often defined as an interpersonal interference or a barrier stalling a movement in a certain direction. It is preferable to view it as a consequence of *choice denial*.

Traditionally, the resisting force is seen as a saboteur to be removed to facilitate the movement of the driving force toward a "right" direction. Yet, what is perceived as an interference may well be a dormant creative force. This strength can be positively energized if brought into contact with new information, skills, attitudes, people, experiments or altered boundaries. Alternatively, the resisting force may exceed the decision-maker in the degree of awareness. Even worse, reality may be an elusive phenomenon which neither possesses! Is the change really desirable?

From whose perspective? If so, could the readiness for change be increased by managing the level of dissatisfaction with the current state of affairs?

7.5.2 Boundaries and source(s) of conflict

The questions addressed so far have in the past contributed to shedding light on the deficit between perceptions and reality. Should further diagnosis be required, this section outlines a process which may assist to locate precisely the boundaries and source(s) of conflict.

The data derived from the perceptions analysis step are often invaluable in drawing the boundaries of the conflict. For instance, Figure 7.2 looks at the population boundaries and distinguishes several levels: individual, dyad, tryad, group, intergroup, organization, clientele, community and intercommunity. The higher the boundary (i.e. the farther to the right of the figure), the less likely that the conflict can be adequately diagnosed and managed. A dyad denotes a special group of two people, e.g. boss and secretary, buyer and seller, teacher and student, doctor and patient, husband and wife, pilot and co-pilot, coach and athlete.

The source of conflict is sought starting from the top of Figure 7.3. Each possible source should be analyzed. Again, the farther down the source is, the less likely that the conflict can be diagnosed and managed.

Both the boundaries and the source(s) of conflict should be combined in grid format as indicated in Figure 7.4. The content should be reviewed with a third party and other significant people. There is rarely a single cause of conflict. An attempt to identify the driving and the restraining forces of conflict should be made prior to engaging in intervention planning and implementation. Force-field analysis can be used to this end.[1]

7.6 Conflict management

Following the above diagnosis, it is possible to explore interventions which can be either etiologic, symptomatic or both. An etiologic intervention either removes the cause(s) of the counterproductive conflict or maintains it when it is productive. The success of etiologic interventions is confined to conflicts diagnosed close to the north west corner of Figure 7.4. There are instances where the manager has to resort to a symptomatic intervention particularly when the issue is diagnosed close to the south east corner.

Think Proactive: New insights into decision-making

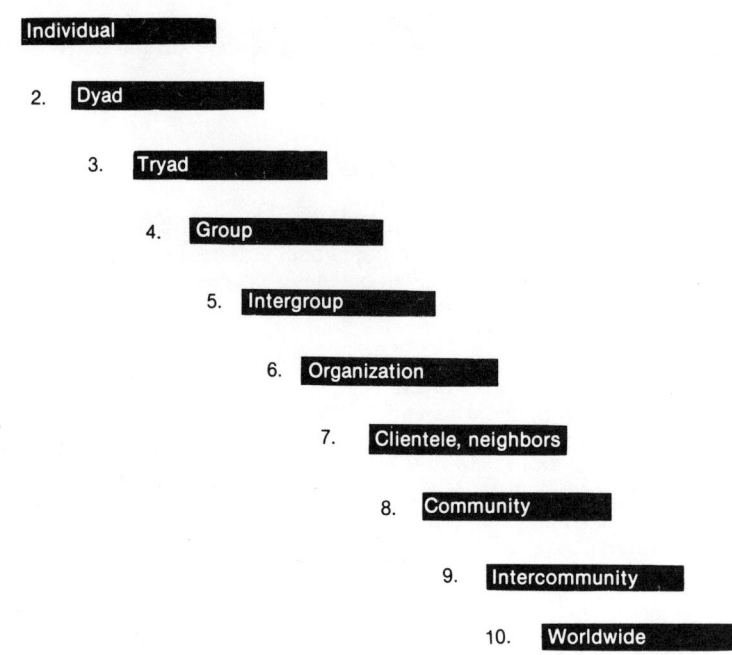

Figure 7.2: Diagnosis of conflict boundaries — the population parameter

Symptomatic interventions will be discussed in the chapter about perception management. Etiologic management of conflicts includes three options: escalation, de-escalation and reinforcement.

Escalation is necessary when the level of conflict is too low to be productive and de-escalation when it is too high. Reinforcement is the process of stabilizing and actively maintaining a productive conflict at a desirable level.

The means of conflict management are almost infinite. The existing driving and restraining forces identified above can be carefully influenced. Alternatively, a new force could be introduced. However, as in physics, every action to move a social system is met with a reaction to maintain the status quo. It is often easier to work smoothly on existing forces prior to applying a new force. As an example, a partial list of

Checklist for Conflict Diagnosis

1. **Mission, superordinate goals & objectives**
   - Lack of explicit agreement on mission, objectives, priorities, urgency
   - Unset or ambiguous goals, fuzzy objectives
   - Mutually exclusive objectives

2. **Role**
   - Poor allocation of responsibilities
   - Conflicting demands or expectations being made by others. e.g. persons **A** and **B** make demands on person **C** which are in conflict, so, if **C** does what **A** expects, he/she will not do what **B** expects
   - Overload: too many expectations of what the person can do
   - Ambiguous definition of job expectations
   - Turf conflicts: disagreement about a job definition

3. **Process**
   - **Decisions** based on status, rather than on location of information and expertise
   - Indirect or poorly timed **communication** about decisions, issues, events; semantic difficulties, distortion; untested assumptions about both agreements and/or disagreements over goals and roles
   - Excessive knowledge of the "opponent"
   - **Reactive** rather than **Proactive** problem solving

4. **Structure, reward system**
   - Poor reporting relationships, interdependencies, reward/punishment system, e.g. when one constituency gains at the other's expense
   - Dependence of multiple groups on a common pool of scarce resources
   - Large organizational group size
   - High degree of specialization and heterogeneity of staff
   - Unequal power/authority balance

5. **Cultural expectations**
   - Ethnic norms, values, belief systems, religions, racial integration, political affiliations and sexual attitudes

6. **Interpersonal climate**
   - Self esteem, status satisfaction
   - Personal attitudes and values
   - Clashes in styles: competitive versus coercive versus collaborative power
   - Differences in approaching problems, e.g. inductive versus deductive

7. **Personality**
   - Behavior, attitude, feelings

Figure 7.3: Sources of conflict
(Compiled with the help of Dr. Kenneth Pollock, Columbia University)

Think Proactive: New insights into decision-making

Problem \ Level	Indi-vidual	Dyad	Group	Inter-group	Organi-zation	Com-munity
1. Superordinate goals Mission Objectives Priorities						
2. Allocation of work role Responsibilities Overload Different expectations						
3. Process/methods — Decision location — Communication — Problem solving						
4. Structure — Reporting — Authority, power — Reward, punishment — Dependencies — Degree of specialization						
5. Cultural — Ethnic norms, values — Belief system — Racial/political affiliation						
6. Interpersonal climate — Respect — Attitude — Styles — Behavior						

Figure 7.4: Conflict diagnosis grid
This exhibit combines selected elements of Figures 7.2 and 7.3.

© Copyright, A.P. Martin, 1983   ISBN 0 86502 000 0

conflict management interventions is provided in Figure 7.5. These interventions should not be considered unless a thorough diagnosis has been performed.

An outline of the preceding steps has been summarized in Figure 7.6.

References and notes

1. A.P. Martin: Validating Perceptions in Issue Management, PDI Press, 1981.

Think Proactive: New insights into decision-making

Figure 7.5: Potential interventions in conflict management

Conflict within acceptable level or productive conflict?

High conflict? Potential interventions to de-escalate excessive conflict

Source is GOAL

CONSIDER REINFORCEMENT

1. Authentic confrontation
2. Interface planning (awareness)
3. Multiattribute utility
4. Delphi
5. Consensus on superordinate goals
6. Reduce intermediate goals
7. Interdependence grids & strategies
8. Power (Catalytic, collaborative, coaching)
9. Compromise
10. Change rewards/penalties
11. Smoothing
12. Authority
13. Arbitration
14. Symptomatic intervention (perceptions)

Source is ROLE

1. Increase feedback, action research
2. Authentic confrontation
3. Responsibility charting (awareness)
4. Negotiate role boundaries
5. Reward cooperation
6. Reduce vetoes
7. Increase support
8. Liaison roles (intermediaries)
9. Switching or role rotation
10. Task forces
11. Power
12. Authority
13. Arbitration, Imaging
14. Perception management

Source is PROCESS

1. Increase feedback, action research
2. Consider laissez faire (selective)
3. Coaching
4. Synergy, team building
5. Encourage distributive leadership
6. Relocate decisions
7. Reduce dissatisfaction
8. Improve communication channels
9. Switch roles
10. Power
11. Avoidance
12. Authority
13. Transactional analysis
14. Symptomatic intervention (temporary)
15. Imaging

Source is STRUCTURE

1. Move control points to sources of information
2. Responsibility charting
3. Increase feedback, action research
4. Confrontation
5. Consider selective laissez faire
6. Cluster conflicting teams under the same hierarchy (interdependence)
7. Consider partial autonomy of selected performers
8. Power (Catalytic, collaborative)
9. Adapt the span of control
10. Improve rewards/penalties
11. Publish succession plan
12. Smoothing, compromise
13. Temporary structures
14. Encourage sponsorship
15. Change leadership (switch roles)
16. Expand resources
17. Avoidance
18. Symptomatic intervention (short term)
19. Appeal system
20. Ombudsman

Source is CULTURE

1. Power (Catalytic, natural leaders)
2. Increase feedback, action research
3. Buffer zones, avoidance
4. Reward cooperation, penalize competition
5. Increase interdependence (Reduce dependence)
6. Encourage sabbaticals
7. Arbitration
8. Symptomatic treatment
9. Imaging
10. Confrontation
11. Forced collaboration, authority (Courts)

Source is INTERPERSONAL

1. Awareness of own polarities (Gestalt)
2. Feedback, action research, Zen
3. Coaching
4. Renegotiate boundaries, Compromise
5. Compatibility tests (FIRO-B, SDI, etc.)
6. Short sabbaticals, special assignment
7. Role models
8. Catalytic power
9. Rewards/penalties (behavior, attitude)
10. Confrontation
11. Creative conflict resolution (Gestalt)
12. Transfer, avoidance, withdrawal
13. Desensitization (!), smoothing
14. Authority
15. Imaging
16. Symptomatic intervention

Conflict management

Source is ROLE
1. Increase feedback
2. Responsibility charting
3. Coaching
4. Negotiate role boundaries
5. Promote confrontation
6. Reduce liaison role
7. Consider role switching

...
5. Synergy, team building
6. Increase intermediate goals
7. Stress adverse consequences
8. Relax penalty schemes
...
12. Power (Catalytic, collaborative)
13. Authority
14. Manage perceptions (symptomatic)

Source is PROCESS
1. Increase feedback
2. Promote confrontation
3. Responsibility charting
4. Synergy, team building
5. Produce Hawthorne and maintain effect
6. Power (Catalytic, collaborative)
7. Coaching
8. Relocate decisions

8. Power (Catalytic, Collaborative)
9. Reduce autonomy, increase dependence
10. Reduce support resources
11. Increase vetoes
12. Reward collaboration
13. Manage perceptions

Source is STRUCTURE
1. Move control location to information sources
2. Increase feedback
3. Responsibility charting
4. Consider selective laissez faire
5. Decrease authority
6. Coaching
7. Publish or improve succession plan
8. Manage perceptions (symptomatic)
9. Consider management by rules
10. Consider span of control

8. Increase dissatisfaction with the status quo
9. Revise communication channels
10. Voting
11. Transactional analysis
12. Flooding
13. Manage perceptions

Source is CULTURE
1. Increase feedback, action research
2. Catalytic power
3. Produce Hawthorne & maintain effect
4. Use cultural polarities
5. Increase interdependence, remove buffer zones

11. Relocate decision points (functional or program change)
12. Power (Catalytic, collaborative)
13. Change leadership
14. Change rewards/penalties
15. Disperse cooperating teams
16. Cluster conflicting units
17. Temporary systems
18. Task forces
19. Matrix

Source is INTERPERSONAL
1. Awareness skills development (Gestalt)
2. Increase feedback (action research)
3. Coaching
4. Change boundaries
5. Compatibility tests
6. Produce Hawthorne & maintain effect

6. Use cross cultural scanning, study tours, social encounters
7. Reward healthy conflict, tolerate restrained confrontation
8. Capitalize on surprise events
9. Manage perceptions

Source is PERSONAL

SEEK PROFESSIONAL GUIDANCE

7. Increase level of dissatisfaction with the status quo
8. Transactional power
9. Transactional analysis
10. Reward healthy conflict
11. Encourage risk

Low conflict?

Potential interventions to escalate insufficient conflict

These interventions can be useful in dealing with conflict. Often a number should be combined either concurrently or serially to get results.

© Copyright, A.P. Martin, 1983   ISBN 0 86502 000 0

Figure 7.6: The Process of Conflict Diagnosis and Intervention

Scanning

1
Dissatisfaction
Tension/Hostility
Frustration
Failure to reach goals

3
Identify specific incidents which may have led to situation (tension)

2
Test and challenge

4
Draft observation grid (Figure 7.1)

Diagnosis

5
Diagnose & draft conflict diagnosis worksheet (Figure 7.4)

7
Experiment (force field analysis)
Probable sources
Assumptions
Design test
Predict outcomes
Predict side effects
Contingency plan
Test & measure
Match most likely cause
Evaluate, verify, explain

6
Graph conflict trend over task life-cycle
Normative model
— Standard desirable
— Mini/maximum expected over task life-cycle
— Check trends in approach avoidance patterns

8
Generalize
Integrate cause(s) & effect(s)
Deviation from norm(s)
Formulate the problem(s)

Intervention

9
Objectives
Acceptable/desirable
Resources, results
Performance indicators
Methods of evaluation

12
Decision
Priorities
(essential, nice to have)
Action plan
Anticipated problems
Contingency plan
Critical mass
Commitment plan
Prework
Responsibility chart
Due dates (milestones)
Controls

10
Alternative interventions (Figure 7.5)
Adverse consequences
Transition side-effects

13
Implementation/transition
Intervention management
— Interfaces
— Adverse effects
— Monitor
— Control

11
Rank options strategies

14
Termination/succession

Evaluation

15
Evaluation
Analysis
Synthesis
Lessons learned
Sharing feedback
Corrective action

16
Post work
Debriefing
Gatekeeping
Feedback to information sources.
If no feedback, explain why not

© Copyright, A.P. Martin, 1983

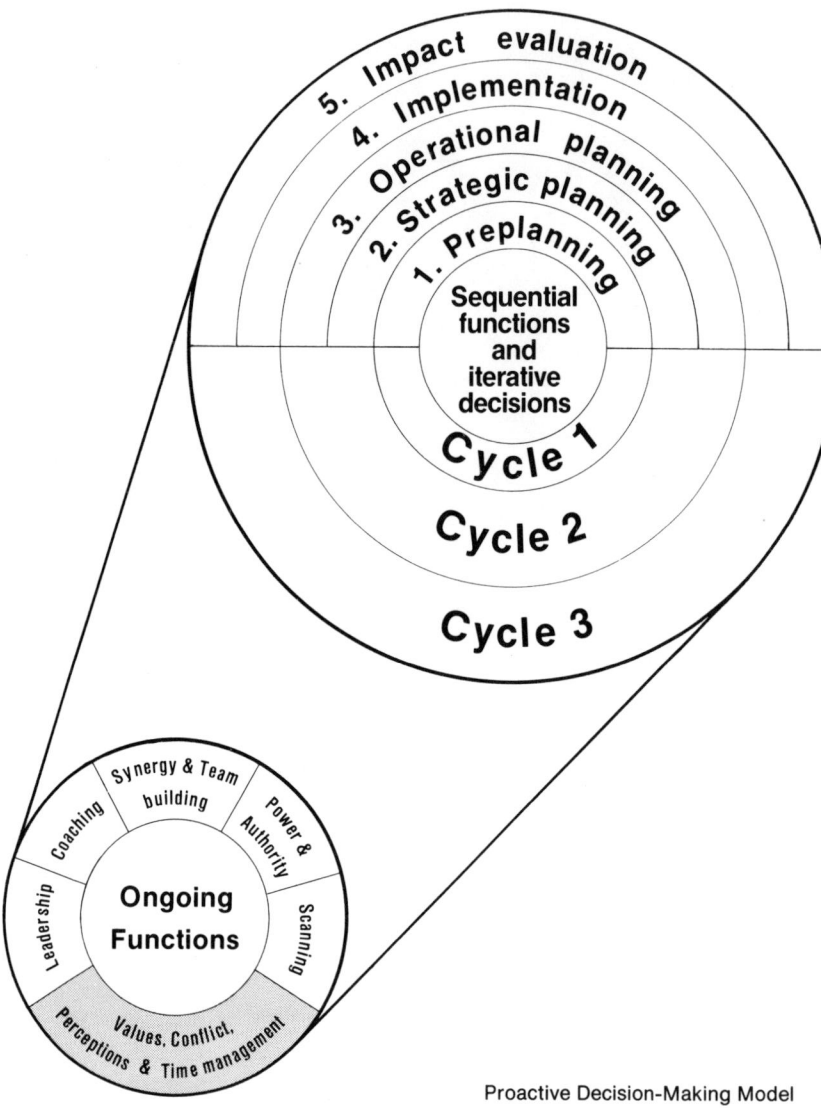

Proactive Decision-Making Model

Chapter eight

Perception and value management

8.1 The need for perception management

For decision-makers, working hard and achieving the best results in program or issue management is a necessary but not sufficient condition for excelling. The stakeholders do not take corporate management effort for granted. Their perceptions should be effectively managed. Otherwise, the program future and even the survival of the executive may be unfairly jeopardized, particularly as a result of surprise events (eg. elections, reorganizations, cutbacks, crises, accidents, etc.).

Managing perceptions should be done ethically. It should not be a shelter system for poor policies. Moreover, it should maintain a high standard of behavior with no tolerance for lies while the demand for the truth should be non-negotiable and above all other concerns.

8.2 Perception management is in!

To appear or not to appear, that is a key question in the inner corporate circles today. Airports, banks, plants, hotels, TV studios, hospitals, shopping centres and even correctional institutions are being renovated (or accredited) to either gain or maintain the confidence of the consumer and other relevant stakeholders. For many, the pay-off is real in market share, profit, staff relations, consumer satisfaction and consequently dividends. A well orchestrated perception management program energizes staff behavior to achieve worthwhile objectives. When these objectives are valued and perceived to be meaningful, people are prepared to sacrifice short term gains and to compromise on some personal goals.

Until recently, governments have not been good at perception management. Some outstanding world leaders such as Valéry Giscard d'Estaing, Lester B. Pearson, Jimmy Carter and Austrian born U.N. Secretary Kurt Waldheim have ignored it at their peril. Now the change is noticeable. Considering the growing importance of this developing area, a few examples will help to illustrate the practice of perception management.

8.3 Walt Disney production

Disneyworld in Florida and Disneyland in California have spearheaded this movement in the industrial world. Patrons are not only entertained, they are taken care of. Time goes by almost unnoticed. Monorail stations are strategically structured to ensure a continuous flow of people. Each segment of the waiting corridor is "bombarded" gently with a wealth of differentiated and useful messages. General information is given at the entrance of the corridor and specific data about the next train station's entertainment activities are broadcast just prior to the end of the waiting line. Staff are trained to maintain a fast pace of change. The rate at which events are unfolding at Disney makes it difficult for patrons to find the time to think. The elaborate staffing policies, professional development programs and project control system account for the company's success.

At Disneyworld, the introduction of E.P.C.O.T.[2] is expected to be a professional masterpiece in perception management and an excellent opportunity for executives to study the process.

8.4 Misperception of technical excellence

In the mid-seventies, a railway company introduced a computerized system to control wheel friction and replace the manual sand dispensers on its locomotives. The new system was automatic and did not require human intervention. Accustomed to pushing the sand button for years, many locomotive engineers mistakenly feared the loss of control and perceived the system as a safety hazard. They complained—legitimately, but in vain. Designers found the grievances unsubstantiated.

Within a few weeks, systematic obstruction of the automated sand dispensers appeared on the horizon. A technologically proven system was the victim of misperceptions and poor implementation strategies. The issue had to be managed promptly.

Perception and value management

Management decided to withdraw the new system and return to the manual sand dispensers to regain the employees trust while a confidential small-scale experiment was authorized. A small sample of locomotives was equipped with both a hidden automatic system and a dummy manual dispenser which was not actually operational. Unaware of the existence of the new system, the experimental group of locomotive engineers continued to use the dummy manual dispenser without ever noticing the difference. Information about the placebo effect was shared with union representatives and local management who had to undertake the sensitive and difficult task of perception disconfirmation.

This is an example where management of perceptions was reactive rather than proactive. Had the designers used Proactive Management in the first place, the implementation would have been much smoother. Both objective and perceived validity would have been considered legitimate *bona fide* issues at the design and implementation stages. A pilot experiment followed by a gradual step by step implementation would have built a critical mass.

The decision-makers could have explored options for voluntary participation in the experiment with a specific reward scheme for the duration of the pilot project. They could have approached either locomotive engineers with a high readiness for change, newcomers to the job, drivers of newly introduced locomotives, or the veterans, i.e. the senior employees in the job with catalytic power. The chances for commitment would have certainly been greater.

8.5 The case of a North American airline company

The client agreed to share with readers the lessons learned from this experience as long as the airline identity and privileged statistical information were not disclosed. Thus, for the purpose of this illustration only, the airline shall be called Activair and the processing time for arriving passengers will be eight minutes.

The Vice-President of Passenger Services received an unprecedented number of complaints from disembarking passengers in Houston airport. Nearly all customers seemed quite satisfied with Activair services throughout the United States except for the unbearable luggage processing time at this one airport. The Vice-President first sought the assistance of the airport transportation authority, but in vain. The Department of Transport "could not understand the passengers complaints since a modern terminal at the airport was dedicated to Activair."

Subsequently, the Vice-President called on in-house support to diagnose the problem and recommend the best intervention. The system analysts took the complaint letters, from which they derived the project objective: "speed up the passenger processing cycle." They formed a small team with representatives from operations research, engineering and transportation planning, then spent a few weeks shopping for alternatives. The team recommended more automation and a greater clustering of luggage expediting crews.

The Vice-President reluctantly authorized the team to test the proposal for a month. The results could not have been worse. Complaints from disembarking passengers skyrocketed and staff grievances went up. Labor reported intolerable stress and high pressure created by the new luggage processing network. Some employees even threatened to quit should the new system's life span go beyond the month test period.

The speed at which the adverse consequences of the experiment unfolded reinforced the Vice-President's suspicion about the validity of the experiment. Activair's reputation was at stake. He approached the author when it became abundantly clear that in-house experts had failed to deal with the issue.

In reviewing the complaint letters, it appeared that most complaints originated from a dozen short haul morning flights which terminated in Houston Intercontinental Airport about eight o'clock weekdays. Two associates were posted at the aiport to observe passengers behavior and time precisely the cycle which started with the plane arrival and finished when the first piece of luggage appeared on the carousel. Luggage processing time was averaging eight minutes nearly every observation day.

The data seemed within the accepted processing time standard of local U.S. flights as well as U.S. bound transborder flights originating from Canada, which are not subject to customs and immigration control at the destination points. In order to further validate the data, the associates discretely spent two mornings at the competing airline terminals and reported similar findings with respect to overall processing time but a sharp contrast in passenger behavior. Most passengers seemed satisfied with the luggage processing procedures.

This finding led to the breakdown of the passenger processing cycle into two discrete subsets: walking time from the gate to the carousel and waiting time at the carousel. While the total cycle was the same, the competitors' old terminals required nearly seven minutes walking time and one minute wait at the carousel. Our client's new terminal permitted the passengers to reach the carousel in about a minute, only to spend the remaining seven minutes waiting. The business rush hour made the perception of waiting time even worse. The solution was forthcoming.

A week long experiment was conducted. The eight o'clock passengers were dropped at one end of the terminal and a carousel was allocated on the opposite end. The escalator speed was slightly reduced and the expediters were instructed to turn on the carousel regardless of whether it was empty or not when the first passenger arrived. It took approximatively six minutes for the first passenger to get to it. The complaints ended. With the reallocation of gates, neither automation nor staff clustering was required.

The first intervention took the passengers' complaints at face value and drafted the objectives while the last intervention had to validate the collected data as well as the objectives through observations and comparative analysis before completing the diagnosis. *A symptomatic treatment was necessary and sufficient,* that is, the intervention had to deal with the passengers' misperceptions of time.

8.6 The bank story

Within weeks after automating personal chequing and savings in Los Angeles, a major Californian bank noticed a positive response from clients in all but one branch, which was located in an industrial district in the San Fernando Valley. The branch staff nicknamed Friday "Disaster Day". Deposits and withdrawals made a quantum jump upwards while the on-line cheque processing cycle, which usually stood at three seconds, approximated thirty seconds on pay days.

The client population, composed mostly of laborers, found the new system's waiting time unacceptable considering the short lunch break and the distance from the factory. Some complained to the branch manager, others closed their accounts and went to the competitor just across the street.

The branch manager summoned the headquarters' systems analysts to speed up response time. The computer people found that Friday's arrival rate of customers had a skewed Poisson distribution, a sort of turnpike effect. They reported that the solution would require a much larger computer at a prohibitive cost. The manager was not satisfied so she called for outside help.

While giving a seminar in Los Angeles, the author was asked informally to advise. To this end, the branch manager was requested to collect data about customer behavior at the nearby competitor's branch which, incidently, was not computerized. Processing time was found to be twice as high but since the cashier was perceived busy all the time, the customers seemed more tolerant than at the client branch where the cashier stood still in front of the terminal for 30 seconds! Again, the customer's perception of time was the issue. Symptomatic treatment was imperative.

In considering several options, the author remembered a similar situation discussed a couple of years earlier at M.I.T. Endicott House with Mr. Myron B. Deily, senior Vice-President of the Republican National Bank of Texas. Deily reported a Mexican branch which used closed circuit TV with Walt Disney cartoons to entertain customers while waiting. Apparently the system was so popular that some customers stayed in the bank a few minutes after being serviced to see the end of the cartoon! Our recommended option combined several features.

The clocks were replaced by green display terminals which gave the time, the weather forecast, the latest sports scores, publicity and interest rates on deposits. Waiting lines were combined into a single line feeding all tellers. Two TV monitors were installed conspicuously in the waiting area. Finally, a partition was erected between the counters and the terminals making the terminal invisible to the customers.

The cashier was therefore always perceived to be busy. With the green displays and the TV monitors, the "demand" for customer time was high. Soon complaints went down significantly and the whole system became a sort of drawing card. The bank popularity went up significantly, a fact which certainly contributed to its increased profitability. As for the on-line banking system, it remained unchanged.

8.7 Management of values

Values are *paradigms;* that is, norms and patterns of beliefs governing our attitudes and behavior. They are in constant transition. Among the major transition forces are peer groups, advertising, technology (e.g. jet set values), institutions, economic conditions and surprise events. In management, nothing could be more mistaken than to consider issues in technoeconomic terms and disregard the profound impact of values. The management of technology is inseparable from the sociopolitical challenges which increasingly confront organizations. Most values are not ordained. They are temporal, relative, territorial and controversial. The controversy may be due to cultural and emotional biases.

Integrity is the positive and most highly regarded value of political leaders and executives. As R. Buckminster Fuller said: "If we do not comprehend and behave spontaneously with the highest, most unselfish integrity, I think man may readily not make it on this particular planet". Successful leaders have a clear idea about their values and the degree to which they are prepared to compromise. Their decisions are mission-driven and often transcend ideologies.

For two decades, Jean Drapeau, the Mayor of Montreal, cultivated an on-going businesslike relationship not only with all federal and provincial Cabinets in power but with the opposition parties as well, regardless of their ideology. Maynard Jackson acted likewise in Atlanta. Proactive leaders are empathic. They are clearly aware of social systems boundaries and have the flexibility and the capability to relate to different value systems.

8.8 Conclusion

The last two chapters provided an overview of the proactive approach to the management of conflict, perceptions and values. These three areas are suffering from the handicaps of social transitions. They are an essential part of every leader's job and should be viewed whenever possible, as an opportunity to excel rather than as a permanent problem to be solved.

References and notes

1. E.P.C.O.T.: Environmental Prototype for the Study of the Community of Tomorrow.

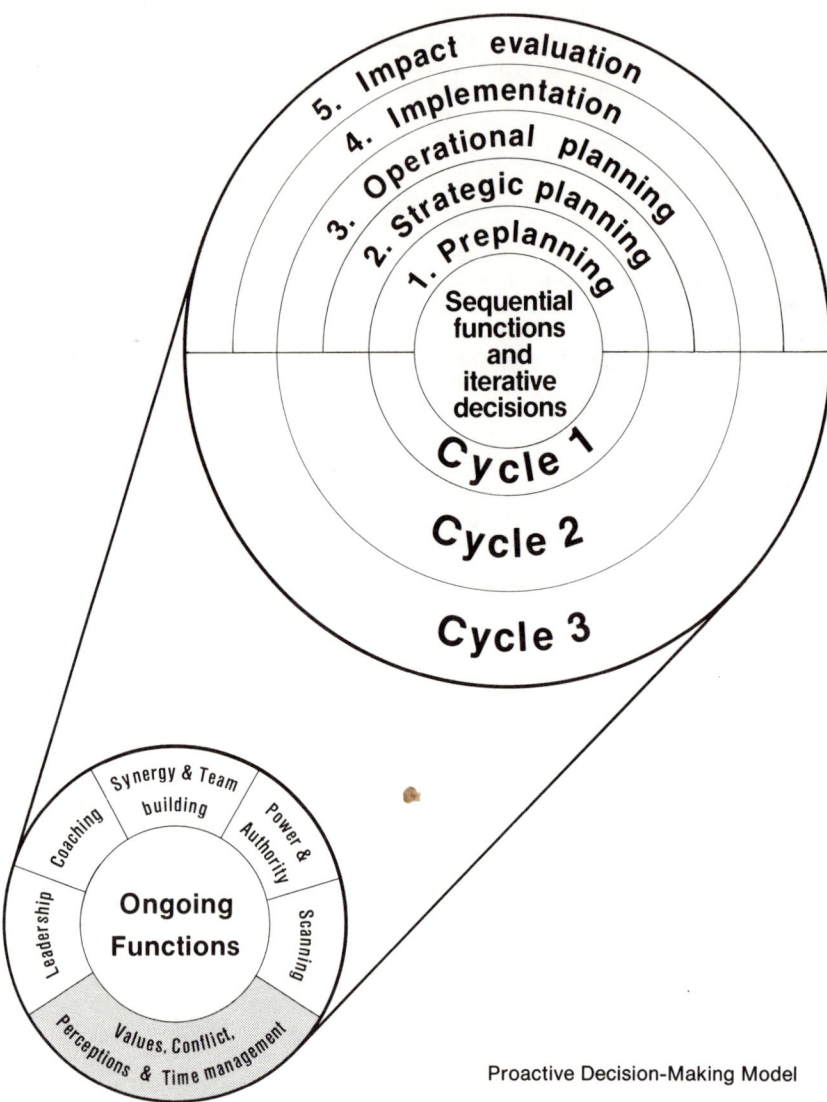

Proactive Decision-Making Model

Chapter nine

Time management

9.1 Introduction

Peter Drucker[1] and Bill Oncken[2] marked a turning point in time management. Until the sixties, the focus on managing time was marginal. Accelerated growth, a booming economy and adequate supply of resources made the steady wastage of management time tolerable. On the eve of the seventies, clouds began to appear on the horizon. Today, major shifts in values combined with a host of new and ambiguous issues have taxed the demand for management time beyond limits. Drucker and Oncken were timely. They at least contributed to a new awareness about the unique characteristics of time management.

9.2 Daily time management

Symptoms of poor time management can still be seen nearly everywhere. These include recurrent crises, overstaffing, stretched meetings, drop-in visitors, and a general maldistribution of efforts toward results. Although the problem is basic, elaborate recipe books have polluted organizations and left managers with a sense of paralysis. As Drucker said, the method is far less important than the approach.

Proactive Decision-Making builds on the characteristics of time which is scarce, inelastic, perishable and non-renewable. The message to leaders and aspiring counterparts is clear:

1. Invest in time planning about 20 minutes every week and 10 minutes daily. List all expected activities, even telephone calls. Indicate the class of activity:
   a. Career development and personal growth
   b. Revenue or service generation contributing to profit or effectiveness
   c. Cost saving activity (efficiency)
   d. None of the above but necessary to survive or get by.
2. Log all work done, both planned and unplanned.
3. Evaluate the results weekly. Determine how much time is spent on each class of activity, the magnitude of discretionary time and planned versus unplanned work, and the size of the backlog, the degree of delegation and the time-wasters. Differentiate between time spent on meeting long term objectives and on fire fighting. Time-wasting is reciprocal. It is essential to make an effort to find out how much of other people's time, particularly our support staff, we waste ourselves.
4. Apply the Proactive Decision-Making process itself to analyzing time-wasting problems and exploring alternative strategies. Part three of this book will be useful for this.

   The Proactive Passport (Figures 9.1, 9.2 and 9.3), available from PDI Press, is a time-management aid designed to combine several functions in a pocket format including a diary, a time log, a calendar and a planning diary for setting and tracking essential objectives and personal commitments. It has been tested to support the above requirements. More about the Proactive Passport can be found in this chapter's appendix.

9.3 Meeting management

Executives should distinguish between information exchange and issue management meetings and social or inspirational encounters. Information exchange meetings vary from rapid feedback and data gathering sessions to elaborate formal briefings or seminars and conferences. They can be frequent and open to a relatively large number of participants as long as problem-solving is either deferred or excluded from the plenary sessions.

9.4 Issue management meetings

The second type of meeting includes problem-solving, policy formulation, opportunity identification, objective-setting, strategic planning, coaching, formative evaluation and decision-making sessions. These issue management meetings should be conducted in small groups. They are

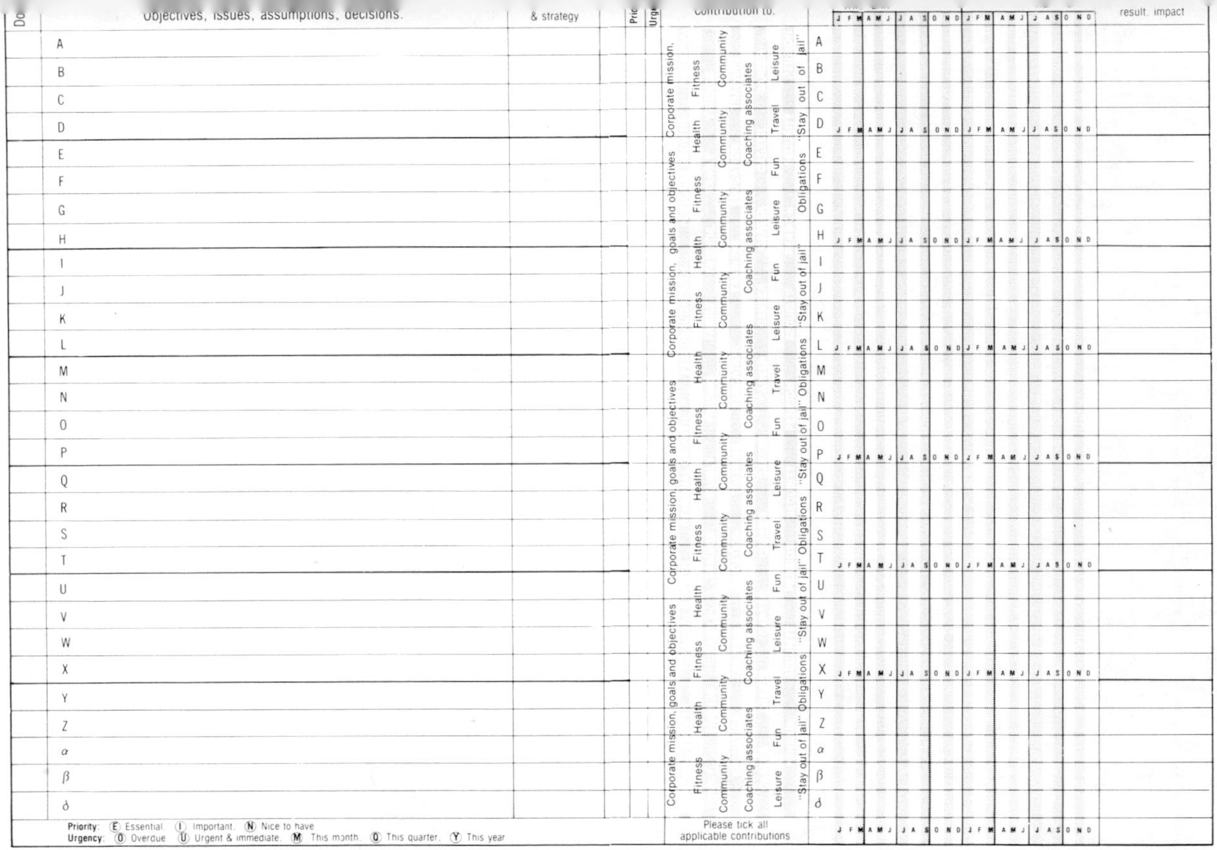

Time management

Figure 9.1: The Proactive Passport: two year objective section

Think Proactive: New insights into decision-making

Essential and important objectives for the month of:

Done		Objectives, issues, assumptions, decisions.	Potential allies & strategy	Priority	Urgency	Contribution to:	PLANNED SCHEDULE		Achievement, result, impact
	A					Corporate mission, Health, Community, Coaching associates, Travel, Leisure, "Stay out of jail", Obligations	1 2 3 4 5 6 7 8 9 10 11 12 13 14 15 16 17 18 19 20 21 22 23 24 25 26 27 28 29 30 31		
	B					goals and objectives, Fitness, Fun			
	C								
	D						1 2 3 4 5 6 7 8 9 10 11 12 13 14 15 16 17 18 19 20 21 22 23 24 25 26 27 28 29 30 31		
	E					Corporate mission, Health, Community, Coaching associates, Travel, Leisure, "Stay out of jail", Obligations			
	F					goals and objectives, Fitness, Fun			
	G								
	H						1 2 3 4 5 6 7 8 9 10 11 12 13 14 15 16 17 18 19 20 21 22 23 24 25 26 27 28 29 30 31		
	I					Corporate mission, Health, Community, Coaching associates, Travel, Leisure, "Stay out of jail", Obligations			
	J					goals and objectives, Fitness, Fun			
	K								
	L						1 2 3 4 5 6 7 8 9 10 11 12 13 14 15 16 17 18 19 20 21 22 23 24 25 26 27 28 29 30 31		
	M					Corporate mission, Health, Community, Coaching associates, Travel, Leisure, "Stay out of jail", Obligations			
	N					goals and objectives, Fitness, Fun			
	O								
	P						1 2 3 4 5 6 7 8 9 10 11 12 13 14 15 16 17 18 19 20 21 22 23 24 25 26 27 28 29 30 31		
	Q					Corporate mission, Health, Community, Coaching associates, Travel, Leisure, "Stay out of jail", Obligations			
	R					goals and objectives, Fitness, Fun			
	S								
	T						1 2 3 4 5 6 7 8 9 10 11 12 13 14 15 16 17 18 19 20 21 22 23 24 25 26 27 28 29 30 31		
	U					Corporate mission, Health, Community, Coaching associates, Travel, Leisure, "Stay out of jail", Obligations			
	V					goals and objectives, Fitness, Fun			
	W								
	X						1 2 3 4 5 6 7 8 9 10 11 12 13 14 15 16 17 18 19 20 21 22 23 24 25 26 27 28 29 30 31		
	Y					Corporate mission, Health, Community, Coaching associates, Travel, Leisure, "Stay out of jail", Obligations			
	Z					goals and objectives, Fitness, Fun			
	α								
	β								
	∂								

Priority: Ⓔ Essential Ⓘ Important Ⓝ Nice to have
Urgency: Ⓞ Overdue Ⓤ Urgent & immediate Ⓜ This month Ⓠ This quarter Ⓨ This year

Please tick all applicable contributions

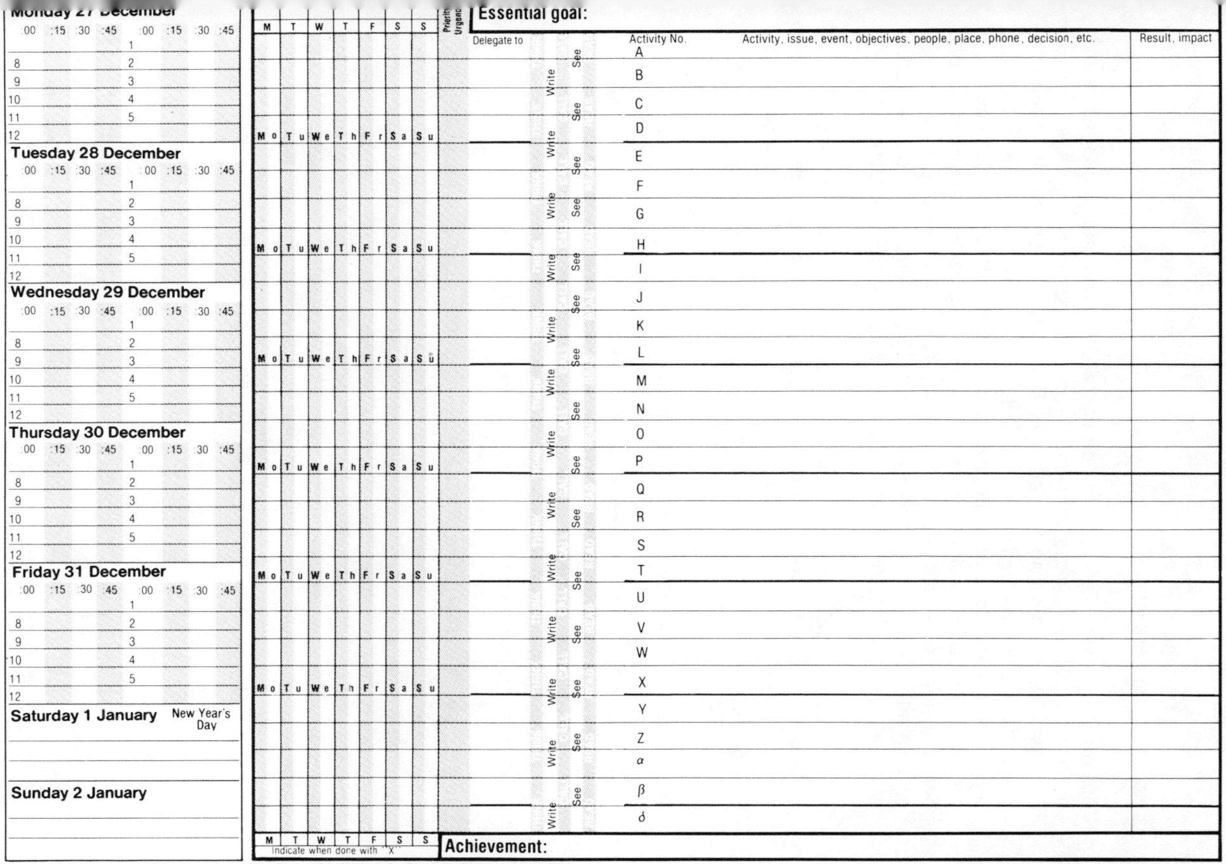
Monday 27 December
:00 :15 :30 :45 :00 :15 :30 :45
1
8 2
9 3
10 4
11 5
12
Tuesday 28 December
:00 :15 :30 :45 :00 :15 :30 :45
1
8 2
9 3
10 4
11 5
12
Wednesday 29 December
:00 :15 :30 :45 :00 :15 :30 :45
1
8 2
9 3
10 4
11 5
12
Thursday 30 December
:00 :15 :30 :45 :00 :15 :30 :45
1
8 2
9 3
10 4
11 5
12
Friday 31 December
:00 :15 :30 :45 :00 :15 :30 :45
1
8 2
9 3
10 4
11 5
12
Saturday 1 January New Year's Day
Sunday 2 January

M T W T F S S
Mo Tu We Th Fr Sa Su
Indicate when done with "X"
Priority Urgency
Essential goal:
Delegate to
Write See
Activity No.
A B C D E F G H I J K L M N O P Q R S T U V W X Y Z α β δ
Activity, issue, event, objectives, people, place, phone, decision, etc.
Result, impact
Achievement:

Available in several formats from PDI, Box 1181. Station B, Ottawa, Canada K1P 5R2

Copyrighted format & style. Pat. Pend.

Figure 9.3: The Proactive Passport: weekly planning section

subject to all conditions previously discussed under the heading of Authentic Leadership, particularly synergy, team-building, and perceptions and conflict management. Participation should be subject to individual preparation.

Business meetings should be carefully planned and managed with behavioral consequences in mind. A comprehensive coverage of the behavioral concerns can be found in Chapter 17 (Impact and Process Evaluation), Section 2. These meetings should be planned in advance with clear objectives and a detailed agenda. The topics to be discussed should be placed in a strategic order. To this end, executives should not only consider priorities but also urgency and the likelihood of winning participant support and getting results. The tentative schedule should be drawn with sufficient contingency time to avoid the attrition trap.

Relevant information about issue management meetings should be circulated well in advance except when privacy or security is an issue. It should include the meeting objectives, agenda, sequence and scheduling of topics, the options available and the role to be played by each participant. The individual's attempt to explore avenues and opportunities prior to the meeting or at least to study the background materials should be a precondition for participation. When this is not feasible prior to the meeting, the first few minutes should be devoted to information exchange, followed by a short quiet period for individual thinking prior to embarking on a group problem-solving or decision-making mode.

Issue management meetings should be carefully coordinated with both content leadership and a high standard of synergy and process leadership. As the time allocated for each topic is consumed, the chairperson could either discretely use the contingency time without interrupting the discussion process or stop the music and explore other alternatives. The options are either to revise the agenda and continue with the issue, make an interim decision and defer action, or recognize the necessity to reach a final decision on the issue immediately. Regardless of the option chosen, the conclusions, their timetable and the responsibility for follow-up should be clearly identified, recorded and shared by all participants to confirm agreement and secure commitment prior to discussing the next topic on the agenda.

By the end of the meeting the participants should be given a duplicate of all conclusions even if in handwritten form. This process was originally introduced by Admiral Rickover in the U.S. Navy. It is now well established in some U.S. and Canadian organizations such as the Quebec Construction Board (OCQ) which regulates construction safety and maintains a large data base for placing all registered construction workers and processing an intercompany pension plan and payroll. According to Mr. Dubé, Executive Assistant to the President, this approach was useful in managing executive meetings and conducting multilateral negotiations with unions and employers.

9.5 Importance of slack time

The necessity for slack resources in industrial engineering is well accepted. Airlines retain a surplus of mechanics at airports to avoid costly plane delays. Oil companies allocate additional repair engineers and technicians to the refinery to prevent multimillion dollar downtime, but virtually all political leaders and senior executives suffer from acute shortage of time and work overload. As an illustration, some members of the Canadian Parliament and of the U.S. Congress work approximately 80 hours per week and visit their constituencies regularly on weekends. The idea of planning slack time for executives is perceived to be almost a sin!

While no one denies the need for slack resources at the working level, it is imperative to also recognize the requirement for slack time at the top. Slack time is a buffer to permit prompt response to unexpected opportunities and ensure high velocity of important decisions when necessary. The greater the uncertainty, risk and the magnitude of unplanned issues, the more slack time should be built into each weekly work plan not only to avoid overload, but also to *capture the moment* and promptly face contingencies.

To this end, political leaders and corporate executives should differentiate between *imperative* and *fill-in* work. Imperative work cannot be postponed and should be dealt with as early as possible daily. Fill-in work is usually performed during the slack time with the understanding that it can be postponed if a new issue is sufficiently important to deserve priority on the contingency time.

9.6 Conclusion

Time management sounds simple. Conceptually, every executive can espouse its principles. However, in order to change behavior, hard practice, concentrated effort and strong determination are required to overcome the enormous pressure and resistance to change.

References and notes

1. Peter Drucker: The Effective Executive, Harper & Row, New York, 1967
2. William Oncken and Donald L. Wass: Management time: Who's got the Monkey? Harvard Business Review, November-December, 1974.

Appendix to Chapter nine

The Proactive Passport[1]

Until recently, managers, executive secretaries and professionals had no alternative but to keep both an agenda and a "do list". Duplication was inevitable. Time logs were difficult to maintain without the assistance of dedicated support staff, a luxury for all but a few decision-makers. Agendas proved inadequate to track the endless changes in schedules, meetings and plans which face busy professionals.

It is the time to rethink your work planning for the best. A new document, the Proactive Passport, has combined a work plan (do list) with the agenda for all management tiers, support staff and professionals. Unlike yesterday's cut-and-dried agendas, the Proactive Passport has several *unique features:*

1. It offers the maximum writing and planning space in a compact set up.
2. The time log of actual versus planned work can be easily maintained without duplication of effort.
3. Each planned activity for the week has a unique reference number which permits rescheduling by simply striking off the single letter code from the original day and time and reentering it under the newly planned day and time. The basic information about the activity (objectives, location, contact phone number, etc.) is recorded only once regardless of how much rescheduling has taken place.
4. For tasks required for a given week or day but for which no specific time has been set aside, the Passport is ideal. It provides for a better use of discretionary time.
5. The Proactive Passport gives users a clear indication about how much discretion they have on their weekly time. By drawing a horizontal line between the plan for the week as of early Monday morning and demands which unexpectedly turned up during the

week, the user can distinguish between discretionary and non-discretionary obligations and may wish to ultimately influence and balance the ratio between the urgent and the essential.
6. The Proactive Passport permits the user to spot at a glance achievement (crosses) versus plans (obliques) each day of the week.
7. The Proactive Passport offers a unique approach for setting essential and important objectives over a two-year horizon and tracking their detailed operational plans and related achievements monthly. It helps the user find out how much time is spent on corporate mission and goals, personal growth, fitness and health, family and friends, career, current job, education and training, coaching aspiring counterparts, community effort, leisure, fun and travel, and "stay out of jail" obligations.
8. When the demand for your time outweighs your availability, each objective and task can be prioritized using a practical generic code. Three columns are provided: one for *priority,* one for *urgency* and one for *delegation.* The priority can be essential (E), important (I) or nice to have (N).

    With respect to urgency, the task can be overdue (O), urgent and immediate (U), due this week (W), month (M), quarter (Q) or year (Y). The *"delegate to"* column permits the user to think about sharing the workload with peers, subordinates, associates, superiors and other allies to keep track of the support resource(s) for the task. This column serves also to indicate tasks transfered to subsequent weeks by entering the "week number" as a reference.
9. The format was designed and tested to facilitate prompt action at a glance. Recording of planned work is done starting from the right page. When planning is over, work is undertaken by scanning from left to right. The leftmost section refers *only* to the most precisely timed activities. They usually include appointments, flight reservations or events with non-negotiable starting time.
10. With respect to *personal messages,* the Passport offers a permanent record. This is an improvement over the throw-away message sheets which usually result in the loss of potentially valuable information, duplication of work and other time-consuming consequences.

The Proactive Passport was developed by the author to help him cope with the demands of running a tight ship of professionals, combined with consulting and lecturing throughout the continent and abroad. Classic agendas could not adequately support his turbulent business environment which for many years included seventy-hour work weeks and air flights to over 40 destinations annually where early breakfast meetings and late night debriefing sessions are a way of life.

The following paragraphs provide practical guidelines to make the user's job easier and keep track of both achievement and time-consuming work.

Early Monday morning, prior to starting work

1. Consult the objective pages for the month and year. Determine the single most important goal for the week.
2. Record this goal on the weekly planning pages in the space titled *Essential goal.* List the tasks needed to achieve it. Enter the priority and urgency if necessary.
3. List other activities, events, issues and obligations to be dealt with this week. Prioritize if necessary.
4. Try to delegate to associates as much as you can using the *delegation* column. Enter a question mark (?) in the vertical column corresponding to the deadline of the delegated job. This serves as a reminder for further follow-up should the associate fail to report progress or work completion.
5. For remaining lines (i.e. work left for you), use an oblique (/) to specify when the tasks are planned to be done. For each weekday you can record the oblique in either the morning column (shaded) or the afternoon column (blank).
6. For tasks which require a specific time such as meetings or flights use the leftmost section of the calendar which contains 15 minute blocks for each weekday. Record the activity number against the exact time.
7. On the right page, draw a line after the last planned task for the week to distinguish between planned and unplanned work for the week.
8. Ensure that some slack time is left for unexpected opportunities.

During the week

9. Keep your Proactive Passport with you. Don't go anywhere without it. Record any new demands on your time below the red line.
10. Cross off (X) the obliques of the tasks on which you have worked (whether completed or not). You now have a rapid feedback time log. Thus, at the end of the morning or the afternoon, you can clearly see the planned (obliques) versus actual work (crosses). Do not cross off the jobs on which you have not worked that day.
11. Reschedule all tasks which have been planned for the day but have not been completed by simply recording a new oblique(s) against the column of the new planned day—a.m., p.m. or both.
12. When someone has promised to either pay, return your call or follow up an assignment on a given day, enter a question mark (?) in that day's column as a reminder for you to ensure that the promise will indeed be fulfilled. If so, cross off (X) the question mark (?), otherwise take the initiative to find out the status of the assignment or the promise shortly after the deadline.

13. Evaluate the results every day by denoting in the last column how much time was spent on each task and to what contribution the effort went. The contribution can be summarized using 'RS' for revenue generation or service delivery tasks, 'SAV' for cost-cutting work, 'COM' for the common objectives of the company, 'PERS' for personal growth, 'FIT' for health and fitness, 'F' for family and friends, 'CAR' for career, 'JOB' for day-to-day job, 'ED' for education and training, 'COACH' for coaching aspiring counterparts, 'HELP' for society and community help, and 'SOJO' for stay out of jail obligations.
14. The use of the columns printed with the verbs *think, write, call, see* and *read* is optional. Ticking one of these columns serves as a short-hand for writing the verb in full. Moreover, these columns permit the user to cluster work at the planning stage. Thus, all calls can be made at the same time simply by scanning the *call* column. Tasks to write reports and memos could also be grouped. It may also be worthwhile to use these columns to evaluate the ratio of time allocated to thinking, reading, meeting, writing and calling others.
15. At the end of the week, review the essential goal, the work done and summarize the week's performance in a point form or a short sentence. To this end, use the bottom row titled *Achievement*.

Note

1. The Proactive Passport is available in English, French, Spanish and other languages. Interested parties can write to PDI Press, Box 1181, Station B, Ottawa, Ontario, KIP 5R2, Canada. Passport and Proactive Passport are registered trademarks of PDI Press. Patents pending.

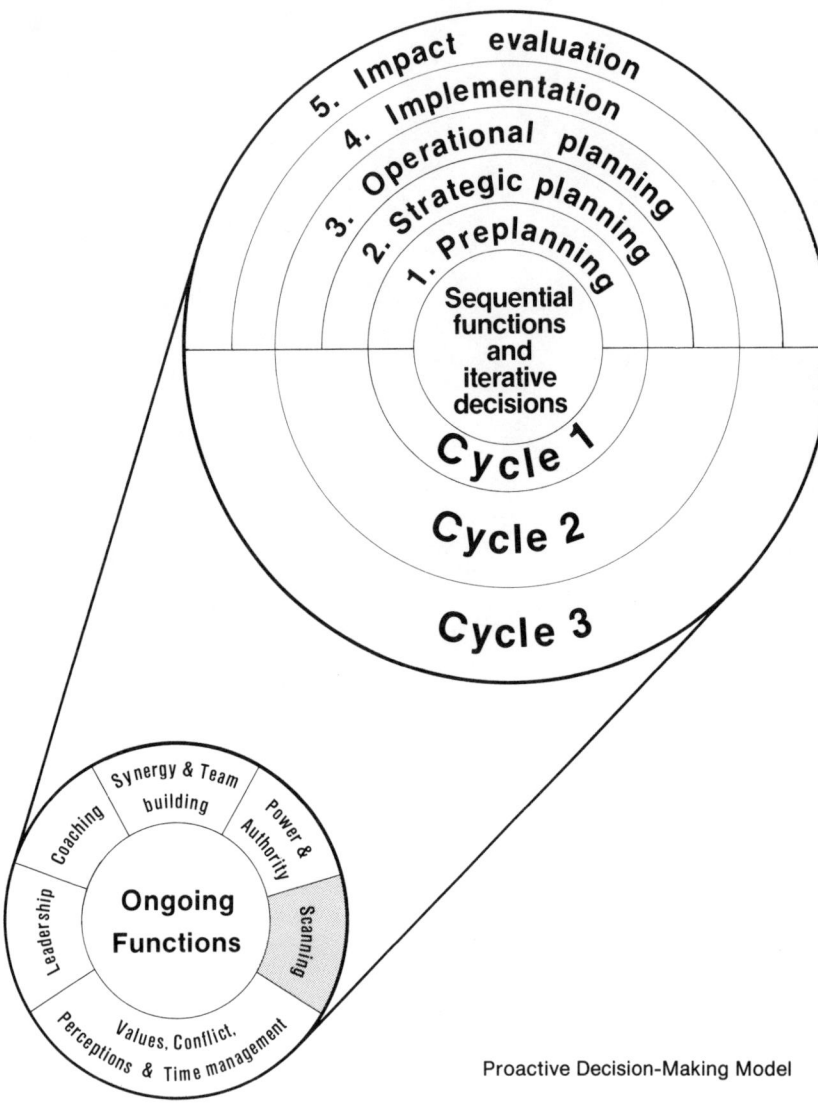

Proactive Decision-Making Model

Chapter ten

The scanning function

10.1 Definition

Scanning is the on-going process by which an organization taps and intercepts the universe of external signals, events, transactions, and surprise developments. The aim is to spot potential opportunities, exploit strengths, introduce innovations and detect threats, weaknesses, rules, attitudes, institutional trends and shifts in social values. The overall objective is to build *awareness,* i.e. collect relevant data to continually monitor factors pertinent to the success of the organization. Scanning is also sometimes called exploratory planning or intelligence gathering.

10.2 Some applications

Scanning is a precondition for preplanning and strategic planning. Thus, it is an important function in the creation of the organization's future plans. Yet, until recently, apart from defense intelligence, only marketers have extensively used scanning (particularly the survey research component) to detect emerging consumer preferences, uncover transitions in competition behavior, and create or improve products or services. Currently, the process is applied to a variety of business and government functions with relative success, as the following examples demonstrate.

Archie Boe is credited with setting up one of the first business scanning groups while presiding at Allstate Insurance. Now, as President of Sears Roebuck & Co., Mr. Boe has built one of America's most effective scanning teams. Sears removed the flammable nightwear from its inventory and replaced them with nonflammable goods before government intervention. Its scanning team was also instrumental in the early removal from its stores of Tris, a flame retardant suspected of causing cancer. This decision came almost a year before government made it necessary while competitors suffered heavy losses from reactive strategies.

Since November 1977, AT&T has formalized its environmental scanning function for the whole Bell System family. The process has already produced dividends. The document "Labor Issues of the 80's" made an immediate impact. In addition, the proactive response to the emerging movement for the rights of the handicapped was timely and the Consumer Guide to the Yellow Pages is quite popular. Apart from these visible innovations, there are other intangible but real benefits. The know-how gained by AT&T's talented managers about the linkages between society and the company has undoubtedly advanced their decision-making capability to a new level of foresight.[1]

Unlike many of its competitors who perceived Reagan's election as a bonanza for business, Atlantic Richfield Co. of Los Angeles predicted that state governments would overtax businesses to make up for lost federal funds. ARCO executives responded proactively to the deluge of state bills and staged a vigorous campaign which led to the defeat of over seventy percent of the bills targeted at oil companies.

Scanning helped a foreign bank in Beirut detect an unstable geopolitical environment eighteen months prior to the 1975 civil war. By regularly scanning a powerful left wing student magazine, the bank manager saw the escalation of isolated violence between local students of the polarized American and Arab universities combined with the underground foreign forces as a recipe for a civil war.

The bank developed a scenario which recognized the impotence of the Lebanese government and the inability of the U.S. to come to the rescue in the aftermath of Watergate. The bank changed its long term lending policies and set up contingency plans to secure exit. In the meantime, competitors remained in the dark with the comforting headlines of the daily L'Orient le Jour.

Another bank, the Bank of America, gained almost two years lead in lending policy before Congress introduced the so-called *anti-redlining* laws. The bank was spared from the antagonism of special interest groups against its less prescient competitors.

S.C. Johnson & Sons, a successful manufacturer of floor waxes and other consumer chemicals, predicted the federal move to ban environmentally harmful fluorocarbons from aerosol sprays four years before the legislation forced others to comply. The company introduced safe substitutes and gained a three year lead over competition.

The scanning function

In July 1982, AMR International surprised its seminar speakers, hotels and other creditors by filing for the 90 days transition period under Chapter 11 of the U.S. Bankruptcy Law. However, anyone close to the scene would have noticed the ailing company problems sooner from the increased time lag in the accounts payable system despite the advanced revenue generated from bookings.

By projecting the most likely consequences of Carter's drive for human rights, a high technology company used its scanning network to predict either the collapse of the Shah regime or the consolidation of an anti-U.S. movement in Iran two years before the opposition forces were let loose. The company offered high incentives to encourage early payments and increased the penalty on overdue accounts. Revenue-rich Iran paid promptly, taking advantage of the high cash discount.

A more detailed description of the current applications of scanning can be found in the Planning Executives Institute's Research Series.[2] As an illustration, W.W. Simmons' *Exploratory Planning—Briefs and Practices* gives an overview of the scanning world. It describes how over 50 corporations and 60 government agencies scan for strategic planning purposes. It also provides a selected list of companies and institutions offering exploratory planning services and gives a short description of existing techniques. The book finishes with summarized curricula vitae of well-known exploratory planners and a selected bibliography of books and periodicals available at the time.

10.3 Scanning resources and organization

Scanning requires a network of part time monitors, a sort of look-out institution. These trained people should come from a variety of sources and backgrounds within and outside of the organization. To this end, some companies such as Internorth, a four billion dollar conglomerate in Oklahoma, rely on voluntary staff. While this practice has some obvious advantages, it can have severe drawbacks such as observer bias and preferences and result in stratified monitoring.

The network of monitors acts as data collection stations. It should be strategically built with both voluntary and appointed memberships to avoid underrepresentation of skills. It should maintain a small permanent secretariat to ensure continuity. Ad hoc observers should participate regularly to avoid homogeneity. Monsanto has a small nucleus of coordinators (called Issue Managers) who run scanning committees of middle managers on a weekly basis.

ARCO has over 25 professionals totally devoted to scanning and issue management in addition to ad hoc observers and part time monitors.

Their diversified backgrounds include constitutional law, petrochemical engineering, aeronautics, advanced technology and multinational affairs. They are organized around five groups: ecology and environment; corporate issues including tax, labor and antitrust; technology and manufacturing process; resources; and trade associations and professional societies. They provide 400 managers and executives with Scan, ARCO's daily bulletins containing a wealth of information about government and surrounding issues. They also monitor and track no less than 100 government and social issues related to ARCO's business on a continuing basis and file special progress reports.

The overall cost of scanning should be commensurate with anticipated benefits. AT&T found it relatively inexpensive. Each monitor devotes approximately 15 person-days of effort spread throughout the year. Incentives should be explicit. Although monitors find the process a rewarding experience itself as it broadens their horizon, they should be rewarded fairly for the task—at least symbolically. Performance evaluation is imperative. When the monitor's work is not evaluated, the problem of scanning coordination and long term quality assurance becomes infinitely more complex.

In addition to corporate monitors dealing with factors that transcend functional boundaries, local units should be encouraged within each function. Actually, all managers ought to invest about half an hour a day to scan for signals relevant to their own business environment. It is part of a learning process to understand the changing context in which the organization is doing business. Scanning is not only a collective responsibility but everyone's job. Careful planning is required to foster interdepartmental cooperation and avoid dysfunctional replication of effort.

10.4 Sources of scanning information

Sources of scanning information range from printed and electronic media, publications and conferences, to survey research. This section gives a cursory treatment of the scanning data most often encountered in modern organizations.

Printed media include newspapers, general periodicals, specialized magazines and newsletters from associations, trade groups, Congress, businesses, universities, governments and research institutions. In scanning newspapers, the monitor should first read all headlines. Then, any stories with some potential business relevance should be skimmed, even if the relevance appears weak. Unlike reading, skimming is characterized by quickly assimilating facts and by skipping over editorials and opinions. Lengthy stories should be skimmed only as far as is necessary to screen articles for in-depth reading.

Unlike news stories, editorial relevance can usually be assessed by reading the conclusion first. Magazine scanning should not be restricted to the most popular periodicals, as many do not reflect the views of agents of change and tend to underestimate the potency of leaders with iconoclastic views. Scanners should distinguish between facts and opinions.

Electronic media include news broadcasts, public affairs radio and TV programs, computerized news services such as the New York Times Information Bank which abstracts a large number of U.S. and foreign papers and magazines, and the Source which provides selected news bulletins and stock information. Other syndicated newswire services include Associated Press, Reuters, Agence France Presse, Canadian Press and United Press International. Financial institutions are increasingly subscribing to newswire services. Defence contractors get the most up-to-date government procurement opportunities through ARPANET. Job opportunities can now be scanned through Telidon with terminals located in selected municipal libraries, university campuses, and high traffic shopping centers. BOSS permits Canadian businesses to reach and be reached by potential importers and exporters throughout the world.

Trust companies, banks, stock brokers and investors can gain from six to eighteen hours' time advantage by tapping into news sources directly. The current instability in strategic regions of the world makes information highly perishable. Considering this fact and the global competition in financial markets, some banks change throughout the day their interest rates on six digit term deposits. In this field, "information avant-garde is only 'avant' until the next newscast", as John McHale said.

Some broadcasters prepare a printed summary of the latest news. The Canadian Broadcasting Corporation abstracts the daily national and international radio news for dissemination to Canadian embassies through the worldwide telecommunications network of the Department of External Affairs, a source many government agencies ignore. The Department of Finance and the Treasury Board jointly produce a daily news Bulletin (Figures 10.1 and 10.2).

Publications include books, monographs, working papers, unpublished dissertations, proceedings, directories and statistical abstracts. Two annual government publications merit special attention. The Statistical Abstract of the United States from the Census Bureau and the U.S. five year Industrial Outlook from the Department of Commerce and their Canadian counterparts provide a wealth of social and economic indicators potentially useful for strategic planning.

| Daily News | **BULLETIN** | de Nouvelles | #119 |
| June 19 | 1981 | le 19 juin | |

Canadian farmers will receive $81 million from the federal Government to compensate them for losses stemming from the 1980 embargo on grain sales to the USSR. The compensation honours a commitment by the former Clark government.
(R. Newman, G & M 19/6)

Closing rate on the U.S. dollar on June 18: C$1.2050.

UNITED STATES The Federal Reserve Board is wary of proposals to establish futures markets for Eurodollar certificates of deposit in the U.S., but at its meeting on June 17 stopped just short of asking the Commodity Futures Trading Commission to prohibit such trading. Chairman Volcker is concerned about the Fed encouraging Eurodollar futures trading at a time when it is publicly favouring more control on the money supply and more productive uses of money and credit. Recognizing that the CFTC might allow the contracts to go ahead despite Fed opposition, the Fed suggested some specific changes for each proposal. (L. Stern, NYJC 18/6)
New financial assets, such as cash management accounts and money market mutual funds, are proliferating so rapidly that it would be "useful" for the Federal Reserve Board to have some regulatory power over any instruments which can be used as transactions accounts, Governor Gramley said in remarks prepared for delivery to the Stonier Graduate School of Banking in New Brunswick. "Such a step seems to me important for reasons of equity as well as for purposes of monetary control". (NYJC 12/6)

WEST GERMANY The Bank of England has been helping to finance West Germany's budget deficit by purchasing D-Mark denominated notes issued by the German Government. The Bank of England has discreetly bought the notes through West German commercial banks during the past year or so. The Bank's purchases are not thought to have been large in relation to the DM 34 billion ($14.3 billion) of direct and indirect borrowing abroad undertaken by the German Government during the last 18 months. (D. Marsh, UKFT 15/6)

GREECE The Currency Committee has increased to 1 billion drachmas (U.S. $17.6 million) the amount that must be deposited in foreign exchange and converted into drachmas by foreign banks wishing to open a branch or branches in Greece. The requirement had been fixed at $10 million per branch. The decision is said to meet Greece's obligation under the terms of its EEC accession to extend equal treatment to Greek and EEC banks. (V. Walker, NYJC 18/6)

ISRAEL The banking system has doubled its branches and agencies abroad in the last five years, from 48 in 1975 to 100 at the beginning of 1981. At present, there are Israeli banks in more than 20 countries on four continents. Banking circles deny vehemently rumours that the expansion abroad is due to Israel's soaring inflation and economic difficulties of the past few years leading to a desire to gradually transfer the assets of these banks abroad.
(M. Dean, NYJC 12/6)

WORLD SDRs should play an increasingly useful, if limited, part in world financial markets, Peter Dreyer writes. Recent developments have made SDRs more attractive both to official institutions and to private investors, and are enabling them to gain wider acceptance. Paul Caron, vice-president of Morgan Guaranty Trust of Brussels, pointed out at a seminar on Monetary problems in Brussels that it is as yet premature to anticipate a meaningful growth for the SDRs. Certainly they will not interfere with the dollar's pivotal role in the international monetary system. So far the volume of bond issues and notes denominated in SDRs has been very modest, but the recent borrowing arrangement between the Saudi Arabian monetary authority and the IMF has clearly enhanced the SDR's status. (P. Dreyer, NYJC 12/6)
A number of major international airlines are nearing agreement on a plan to avoid currency rate turbulence by linking air fares and cargo rates to SDRs. The plan is aimed at removing as much as possible currency rate fluctuations as a factor in airline revenues. (G & M 19/6)
The Federal Reserve Boards' approval for New York to become an international banking facility, (NB#112) is regarded by some international bankers as one of the most significant developments in the Eurocurrency markets. Deryk Vander Weyer, deputy chairman of Barclays Bank (U.K.), has warned that the main threat to London in the next decade must surely come from New York if it goes ahead with its plans for an offshore banking centre. Eric Carter, National Westminster's deputy group chief executive in charge of international operations, feels that the New York development will not damage London's role. Barry Linsley, head of Chemical Bank's European treasury operations, shares this view. He believes it will have an immediate impact on U.S. banks' Nassau and Cayman Isle Operations.
(W. Hall, UKFT 12/6)

Figure 10.1: First example of Daily News Bulletin

| Daily News | **BULLETIN** | de Nouvelles | # 124 |
| June 26 | 1981 | le 26 juin | |

The now-defunct AIB probably did "long-term harm" to industrial relations by reinforcing the idea that wage increases should provide some measure of protection from inflation, Thomas McCormick, former research director with the board, has told an economic outlook conference organized by Data Resources of Canada. The current "acceleration in wage rates" has encouraged speculation that some form of controls may be imposed again. He acknowledged that during the 3 1/2 years of wage and price controls, the AIB's impact on wages "was relatively large, but on prices there was very little effect at all". David Wilton, economics professor at the University of Guelph, predicted that the next budget will contain anti-inflation measures to supplement the tight-money policy being pursued by the Bank of Canada. However, he adds that the odds are against a repeat of the anti-inflation programs but sees the introduction of a tax-based incomes policy (TIP). (V. Galt, G&M 26/6)
High interest rates may be a boon to the banks but credit union officials say their profits are being squeezed by the high cost of money. However, Canadian Co-operative Credit Society Chief Executive George May said on June 25 that the situation is improving. "In another six to nine months, credit unions will be in a very similar position to the banks — insulated from the high rates." (CP 25/6)
The Province of Manitoba will lose 1,000 hog producers and $200 million in economic activity if the federal Government establishes a national pork marketing board, provincial Agriculture Minister Downey has told the annual conference of the Canadian Feed Industry Association. (R. Newman, G&M 26/6)
Closing rate on the U.S. dollar on June 25: C$1.2012.

UNITED STATES The Federal Reserve Board asked Congress on June 25 for restrictions on money market funds so that people who use their funds as chequing accounts would receive lower interest rates. Chairman Volcker does not favour any restrictions now on funds that are used as traditional savings accounts; however, to the extent that the funds are used as a high-interest chequing account, they should fall under the same reserve requirements set for regular banks and savings institutions. (CP 25/6)

JAPAN Six months after the country liberalized its foreign exchange laws, foreign currency deposits held by Japanese residents and so-called "impact" loans have increased over 45% each, but the jump is still less than government officials had anticipated. There had also been concern that deregulating impact loans would subject Japanese banks to increased lending competition, but this has not yet happened to any great degree. (CP 25/6)

Exports played a crucial part in economic growth in 1980, according to the Economic Planning Agency in Tokyo. Domestic economic activity contributed only 24% of the total GNP growth, with the rest attributable to the export sector. Foreign earnings grew by 68.4%, reflecting a 20.7% rise in the real value of exports. Imports remained at about the same level over the year and showed an 8.1% decline in real value. The EPA's official forecast for GNP real growth in the year to March 31, 1982, is 5.3%. (R.C. Hanson, UKFT 19/6)

POLAND The outline of a compromise for rescheduling $2.37 billion of Poland's commercial debts due in 1981, has been agreed upon by 19 international banks at a two-day meeting in Paris. The banks represent 460 creditor banks to which Warsaw owes about $15 billion. The package proposed a moratorium on payments of principal between March 26 and December 31, 1981. This would give all the banks time to discuss European and Japanese recommendations to extend repayment of this year's outstanding loans over seven or eight years beginning in January 1982. (CP 25/6)

WORLD The pound and the dollar are expected to fall against the DM as West Germany's low inflation rate and narrowing current account deficit force a correction of the disequilibrium on the foreign exchanges, the London Business School says in its Exchange Market Outlook. It notes that the pound and the dollar are overvalued at current levels, and that Germany enjoys a "huge competitive advantage". (D. Marsh, UKFT 19/6)

Figure 10.2: Second example of Daily News Bulletin

The U.S. Congress publishes about 3,000 briefs on the issues facing the nation *every month*. They provide insights into proposed bills which may affect the future. Several companies, particularly in highly regulated sectors, have developed effective tools for scanning and screening congressional briefs to spot the emerging issues which may impact on the corporations' future. For instance, an analysis of the volume of bills over the past two years clearly indicates a priority shift from the issues of the seventies such as minorities' rights, unemployment and environmental health to the rights of the handicapped, inflation and energy respectively.

Business and trade directories can also be illuminating, giving insight into issues relevant to professional groups. Columbia Books of Washington, Gale Research Co. of Detroit, Dun & Bradstreet, the Conference Board and the Chambers of Commerce compile membership statistics and planned activities of 8,000 active national trade and professional associations and labor unions throughout Canada, the United States and Mexico and a selection of counterparts overseas. State-of-the-art symposia, trade fairs and conferences provide early warning signals on precursor jurisdictions where national issues emerge first. Margaret Stroup, Director of Scanning at Monsanto, found it to the company's benefit to track "precursor" states which include Connecticut, California and Michigan.

Scanners should pay particular attention to *early adopters* of change. Sweden has been a catalyst in institutional reforms. The Netherlands has been the silent champion of international aid. Japan is a pace setter in robotics. Milan is now leading Paris in many segments of the fashion world. Bureautics[3] is coming of age in the corporate offices in Silicon Valley (California). Small firms merit a close watch. They tend to introduce innovations faster as they have nothing to gain by delays.

Another potent source of scanning material is *survey research.* In *Images of the Future,* Fred Polak demonstrates that what the public thinks will happen has a definite impact on what does happen. That is why opinion scanning is an important ingredient of Proactive Decision-Making.

Syndicated studies are readily available to show the opinion currently held by the public on corporate and sociopolitical issues. In some instances, it is possible to examine the views of sub-groups by income, age group, geographic area, sex, ethnic or political affiliation, educational background and occupational category.

Most public surveys suffer from respondent bias, particularly when the question has a prospective dimension. Validity and reliability tests are imperative, as a recent Gallup survey indicated. A significant number of U.S. respondents interviewed about the international economic outlook could not define the European common market. Many believed the EEC to be "a supermarket where Europeans go to shop"!

In general, people do not know enough about the choices of the future and are only concerned with immediate personal change. Sometimes, more reliable information could be obtained by surveying policy-makers. To this end, data are available about the attitudes and opinions of influential members of society. In the United States, Canada and Western Europe, business and labor leaders, government executives and legislators, experts and change advocates are periodically surveyed.

Among the organizations offering syndicated services, many have gained acceptance by strategic planners. Some household names are Gallup, Yankelovich, Louis Harris, Cambridge Reports Inc., the Opinion Research Corporation, the Roper Organization and the Conference Board. Other think tanks in the field include the Stanford Research Institute, M.I.T. Systems Dynamics Group, the Rand Corporation, the Hudson Institute, Arthur D. Little, the Center for Future Research of the University of Southern California, the Frazer Institute of Vancouver, the Survey Research Center of the University of Michigan, Batelle, the Dutch TNO, the French International Association of Futuribles, the International Institute for Applied Systems Analysis in Laxemburg (Austria), the C.D. Howe Institute of Montreal and the Scandinavian Employers Research Councils. OECD and government agencies throughout the Western world disseminate a wealth of social indicators and economic predictions.

The general data from syndicated studies should be supplemented with *special surveys* to provide measures on sensitive questions which are proprietary to the organization. On critical questions, *tracking studies* should also be conducted frequently to monitor changes in attitudes, perceptions or behavior over time. Figure 10.3 shows longitudinal data indicating changes of the most important job values over time for American male workers interviewed by the Survey Research Center of the University of Michigan. The data from this tracking study can be used by human resources specialists including job designers, career counsellors, manpower planners, recruiters and corporate management.

The opinion-scanning system should include community opinion, clients, competitors, regulators, unions, professionals, trade groups, catalysts, potential clients, suppliers, *neighbors* (businesses, institutions and households) and *former clients*.

Survey research costs to study issues related to *rare occurrence events* are prohibitive. Examples are the incidence of cancer at low level radiation (e.g. Denver City residents, airline crews), the deterrence effect of capital punishment, inadequate compliance with affirmative action

Think Proactive: New insights into decision-making

	Steady income	No risk being fired	Lots of free time	High income	Chances for advancement	Work Important	Total
All respondents							
1965	46%	9%	3%	10%	11%	21%	100%
1972	35	12	3	10	11	29	100
1977	20	8	4	12	13	43	100
Blue-collar workers							
1965	52	12	3	11	9	13	100
1972	45	15	2	11	12	15	100
1977	30	9	4	14	17	26	100
White-collar workers							
1965	37	6	2	9	14	32	100
1972	24	8	3	9	10	46	100
1977	17	6	4	8	12	53	100
Younger workers (under 30)							
1965	41	9	2	13	18	17	100
1972	27	12	2	15	17	27	100
1977	16	5	4	15	19	41	100
Older workers (over 30)							
1965	47	9	3	9	10	22	100
1972	38	12	3	8	9	30	100
1977	22	9	4	10	11	44	100

Question: "Would you please look at this card and tell me which thing on this list about an occupation you would most prefer (Interviewer shows card): Income is steady; Income is high; There is no danger of being fired or unemployed; Working hours are short, Lots of free time; Chances for advancement are good; The work is important, gives feeling of accomplishment."

Figure 10.3 The most important job characteristics
(for American male workers)

Source: National cross-sections interviewed by the Survey Research Center of the University of Michigan.

legislation, civil aviation safety, the side effects of new treatments or pharmaceutical drugs and restrictive trade practices. In these cases, Baysian decision theory is being applied to scan and identify emerging threats and opportunities. It capitalizes on prior knowledge and generally requires fewer data than classical survey research methods. However, the design, data collection, analysis and interpretation of the results is complex for both methods. Complexity constitutes a problem even for competent and experienced analysts.

10.5 Scanning tips

1. Scanning can be a total waste of time. With the information explosion and limited time, the dilemma of what to scan and what not to scan is forever present.
2. As with other skills, professional development and *coaching* combined with action research and regular practice are necessary. Professional development includes the participation in formal training and informal networks of colleagues who share an interest in building solid scanning expertise across organizational boundaries.
3. *Action research* is the on-going review of the scanning process itself and the flexibility to experiment with new patterns of thinking (paradigm shifts).
4. At the corporate level, an *inventory* of "who scans what" should be kept up to date and subjected to regular reviews. In general, corporate executives are surprised to find out how uniform their reading menu is. Apart from the New York Times, the Wall Street Journal, Time Magazine, Business Week, Harvard Business Review and Fortune, managers rarely read more than a handful of publications outside their industrial sector or professional field.

10.6 The scanning process

1. After skimming all available information, the monitor should screen what seems relevant for in-depth reading or analysis.
2. Relevant stories should be read, integrated with survey data and abstracted, preferably in a comprehensive point form with a clear reference to the source.
3. Cross-referencing by topic of business interest, potential influence attributes and possible impact should be added.
4. Information abstracts of the current business environment should be promptly recorded in an automated data base.
5. The data should be readily and selectively accessible to legitimate interested parties and kept to a manageable size. Procedures should

be established for selecting and transferring segments of information to an off-line storage media which in turn should purged periodically. The cost of system development is now relatively inexpensive. Ever since the late sixties, when IBM developed KWIC (key word in context), a *"user-friendly"* software for scanning textual data bases, trademarked support in this field has been mushrooming.

10.7 Screening techniques

Experts have developed practical tools to assist organizations in detecting new forces and studying potential implications. This section provides brief illustrations of the most widely applied methods.

New York Telephone uses *Future Wheels* and *Synectics*. *Future Wheels* (Figure 10.4) describe the possible immediate and long term implications which might occur both directly and indirectly as a result of a decision, an event, an innovation, a new policy or information disclosure. It is a network of circles. Starting from the central node describing the event, each generation of circles outlines the immediate implications that would result from the previous order of events.

Future Wheels are developed as a team effort in a synergistic work climate. The description of each event or implication should be succinct, to facilitate communication with other decision-makers and also for future reference. The team should indicate the probability, the desirability and the time horizon of each implication, then differentiate among the possibilities under its organizational control, identify the stakeholders controlling the remaining events and their relationship to the company (F_1: family, F_2: friends, F_3: foreigners, F_4: foes, F_5: fools). Influencing strategies could be explored at this point or developed during the strategic planning exercise if necessary.

Synectics is a process to increase the creative capacity of team members in dealing with a given issue. Originally developed to foster technological innovations, Synectics is now also used for sociopolitical change. Under the direction of George Prince, New York Telephone developed a training film to make the process available not only to management, but also to technicians and support staff, and derived several benefits. A detailed coverage of how Synectics works is beyond the terms of reference of this book. Further information can be found in William J.J. Gordon's monograph entitled *Synectics* and published by Collier Books of New York.

The scanning function

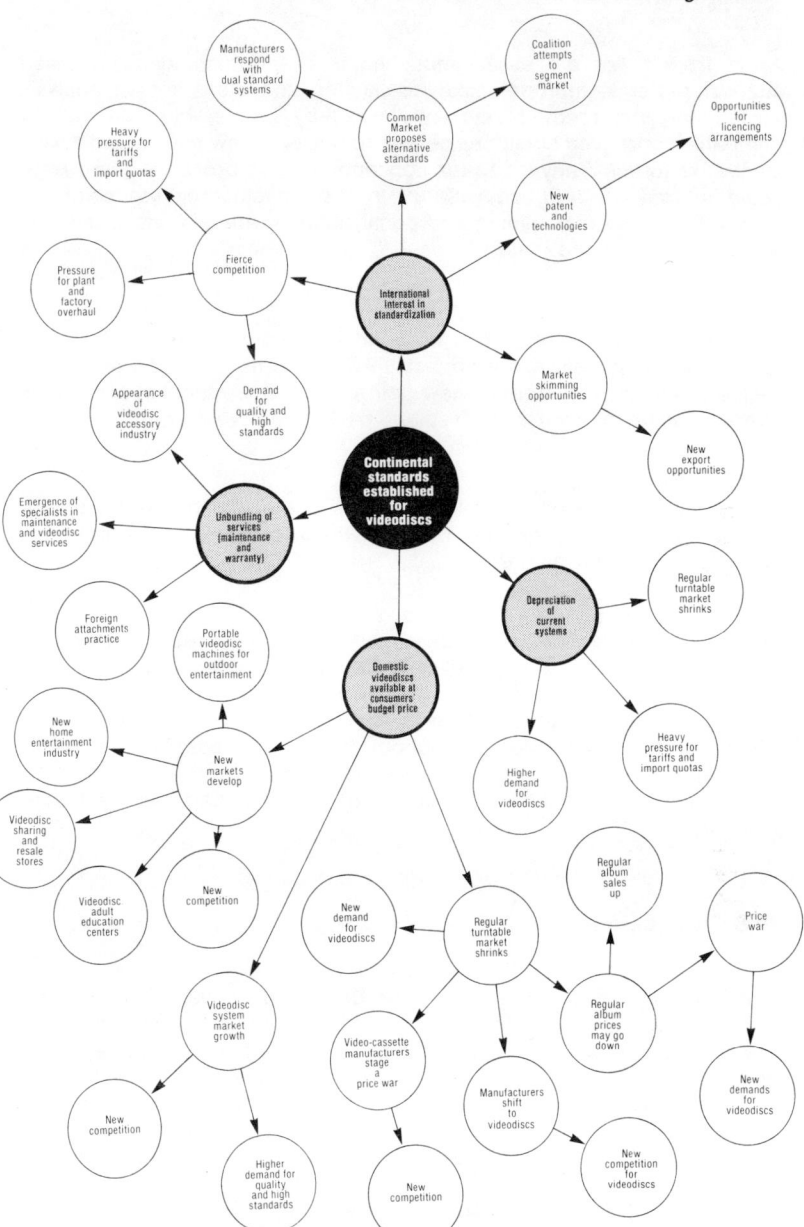

Figure 10.4: First draft future wheel exercise on standard videodiscs

Apart from these processes, modeling, scenario techniques, decision support systems, morphological forecasting and cross-impact analysis are among the methods currently used by banks, high technology companies and even small businesses to uncover new trends and reveal innovative forces. They led to the concepts of word processing and *large scale integration (LSI)* as well as to the development of color TV components and new mining and construction materials and processes for converting ores to metals.

Cross-impact analysis studies show how a change in one part of a sociotechnical system might impact on others. The method was instrumental in the development of new petrochemical products at Monsanto where it has been extensively used and partially automated.

These methods are not a precondition for screening the future. Sometimes simple grids or decision trees can help to explore several growth paths to secure new markets.

As an example, a software supplier marketed its new report generation system starting from a local police force where the degree of readiness was quite high. Capitalizing on that success, the marketing manager developed a horizontal growth plan aimed at approaching neighboring municipal police agencies throughout the West Coast. A year after penetrating that market, he drew a vertical growth grid to enter state and federal law enforcement agencies with existing and new software products.

10.8 Conclusion

With the assistance of the techniques described above, the permanent scanning secretariat should access the data base of the current business environment regularly to search for new information patterns, assumptions, event interdependencies, detect new forces and draft the findings for review and discussion by the monitoring network and the executives. The effort should result in a short bi-weekly or monthly *Business Outlook*. In addition, *Issue Briefs* in a condensed format providing alternative projections or scenarios of events should be prepared for major forces or issues in sight. Worst, best and most likely scenarios are usually found in most issue briefs. These two documents are prerequisites for the interface planning and strategic planning exercises described in the forthcoming chapters.

References and notes

1. American Telephone & Telegraph Co: The Bell System Emerging Issues Program, April 1980, 295 N. Maple Avenue, Basking Ridge, New Jersey 07920, USA
2. The Planning Executives Institute 5500 College Corner Pike, Oxford, Ohio 45056, USA
3. Bureautics: Word increasingly used to describe the methods and techniques for analyzing and implementing a cybernetic approach to office work, including office automation.

The on-going functions
- Leadership
- Synergy
- Team building & coaching
- Power
- Authority
- Scanning
- Management of values
- Conflict management
- Perception management
- Time management

The sequential iterative functions
- Preplanning
- Strategic planning
- Operational planning
- Implementation & control
- Termination/succession/abortion
- Impact evaluation

The options
- Wait and see
- Compliance
- Active
- Proactive

Proactive management functions

Part Three

Proactive Decision-Making: Sequential iterative functions

The last part of this book is a step by step framework for objective-setting, planning, organizing and controlling. It presents an innovative approach for managing contemporary issues that has been effective in filling the gaps that exist between present methods.

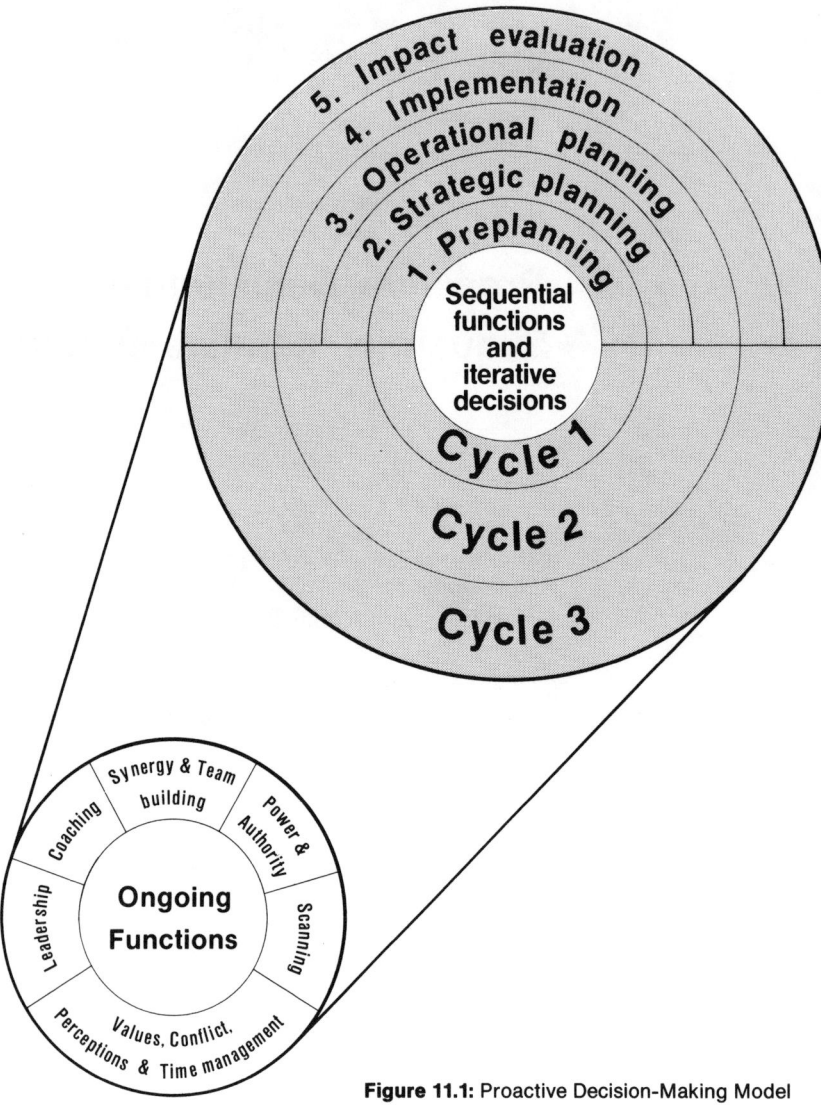

Figure 11.1: Proactive Decision-Making Model

Chapter eleven

Sequential iterative functions

11.1 Introduction

The on-going functions have now been dealt with in sufficient detail. The second class of activities, namely the sequential iterative functions, will form the balance of this book. As indicated in Figure 11.1, the sequential model distinguishes among several phases.

1. The *preplanning* phase includes issue identification, mission-setting and review, stakeholder identification, objective formulation and systematic validation.
2. The *strategic planning* phase includes issue and stakeholder analysis and mobilization strategies (strategic capability assessment) and the definition of work including production, marketing systems and processes, risk and contingency plans, commitment planning, responsibility charting, termination planning, and abortion and succession strategies.
3. The *operational planning* phase includes estimating, scheduling, resource allocation, budgeting, financial planning and information systems development.
4. The *implementation* phase includes resource mobilization, prework such as constituency education and involvement, and work and progress management.
5. The *evaluation* phase is both summative and formative. It includes data collection, data analysis, formal reporting, debriefing and informal feedback.

These phases are arranged in three basic cycles as shown in Figure 11.1. Key decisions should be made before crossing the boundaries between cycles since each transition to the next cycle requires a greater degree of commitment and a significant increase in resource allocation. Iterations within cycles 1 and 2 are generally less expensive and more desirable than a premature transition to implementation. As a rule of thumb, preplanning requires about three iterations while two iterations are necessary to validate the strategic planning information.

The decision to implement leads to a point of no return. Unless a consensus exists with respect to both the quality and the acceptance of the undertaking, success is unlikely. Planning iterations will not guarantee consensus, but serve to reorient the debate in light of new facts.

11.2 How much time should planning take?

Judging from previous client assignments, preplanning sessions last about two days while strategic planning activities vary from a few hours to six weeks. However, once the process is on-going, the effort to update the information base is relatively smaller.

A telephone company reported a two year continuous strategic planning effort. Such an extended period of time is unnecessary because the environment will change regardless of how perfect the data collection effort is. The capability to work with imperfect data is a mark of effective decision-makers.

Throughout the United States and Canada, most corporations who have opted for this approach conduct a regular monthly review of the preplanning and strategic planning network, in addition to ad hoc sessions in response to emerging new trends or unanticipated issues.

11.3 Who should participate?

In complex organizations, information exists in bits and pieces in multiple locations. To pull it all together, teamwork may be beneficial. The potential can be best realized if the process of team-building is undertaken wisely. In order to be effective, group work should be preceded by individual effort. Then, sessions should be held with three to six active participants at a time. Larger groups should be divided into multiple parallel units with members selected to avoid clustering along functional expertise. In order to get more synergy, the results of each unit should be fed back to the full membership for a final iteration of the problem formulation and intervention phase.

The scanning function

In Canada, all issues requiring ministerial approval are debated in small Cabinet committees. As an example, the Cabinet Committee on Priorities and Planning chaired by the Prime Minister reviews its mission and strategic plan regularly with a nucleus of senior Cabinet members and circulates the minutes for approval on a non-objection basis well prior to meeting the full Cabinet. The weekly Cabinet meetings are mainly devoted to controversial issues. The remaining topics are listed in an annex to Cabinet Agenda and are not discussed. However, the conclusions of the annex are ratified during the meeting, as if they were part of the Agenda. It has been said that this process has contributed to the velocity of Cabinet decisions.

With respect to structure, several business organizations, such as Teleglobe, have set up a formal issue management function reporting either to the Vice-President Corporate Planning, Vice-President Public Affairs or directly to the Chief Executive Officer. Others such as Internorth have opted for a task force with support from a full time one-person secretariat.

11.4 Some caveats

A brief and partial description of the sequential functions model (Figure 11.2) follows. The rationale for each step and a detailed interpretation is outside the scope of this book. Although presented in a linear form, the model is both a sequential and an iterative process with multiple purpose heuristics developed to meet the user's needs. It should be adapted to the specific problem at hand, rather than applied cookbook fashion. *Absolute adherence to the framework may, in some instances, be harmful to users.*

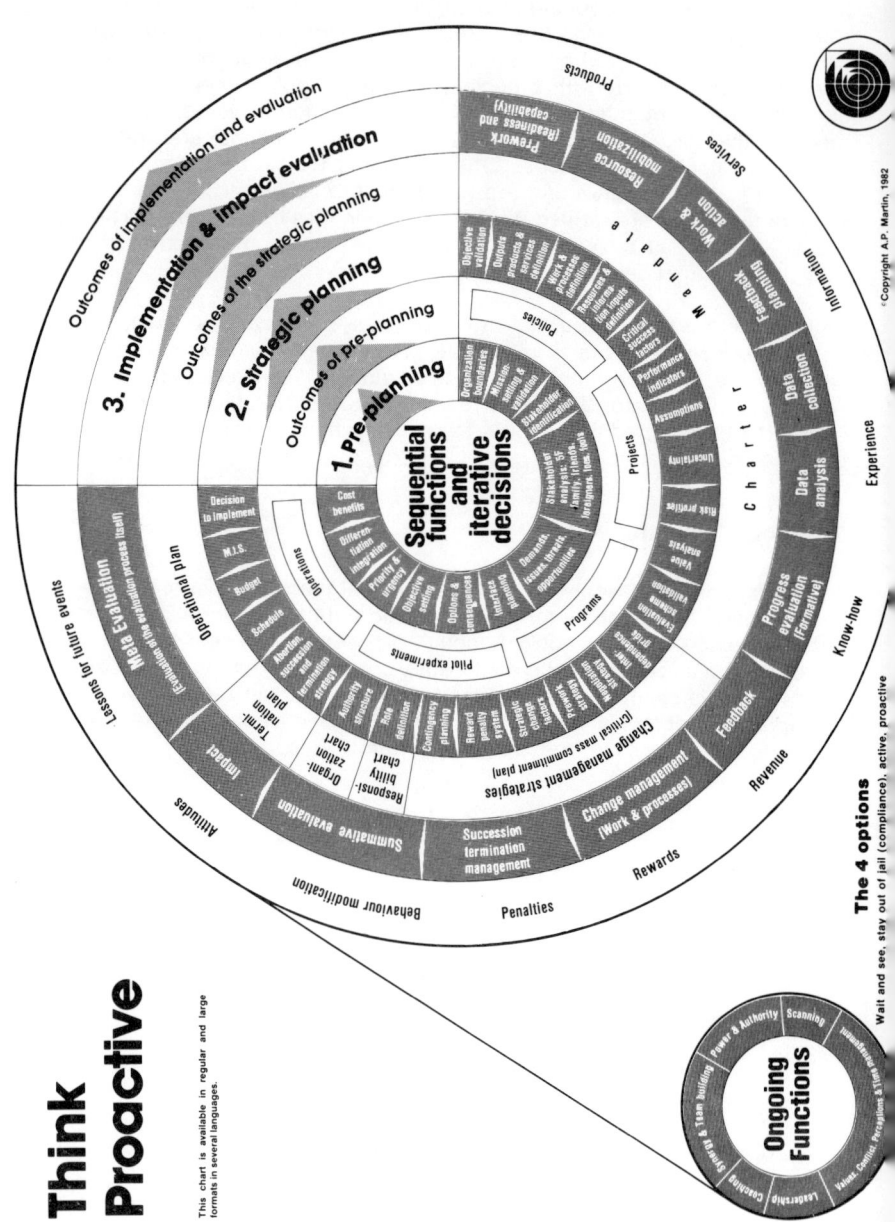

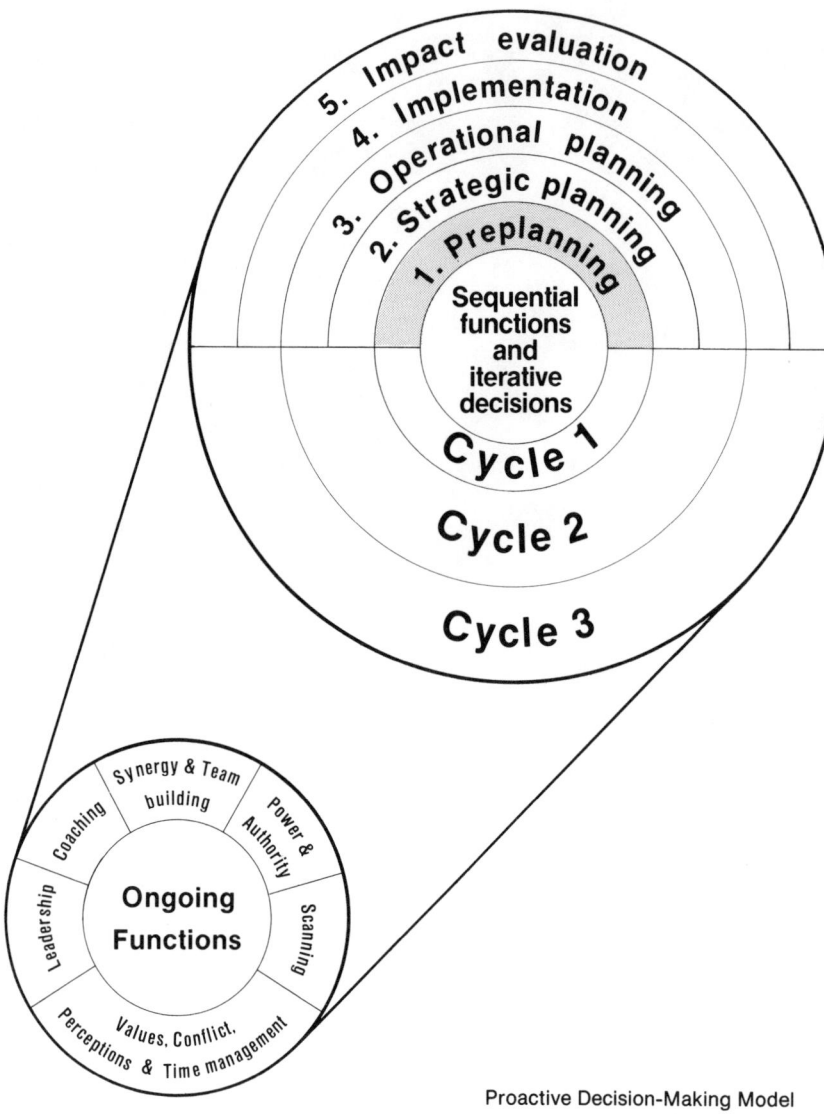

Proactive Decision-Making Model

Chapter twelve

The preplanning phase

12.1 Introduction

The energy or effort devoted to the development of future products and services is often in conflict with maintaining present performance, as both compete for scarce resources. Bread and butter needs are met by present performance, but unless due attention is paid to the future, survival may be gravely threatened. The preplanning phase helps to induce organizations to systematically take the foreseeable future into account. It includes the following steps: mission-setting, issue identification and interface planning, objective-setting and validation and, finally, differentiation and integration. There are up to four outcomes of this process, namely policies, operations, projects and pilot experiments. A comprehensive description of each step and a definition of each outcome follow.

12.2 Mission-setting or review

The core mission of an organization is different from its objectives. The mission is the reason for being. Virtually no organization wants to put itself out of business. That is why the mission's time span is normally indeterminate (i.e. neither finite nor infinite) while objectives have a finite life cycle.

A dramatic example to illustrate sharply the difference between mission and objectives would be to look at the mission of the Amerindian community in America. Prior to the 18th century, the mission was survival. Each time a white man was shot, the Indians achieved an objective which contributed to this mission. Nowadays, the mission remains survival but, fortunately, the objectives to support it have changed altogether. Advocacy groups and court battles have replaced violence, hostility and war.

The mission can be seen as the superordinate goal to which the "organization and its members dedicate themselves". It is a choice. It is not universal. It is fragile. It cannot exist without infringing on someone's boundaries (by necessity, not by desire) because social systems are not mutually exclusive entities.

The real corporate mission may conceivably be remote from the publicly announced raison d'être (Figure 12.1). That is precisely why the corporate mission should, whenever feasible, be clearly communicated to each management tier—to avoid confusion. The emphasis should be on a concise *working mission.* For business organizations, it should be expressed in terms more useful than the simplistic, sometimes naive statement of "maximizing profits". As an example, The New York Times' current mission *to publish a non-partisan newspaper* is as old as the paper itself, although the need to be profitable has never ceased to be a "cardinal concern" of the Ochs-Sulzberger heirs since their grandfather Adolph S. Ochs rescued The Times from bankruptcy in 1896. Ochs drafted a detailed working mission which guided the paper's publishers and editors for nearly a century:

"It will be my earnest aim that The New York Times gives the news, all the news, in concise and attractive form, in language that is parliamentary in good society, and give it as early, if not earlier, than it can be learned through any reliable medium; to give the news impartially, without fear or favor, regardless of any party, sect or interest involved; to make the columns of The New York Times a forum for the consideration of all questions of public importance, and to that end to invite intelligent discussions from all shades of opinion."

As for governments, the working mission should be articulated to reflect the specific mandate of the agency at the time as perceived by its leadership. Although the legislation would be the major "food for thought" for drafting the mission, it should be complemented by up-to-date personal judgment and conscience if necessary. This does not mean that the agency leader's opinion should prevail over Parliament or Congress, but rather that the present mission may indeed differ from the outdated legislation giving rise to it. In that case, one of the outcomes of the process may well be to propose modifications to existing laws to reflect either major shifts in public support or social needs.

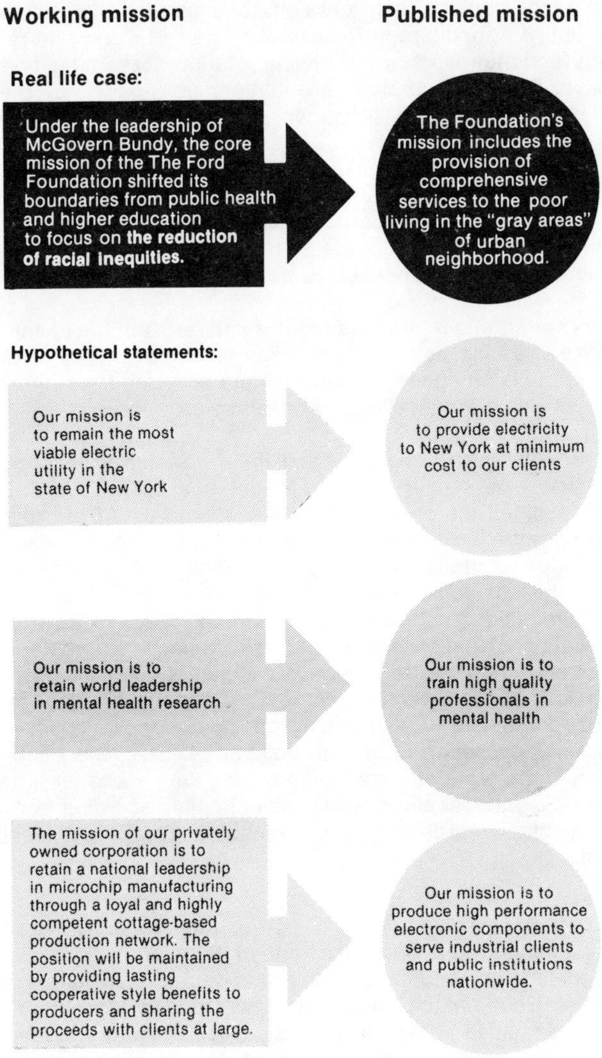

Working mission

Real life case:

Under the leadership of McGovern Bundy, the core mission of the The Ford Foundation shifted its boundaries from public health and higher education to focus on **the reduction of racial inequities.**

Published mission

The Foundation's mission includes the provision of comprehensive services to the poor living in the "gray areas" of urban neighborhood.

Hypothetical statements:

Our mission is to remain the most viable electric utility in the state of New York

→ Our mission is to provide electricity to New York at minimum cost to our clients

Our mission is to retain world leadership in mental health research

→ Our mission is to train high quality professionals in mental health

The mission of our privately owned corporation is to retain a national leadership in microchip manufacturing through a loyal and highly competent cottage-based production network. The position will be maintained by providing lasting cooperative style benefits to producers and sharing the proceeds with clients at large.

→ Our mission is to produce high performance electronic components to serve industrial clients and public institutions nationwide.

Figure 12.1: Statements of working missions and published missions

© Copyright, A.P. Martin, 1983   ISBN 0 86502 000 0

In this context, one can cite endless examples of government agencies which did not confine their mission to legislation. For instance, the Department of Agriculture in Pennsylvania gained worldwide recognition in setting food standards and licensing food processors beyond its state jurisdiction. Even French chefs are sometimes required by their distinguished clientele to register their onion soup croutons with Pennsylvania!

Likewise, the U.S. Department of Agriculture through its Graduate School of Management offers courses in virtually every aspect of public administration and attracts participants from governments and non-profit institutions across the land. The additional revenue permits the department to sponsor far-reaching activities.

Elsewhere, international development agencies throughout the Western world have used the petrodollar tricooperation route. They managed to sponsor projects and generate jobs without suffering from the handicaps of cost-centered budget ceilings imposed by parliaments.

Among airlines which have extended their missions to markets beyond the traditional passenger and air freight operations, Air Canada has prudently avoided the cheap charter league and opted to profit from its strengths in more lucrative areas. The company's excellent safety record and worldwide reputation in jet engine overhaul and aircraft maintenance led major airlines such as Air Florida and CP Air to seek its expertise on an on-going basis. Air Canada is also a recognized leader in the design and marketing of passenger reservation systems, automated resource allocation and computerized diagnosis methods and other data processing services. The revenue generated from these high technology programs combined with the efficient operation of courier services (Airvelop) has exceeded 60 million dollars. Likewise, the Department of Education in the state of Texas has become the pacesetter in textbooks for most U.S. and Canadian public schools, thus accruing both tangible and intangible rewards from educational institutions throughout the continent.

These illustrations should not prompt decision-makers to expand their mission without extreme prudence. Indeed, there are organizations which would benefit much more from strategic retreats. Expanded missions can be disastrous for the unwary as news headlines constantly remind us. Companies such as Admiral, Abacus, White Motors, Laker, Braniff, Dome, Telefunken and Massey Ferguson merit a corporate Remembrance Day.

Whether the decision-maker is in a position of power to change the mission or not, a *mission-setting or review exercise should be performed no less than once a year*. The purpose is at least to clarify perceptions and make assumptions explicit. Otherwise, each manager would be working from an implicit untested perception of the actual mission, something not uncommon among a significant number of corporate and political leaders, particularly when the published mission was originally formulated for public consumption.

12.3 Mission-setting process

The process of mission-setting and review should not be undertaken in a group mode unless the key participants have made a genuine attempt to draft the mission individually. This four step process marks the beginning of preplanning.

1. Indicate the relevant *boundaries or organization level* (unit, division, department, branch or company) to which the effort is being applied.
2. Draft *the core mission,* in which sectorial, functional, demographic or geographic boundaries should be clearly expressed whenever relevant.
3. Present the draft to a trusted third party with *no* vested interest in the outcome of the process to get unbiased feedback. Ideally, the third party should come outside the organization boundaries to experiment freely with both the advocacy and the adversary roles. Daniel Carroll, President of Gould Inc., actually set up "green and red teams" to this end.
4. Conduct a *relevance test* with the dominant coalition. Consult the relevant decision-makers from the dominant coalition, which normally includes several management tiers. Ensure that the selected boundaries are either real or by deliberate choice (ie. *not self inflicted*).

Judging from past experience, managers rarely agree wholeheartedly on a single definition of the core mission. This is a good sign. Apart from different values, it reflects a rich information base to start with. In Proactive Decision-Making, gatekeeping[2] is therefore important to ensure that good ideas are not abandoned for the sake of unanimity or popularity. That is why consensus is not a precondition of the preplanning phase. Indeed, the process can be carried through separately for each of the disagreeing parties resulting in a wealthier data base for subsequent iterations and discussions.

It takes a strong leader to resist undue pressure for conformity, homogeneity and cohesiveness while the potential for conflict and creativity still exists. With sufficient time, the participants can share, clarify, elaborate, and summarize each other's perceptions to generate a greater synergy. Although this approach seldom reduces disagreements to zero, it has often led to increased commitment and a more genuine appreciation of the nature and the magnitude of the difference. However, if an agreement cannot be reached after several iterations, consensus should be sought. Failing that, other means of influence such as authority should reluctantly be used as the process offers technology, not miracles![3]

Mission statements are not universal, nor are they meant to be. James McFarland of General Mills opted to make his corporation "a great company", while McColough of Xerox stated a more specific *raison d'être,* namely "the architecture of information".

For each organization, the mission will vary depending upon the current leadership's perception of the organization's reason for being in a constantly changing world. The case of Bombardier illustrates the point. The company led the worldwide growth of the new snowmobile market with the "Ski-doo" which became a household name in the early sixties. The organization's mission was clearly identified with the winter sports market. On the eve of the seventies, a new president changed Bombardier's mission to the much broader field of transportation. The company is now offering a variety of products ranging from the "Ski-doo" to railway locomotives, subway vehicles and even diesel engines.

It is worthwhile to stress that similar organizations working in the same sector rarely have the same mission. At the November 1974 World Food Congress in Rome, a Secretary of Agriculture sought to adapt, with the help of the author, the mission of the Swedish Department of Agriculture and Food for his own country. After a brief consultation with the Swedes, it was discovered that their agricultural mission statement was drafted with the active participation of the Department of Defence.

The client was surprised but should not have been. Sweden depends on foreign markets for food imports. It is a neutral state. Thus, in the event of an East-West surprise war, no one is expected to come to the rescue. The domestic food needs cannot be met unless the mission of Agriculture is designed with emergency measures in mind. That amply justifies the contribution of the Department of National Defence. Unlike Sweden, the geopolitical environment of our client was totally different. While the mission of Swedish Agriculture could certainly be considered as food for thought, it cannot be construed as an institutional model for others.

12.4 Interface planning

The result of the mission-setting exercise is a descriptive statement of the raison d'être. As a social system, the organization is subject to a

The preplanning phase

continuous pressure from its environment. As an open system, the corporate boundaries are fragile and subject to space invasion attempts.

Interface planning is a boundary management instrument. It bridges preplanning with strategic planning. It is a powerful process to build awareness, *identify new opportunities and threats,* create attractive markets, assess the nature, the magnitude and the impact of issues and external demands, project their respective trends and explore alternative response options. *It attempts to unlock the latent energy of the stakeholders whose vested interest in the mission can range from survival to mere intellectual curiosity.*

Stakeholders are grouped into five categories nicknamed the 5F. As previously indicated, the *family* includes those who see our mission as essential to their own survival. The *friends* see it as important but not essential. The *foreigners* are neutral and often indifferent. They include academics, media analysts and the public at large. Their vested interest is often intellectual curiosity. The *foes'* vested interest is annihilation of the organization. The *fools* are eccentrics with illusive loyalty. Their vested interest is unpredictable, often fluid and fragile. Their behavior is erratic and could even include self-destruction. However, they often think they are acting for the common good and are unable to divorce their minds from the dramas and traumas of the issue. They can be anybody ranging from the president to the zealous change advocate.

Interface planning is participative and it requires the active commitment of senior management. It is an iterative sequential process which should be performed in three stages: first prepare a draft version of the plan (refer to Figures 12.2 and 12.3), then review it and, lastly, finalize it.

At the corporate level, the process should be reviewed regularly throughout the year to ensure that emerging issues and recent developments have not been ignored. Indeed, a major airline has benefited from a systematic monthly review of the interface plan with the participation of its executive committee. It made some gains by capitalizing on the new deregulation opportunities while competitors were still suffering from the loss of lead time.

Interface planning bridges the gaps between the core mission of the organization and the objectives of its programs. Most objective-setting methods focus so much on the future that they lose sight of the current state of affairs. *Interface planning starts with a systematic diagnosis of the present* to ensure that no current issue has been overlooked. It leads to greater insights in exploring alternative objectives and less fuzziness in goal statements. A comprehensive list of interface planning activities follows.

Stakeholders	Current demands
Senior Pilots	1. Accreditation review system 2. Higher pay index and parity with Eastern Airlines 3. Paternity leave
Competition – CP Air – Pan-Am – KLM – B.A.	4. Greater share of polar routes (Burbank-Seattle, Vancouver-Frobisher Bay) 5. Renegotiate joint service contracts in Lagos, Johannesburg 6. Reciprocity deals in passenger check-in in Rotterdam and Miami 7. Passenger referrals on Far East routes 8. Price war on Atlanta-Gatwick route
Suppliers – Fuel Co. – Boeing – Lockheed – Douglas	9. Discontinue block purchasing 10. Shorter notice on jet fuel price hikes from 90 to 60 days 11. Phase-in the new B757 fleet within 12 months 12. Acquire the new preventive maintenance software for the B747 13. More 1011's will do 14. Unbundling of software networks 15. Give DC10 more visibility
Passengers	16. No more DC10 17. Roundtrip discounts on transamerica long haul flights 18. Shuttle service New York-Ottawa 19. Handicapped priority seats on each plane
Hotel X	20. Be our travel companion for the 90s
Labor	21. Flexible hours for ground personnel 22. Fifteen percent hike on the per diem allowances of flight attendants 23. Eighteen percent salary hike
Regulatory Agencies – Kennedy – FAA	24. Respect midnight curfew, fly to Newark after midnight 25. Ninety days to comply with Eurobus safety standards 26. Phase-out second generation DC6 from the freight fleet

Etc.

Figure 12.2: Hypothetical Demand System for Activair Airline

1.	Time horizon:	— Two years
2.	Stakeholders:	— Senior pilots
3.	Stakeholder's class:	— Family (F_1)
4.	Current demand:	— Accreditation review system
5.	Current response:	— Joint accreditation task force
		— Draft recommendations due in six months
		— Conclusions expected to meet most expectations of senior pilots
6.	Response category:	— Active
7.	Current level of dissatisfaction:	— High dissatisfaction reflected in absenteeism and rate of grievances
		— High readiness for change
		— Temporary hostility and fears among junior staff will dissipate with the publication of the task force report
8.	Equilibrium:	— Fragile if current perceptions about the secrecy of task force work continue
9.	Projection of demand:	— Senior pilots may work to rule if current response does not lead to a breakthrough
10.	Potential demands:	— Opportunity for Activair to foster a universal accreditation review standard
11.	Best demand:	— Senior pilots recognize that Activair has the best accreditation review scheme
12.	Best versus projected:	— Current response should shift from active to Proactive to minimize chances for the projected trend and increase the likelihood of success of the best demand
13.	Realistic demand:	— Pilot union presses Activair to ratify the new procedures promptly
14.	Strategies—Acts:	— Proactive option:
		— Higher visibility of task force. Use Activair magazine and the Pilot Newsletter regularly
		— Create the impression that Activair Board of Directors may delay the final approval of the recommendations. This would lead to the creation of the realistic demand
15.	Most likely outcome:	— Greater cooperation between management and pilots
16.	Costs/benefits:	— The cost for the Review system is not an expense but an investment. It could lead to less absenteeism, fewer grievances and more loyalty
		— Adverse consequences could be felt during upcoming negotiations with senior flight attendants. The process may also lead to a two tier system among pilots which could be undesirable if reinforced by Activair
		— The corporate posture clearly identifies with U.S. and other host countries interests in promoting high standards for civil aviation above and beyond existing FAA and ICAO regulations
17.	Planning iterations:	— Retain the Proactive option
18.	Priority:	— Essential, urgent
19.	Objectives:	— Ensure the success and the legitimacy of the Accreditation Task Force. Explore the feasibility of advocacy advertising to increase the task force profile without adverse consequences

Figure 12.3: Hypothetical interface plan for a single demand

© Copyright, A.P. Martin, 1983   ISBN 0 86502 000 0

12.4.1 Scenario of the current state of affairs

1. **Select a reasonable planning time frame.**

   Investments to build pipelines, refineries, aluminum smelting plants, etc. take decades to break even. Fundamental decisions to build or stay put require a thorough understanding of the market forces, the organization's strengths and ability to build and keep powerful allies among the 5F's. This process takes place through the management of domestic and international issues which can be of interest to the organization.

   Although the life cycle of these issues ranges from two to eight years, it is often sufficient to limit the planning to a foreseeable time span, generally from one to five years and to update the plan continuously by expanding the horizon on a quarterly basis.

2. **Identify *all current sources* of demands, opportunities and issues.**

   The sources should include the clientele, suppliers, neighbors, agents, creditors, potential buyers or divestiture candidates, employees, geopolitical groups, the dominant coalition, the formal authority and the current power base including coercive, competitive, collaborative, synergistic and compliance forces and other *stakeholders* (both internal and external). The on-going scanning exercise, described previously, should provide relevant data with respect to the external environment.

3. **Classify the stakeholders into five groups.**

   These include the family (F_1), the friends (F_2), the foreigners (F_3), the foes (F_4) and the fools (F_5).

4. **Draft the existing opportunities, pressures and the present demands.**

   These are exercised on mission by individuals, groups, organizations or constituencies identified above. All demands and issues should be considered, regardless of their legitimacy. These could be legal or not, formal or informal, external or internal, solicited or unsolicited, soft or hard, accepted or not, discreet or public, direct or indirect. It is very important to relate pressures, demands and opportunities to sources, i.e. to people or organizations, otherwise the issues would remain an abstraction of reality (Figure 12.2).

5. **Define the present response system in narrative.**

   Outline how each issue is currently managed. Briefly indicate the type of work, processes, resources, decision-making structure, and reward system(s) now devoted to the issue.

6. **Categorize the type of response.**

   From the above description of responses, indicate whether each current issue and demand is ignored, faced with the minimum

The preplanning phase

response to get by, actively or proactively addressed. Identify the intended and unintended beneficiaries of the current response system.

7. **Identify the level of dissatisfaction with the status quo.**

   What is the present equilibrium position? Consider the current forces for change and the latent or hostile resistance, as well as potential forces that may emerge in the future.

8. **Assess the stability of the equilibrium of the present demand-response interface.**

   Whether the equilibrium is fragile or quasi-stationary, the assessment, however imprecise, is necessary. To this end, the process of force-field analysis[4] could be used to get a "snapshot" picture of the potency of the major forces in action and to recognize the power balance as well as the connection between issues. Each issue direction will usually have advocates, opponents, sympathizers, beneficiaries and uncommitted parties—a sort of silent majority to be tapped.

9. **Project current demands over the planning horizon.**

   This projection assumes no change in the present response system and a plausible sequence of future events. The purpose is to explore what would happen to the issue if the present management policies, structure, systems and decisions remained unchanged.

12.4.2 Exploring alternative scenarios for the future

10. **Draft the potential new sources of demands, opportunities and issues.**

    This is a description of possible future scenarios which include new technology transfers, innovations, new institutions, etc. To this end, use the most current information from the on-going scanning and screening processes described previously under the Scanning Function chapter. The potential demands for each source should be drafted. Consider all stakeholders including the family, the friends, the foreigners, the foes and the fools. Demands for new products or services, opportunities for acquisition, joint ventures, divestitures or internal development should be *broadly* explored at this point.

12.4.3 Analysis of preferences

11. **Outline the best system of demands and issues from the organization perspective.**

    Among the possible futures described above, single out the most desirable scenario(s). This scenario should deal with capability by capitalizing on strategic resources in a *blind,* covert or overt fashion going from F_5 to F_1, if feasible.

12. **Compare the above system with the projected trend.**
    If the best and the projected trend converge at the same destination over the planning horizon, that is fine unless we face surprise events (a topic to be dealt with in strategic planning). In most cases, the best conclusion is to continue with the present response system and issue management process unchanged. Otherwise, proceed to the next steps.

13. **Test perceptions and social values.**
    Look at the hypothetical sequence of events that could lead to the best demand and assess the likelihood of sociotechnical success. What is the extent to which the pursuit of the best system of demands would serve the public interest?

    If the projected system cannot be reoriented toward the best system within the planning horizon, determine *the realistic system of relevant demands, opportunities and issues.* The word "realistic" means more likely to serve both the organization and the public interest.

14. **Define instruments for deliberate pursuits of the realistic future.**
    To this end, determine available *acts* and *strategies* to move the present trend towards the realistic demand and opportunity system. In this context, a strategy is a *pattern* of acts that blend together toward a common goal. These acts ought to include information dissemination to change perceptions, work, cross-influences, power, authority, rewards, penalties, structure, decisions and communication networks. Information can be disseminated in descriptive, normative, maieutic or *subjunctive* form.

    Acts should be formulated with the four proactive options in mind, i.e. wait and see, compliance, active and proactive stance. Each option requires energy and in turn creates energy which can be either positive or negative. The direction of the energy and its adverse transition effects should be clearly understood.

    Sometimes, the most effective strategy is to overreact immediately and absorb the adverse consequences for a while, then to relax the response mode when the social system is ready for a new equilibrium position. This is what a utility company did in an eastern state in 1980. Electricity bills were higher than necessary for eleven months. Then December was free for all, an astute move which was welcomed as a Christmas gift.

    There are also instances where the momentum created by one source of demands can be strategically used to respond to another source of demands, each of which may be in conflict with the other. For instance, anti-combine agencies used to invest a great deal of effort to justify their decisions to the mighty business establishments. Nowadays, they can readily use the pressures from small

The preplanning phase

business to do more and big business to do less as an indication that they are doing the job! That is why grids can be helpful in determining how one force may impact on the other(s): delay, remove, accelerate or intensify its effects.

Explicit strategies should be explored to: (a) build closer alliances with family members; (b) move the friends into the family group; (c) influence the foreigners to become at least friends (if not family) with "linkage" opportunities, as brewers have moved car racers and other sport professionals from indifferent foreigners to friends. Some foreigners have the integrity and credibility to form a network of potential sensors for the on-going scanning function; (d) seek alliance opportunities (friends, family) with foes. If this is not viable, either ignore the foes or strategically neutralize their behavior, moving them into the foreigners group. A deterrence capability against residual foes should be designed to prevent preemptive strikes; (e) friendly avoidance strategies should be explored to distance the fools from power centers and decision-making arenas.

The focus should be on goals and issues, not on personalities. Humiliation of foes should be avoided by providing a window of retreat and "even setting the pace for cooperation at a later date".[5]

Four perception factors tend to condition the success of a strategy with each group of stakeholders. These factors are nicknamed the 4C's: *complementarity, clarity, continuity,* and *consistency.* Five additional C's apply to opponents (the foes and the fools) for whom the strategy should be *covert, confession* permissive, *concentrate* on the single most important objective, have a *concession* baseline to permit withdrawal of resources from non-essential goals, and have a built-in *cache* to exploit opponent weaknesses when necessary.

15. **Identify the most likely outcomes.**

16. **Project the benefits/costs.**
    Evaluate the feasibility of each of the four proactive options and each available act from technical, monetary, geopolitical, institutional and psychosocial perspectives. Economic viability is necessary but not sufficient. A legitimacy test from all stakeholders' perspectives is also required to complete the cost benefit feasibility. Finally, the cost benefit analysis should not overlook the extent to which the strategy identifies with the interests of host jurisdiction (municipal and state government) and provides the comfort level required by neighbors.

17. **Repeat the process if necessary until a satisficing[6] cost benefit projection has been reached with respect to each act/option combination.**

18. **Assign tentative priorities to the most effective acts.**
    Priority will be defined as the degree of contribution to the mission. Urgency will reflect the timing of that contribution. No organization can muster the resources to pursue all desirable acts and strategies. In fact, the fewer the number of acts and goals, the better the chances for achievement. A priority scheme should help in selecting the most viable acts.

    Instead of using a linear numbering system, a two dimensional grid (Figure 12.4) is used to assess priorities. Vertically, the acts are classified under three categories which constitute practically what all organizations do:
    a. revenue or service activities: efforts which generate a revenue or improve a service;
    b. cost/resource savings activities: efforts which achieve efficiency;
    c. compliance and survival activities: efforts which achieve neither of the above but which are required to survive or get by.

    Horizontally, priorities and urgency are assigned. Under the priority column, acts can be either essential, important, desirable or nice to have. Under urgency, acts are either overdue, urgent, immediate but not urgent or time dated within the planning horizon or beyond it.

19. **Draft objectives with the most viable option for the foreseeable future and review priorities as specified in the following section.**

12.5 Objective-setting and validation

Objectives, goals and purpose will be used interchangeably in this book. Objectives exist to support the core mission. They refer to destination points to be reached as a result of moving from the present to the best system of demands identified during the interface planning exercise. Using the priorities from the exercise, the objectives are formulated with respect to every constituency and demand. In addition, the objective should be measurable to the extent necessary and sufficient to energize behavior rather than control it, with a moving and dynamic rather than a static target.

For public institutions, objectives should, when possible, be formulated from a client-centered perspective. A good product or service does more than simply reduce a single problem. It should be timely and available when needed, accessible (cost, location, eligibility criteria) and result in minimum side effects. This requirement is necessary but not sufficient to avoid the single perspective trap. The aspirations of the relevant power group as well as other stakeholders should be considered throughout the exercise.

The preplanning phase

Acts/Decisions	Priority	Urgency
A. Revenue/Service generation		
1 —	Essential	Overdue
2 —	Important	Urgent
3 —	Desirable	Immediate but not urgent
4 —	Nice to have	
5 —		
6 —		
B. Cost/Resource savings		Due this month,
1 —		this quarter,
2 —		this year
3 —		etc.
4 —		
5 —		
6 —		
C. Compliance and survival		
1 —		
2 —		
3 —		
4 —		
5 —		
6 —		

Figure 12.4: Priority assignment

Judging from experience, middle managers tend to take for granted the objectives set by upper management and work religiously toward their achievement. That is why many objectives are conflicting, fuzzy and often inoperable. Regardless of the authority and power of the individual or client groups formulating goals, de facto acceptance of stated purpose could be a burden if not a disservice to the entire organization. Furthermore, behind every unqualified agreement probably lies some misunderstanding! Performers should probe and validate the objectives before accepting responsibility for them.

The process of validation includes clarification of semantics, genuine misperceptions, paradigm traps, and hidden agendas and a scrutiny of underlying values and subjective validity.

Objectives are sometimes expressed in a non-threatening format with public consumption in mind. Hidden agendas may be set, as dramatized by the anecdote in Figure 12.5. In other instances, the word set used is quite remote from the intended terminology either through oversight, cognitive choice or inappropriate understanding of the needs. Understanding the beliefs and values underlying the objectives is also imperative to provide a reasonable assurance that outcomes are in conformity with the superordinate goals of the community. Questioning an assignment is a healthy practice. It helps to clarify the mandate, reduce ambiguity and build joint ownership. The questioning of clients should be done cautiously. To this end, the process of *empathic rehearsal* which is exemplified by Detective Columbo in the famous television series is highly recommended. Columbo always considers his client(s) innocent unless proven guilty. He starts where the system is and restricts his language repertoire to the elementary level.

Ms B. Brown, a shrewd business person, was not amused to be classified by Dun & Bradstreet as a non-borrowing account. So she asked her banker for a $10 loan in the mid-sixties. Although the bank manager found it odd, he granted Ms Brown a loan at 8%, because she was such an important customer. The wealthy woman readily agreed but insisted that she wished to post her jewelry and government bonds worth $100,000 as a security. The banker said no collateral was necessary but the customer insisted.

At the end of the year, the loan and interest were duly paid off, but the banker suggested that it was rather strange that she had gone to so much trouble for such a small loan. To this the rich lady replied, "But how else could I have a safety deposit box for just 80 cents a year?"

Figure 12.5: Hidden versus stated objectives
Adapted from SBA's Instructor Kit, Washington, D.C.

Finally, the announcement of objectives may invite opposition, help competitors or create rigidity. That is why the objectives, once understood, may have to be redrafted in non-threatening terms, broadly stated or even kept secret for strategic reasons.

12.6 Differentiation and integration step

Decision-makers, particularly in manufacturing industries, have a tendency to integrate objectives and decisions more than necessary and often prematurely during the planning process. Yet, success generally requires a differentiated approach for each market segment or public constituency, particularly with respect to delivery of services, health care, public relations, promotion and product acceptance. While arbitrary integration can have far reaching consequences in back up costs, lost sales or public support, excessive differentiation may be expensive in production and processing cost. No company can pursue more than a few objectives simultaneously. Thus a balanced approach is often indicated.

To this end, the objectives and the acts to influence the movement of present trend toward a desirable equilibrium should first be differentiated, based on effectiveness and equity requirements. The goal is to define the issues sharply and achieve the greatest impact. Then, based on efficiency and economy of scale requirements, attempts to integrate these should be undertaken subsequently while maintaining the differentiation *at least* above a standard performance criterion. Acts include work, power, structure, authority, rewards, penalties, communications and strategies to link the family and friends closer to the mission, bring some foreigners on board, upgrade foes and neutralize fools. The objectives should be redrafted to reflect the results of this step and classified as indicated below.

12.7 Outcomes of the preplanning phase

The objectives set previously are grouped under four categories that constitute the outcome of the preplanning phase: policies, operations, projects and pilot experiments. The classification criteria for each follow:

12.7.1 Policies

Under the *policy* heading are listed objectives related to either a new *standard of behavior,* attitudes toward external and internal forces where *consistency in organizational stance is necessary,* guidelines to resolve potential conflicts among goals or head off inappropriate competition among managers, situations requiring prompt and predictable response and *routine* decisions which can be formulated in advance to minimize duplication of executive effort.

Policies increase the velocity and the capacity of the organization's decision-making network. Systems and Procedures are instruments to put policies into practice.

12.7.2 Operations

Under the *operations* heading are objectives related to *current profitability* and on-going *bread and butter* production or service efforts where effectiveness, efficiency and economy of scale are critical. A large share of the productive resources of most organizations is devoted to operations.

12.7.3 Projects

Under the *project* heading are objectives related to institutional *changes,* technological and organizational *transitions* to sustain a viable organization or social system in the long term.

By their nature, projects are in conflict with current operations as they compete for scarce resources, a fact which tend to make them a sort of "second class" citizen under minority governments or vulnerable corporate leaders who are interested in a myopic reduction of costs. Nowhere is the need for perception management greater than in project planning and implementation. Projects are characterized by latent fragility, uncertainty, integration of multidisciplinary skills, a finite life cycle and non-repetitive tasks. Projects facilitate on-going changes and focus on results.

Unlike short-sighted firms, organizations like IBM and General Electric maintain a healthy portfolio of projects in the work-in-progress "pipeline", far exceeding what they can implement in the foreseeable future. In this context, projects can also be seen as a sort of "corporate life insurance" policy.

Unfinished projects result in a high emotional, social and monetary opportunity cost. That is why projects with a high probability of failure should be classified independently as pilot experiments—the subject of the next category.

12.7.4 Pilot experiments

Under the *pilot experiment* heading are objectives related to either perception testing, strategies with multiple options when the real impact is unclear, or high risk activities with uncertain results. The rationale for this category is to avoid creating false expectations. In the technical jargon, this category is sometimes called *Research less Development.*

The preplanning phase

Trial and error is permitted particularly in areas distant from traditional bread and butter lines.

While projects focus on results, pilot experiments focus on *learning and risk management*. Tested experiments with a manageable risk should be reclassified elsewhere above or "stockpiled until their time comes", as a senior executive at Xerox once remarked.

12.7.5 Notes

Multiple projects sometimes form a *program*. However, the word program is extensively used but not universally understood to reflect the same concept. Governments use it for a combination of operations, projects and policies. Companies such as Procter & Gamble use it for product grouping.

Under normal conditions, policies lead to pilot experiments. Pilot experiments produce projects. Projects lead to operations and new policies and so on. However, in real life, anything is possible. Each category requires a different diagnosis and strategic planning approach as outlined in the next chapter.

12.8 Illustration: CWG Inc.

This example illustrates how a company successfully applied interface planning to deal with a major corporate crisis. For several years, City Wood Grains Inc. (CWG), a small manufacturer of plastic laminates, competed successfully, giving customers 48-hour delivery. As the company grew, orders became more diverse in grain, color, shape and form. Unable to cope with the workload increase, the production scheduler asked management for additional staff. The director of personnel was reluctant to yield without validating the request. An analyst was assigned to diagnose the problem, set objectives and suggest solutions.

12.8.1 The classical intervention

After a month of ground work, a preliminary report indicated the manual scheduling system to be the culprit. In the report, it was forcefully argued that staff additions would be only a bandage, not a long term cure for the problem. The author recommended the creation of a project team to design a linear programming system. The latter would meet dual objectives: namely, minimize the loss from plastic laminate cuttings and speed up scheduling through computer automation.

The cost of system development, software programming and hardware interface was estimated in the range of $73,000 over a nine month period. The project was approved, given a high priority by the President and assigned to the system analyst with the production scheduler, a programmer and an industrial engineer acting as regular members of the task force.

The system design and specifications were promptly produced. A packaged program originally designed for scheduling pulp and paper mills was purchased from a mainframe computer manufacturer. The project seemed to progress on time until the seventh month when the software modifications to accommodate the idiosyncrasies of plastic laminate production were due for testing.

12.8.2 The crisis

The team requested a six week extension of the project deadline and was already on the verge of a cost overrun. At the same time, the company was hit by *a surprise event*. A foreign shipment of plastic laminates was unloaded in the West Coast. Japan Inc. came up with a new production technology which permitted continuous mill runs.

12.8.3 The interface planning diagnosis

A complete and urgent review of all company projects and operations was commissioned by the President. Using the Proactive Model, an *interface plan* was drafted. Subjective and objective validity of corporate policies was analysed. In studying the external demands, differentiation was used particularly for large and small customer orders.

It became clear that the marketing policy which advertized 48-hour turnaround to everyone was among the causes of the company weakness and the source of scheduling deficiencies. The policy also led to arbitrary integration, poor product line positioning, and the slowdown of the production machinery far below the economy of scale capacity. Thus, marketing problems were compounded by production inefficiencies and vice versa.

Using the 5F classification, new marketing strategies were explored based on customer needs (differentiation). Wholesalers (family) required fast delivery on four common grains (walnut, satin, suede and butcher block) in two sizes (four by eight and two and a half by eight feet). Industrial clients (friends) were mostly interested in volume discounts. Among these, manufacturers of buses, furniture and small aircraft used call for tenders giving two to twelve weeks lead time.

As for households (foreigners) and retailers (friends), they were found to order a full spectrum of sizes, grain and finishes. However, the total share of direct sales to household and retail businesses was about 9% of the company revenue and contributed only 6% to its profit margin despite the retail mark-up.

In exploring alternative marketing strategies for household and retail orders, it was observed that almost all of these direct orders were either a company specialty or replacements of damaged kitchen furnishings. In other words, these customers would generally not find a good grain match from competition and may wait a week or even more to get a replacement for their partially burned kitchen tops! The 48-hour service was not justified.

12.8.4 The proactive intervention

A new marketing policy was drafted. A product catalogue was prepared. Delivery would be within 24 hours for stock items and one week for specialty and household orders with a higher premium for shorter lead time. Industrials would be negotiated. A new scheme of discounts was set for regular standing offers on items readily available in stock.

The marketing plan was complemented by a new optimum inventory and production policy (integration). Every morning, the plant would go into production to replenish its inventory calculated based on a stochastic model of economic order quantity. Industrials would be processed either on late afternoon runs or during the second shift. Household orders would be used as fill-ins or produced weekends when fill-in time was not available weekdays.

The President participated actively in the development of the new policies. A pilot survey designed in maieutic fashion to mask the intentions and the identity of the client provided CWG with quasi-experimental feedback and led to further streamlining of the strategies. Then, the President invited wholesalers and industrials to a cocktail party to announce the improvement in the delivery of stocked items from 48 to 24 hours and to introduce the standing offer discount scheme. The original automation project was replaced by a small simulation package for resource allocation offered by IBM (friend) on a complimentary basis (strategic resource).

12.8.5 The immediate impact

In contrast with the cookbook solution offered earlier, the total cost of the preplanning review including the design of the new marketing catalogue, the pilot experiment and the courtesy cocktail meeting came to less than twenty percent of the computer system route.

As for the benefits, the company gained more business with wholesalers and industrials. The 24 hour delivery was instrumental. Nothing could beat the perception of being more helpful!

In addition, the standing offer discounts gradually reduced the extreme fluctuations which existed before with batch volume discounts. A smooth production run was established.

The volume of household and retail business did not suffer, despite premium billing. Moreover, profit from this class of orders went up by 31%.

12.8.6 The follow-up benefits

The interface plan exercise was repeated regularly. It led the company to shelter its markets from foreign competitors (foes) and to consider new business areas. Computer and high technology companies were offered help. They considered using plastic laminates for furniture supporting their desk top terminals and printers. Railways and shipbuilders joined the customer ranks. Special products were sold to the military and to the builders of hotels and conference centers.

The foreign market was penetrated in a creative way. The small company found that publicity had far more appeal and credibility than advertising when entering markets where competition is already intense. It focussed on foreign areas where plant and office equipment are badly in need of replacement. Within two years, the company opened a new plant in another metropolitan city to meet the steady increase in domestic and export demand.

12.9 Conclusion

Preplanning takes time. Its iterations can be frustrating. However, its benefits are immense, particularly when an on-going scanning function is well established to support it. This chapter provided a step by step description of preplanning activities and ample examples from business services, industry and governments about how the process works. The next chapter will use the outcome of preplanning as a prerequisite for strategic planning.

References and notes

1. The case of Massey-Ferguson is of interest to decision-makers who equate mission with maximum dividends to shareholders. For several years, Massey's executives did what was normally expected in letting the wishes of the major shareholder (Bud McDougald of Argus Corporation) dictate Massey's future despite marketing and engineering advice to the contrary. When Massey became unprofitable, Argus wrote it off by giving its shares to the employees. Now management have to face a powerful group, the "subordinate turned owner".
2. Ed Schein: Process Consultation, Addison-Wesley O.D. series.
   A gatekeeper is someone open to a new idea regardless of the role and background of its source, eager to give recognition and to credit people even for a partial contribution, ready to single out dysfunctional behavior and prevent it from interfering with synergism.
3. Adapted from Ward Edwards and Peter C. Gardiner: Public Values: Multiattribute Utility Measurement for Social Decision-Making, pp. 1-38 in Martin F. Kaplan and Stevens Schwartz (eds.) Human Judgment and Decision Processes, Academic Press, New York, 1975.
4. A.P. Martin: Validating Perceptions in Issue Management, PDI Press, 1981.
5. Expression adapted from Henry Kissinger, "Random Reflexions" Time Magazine, March 1982.
6. From Herb Simon:
   A satisficing solution is an appropriate solution short of the optimum but to which a firm commitment can be expected.

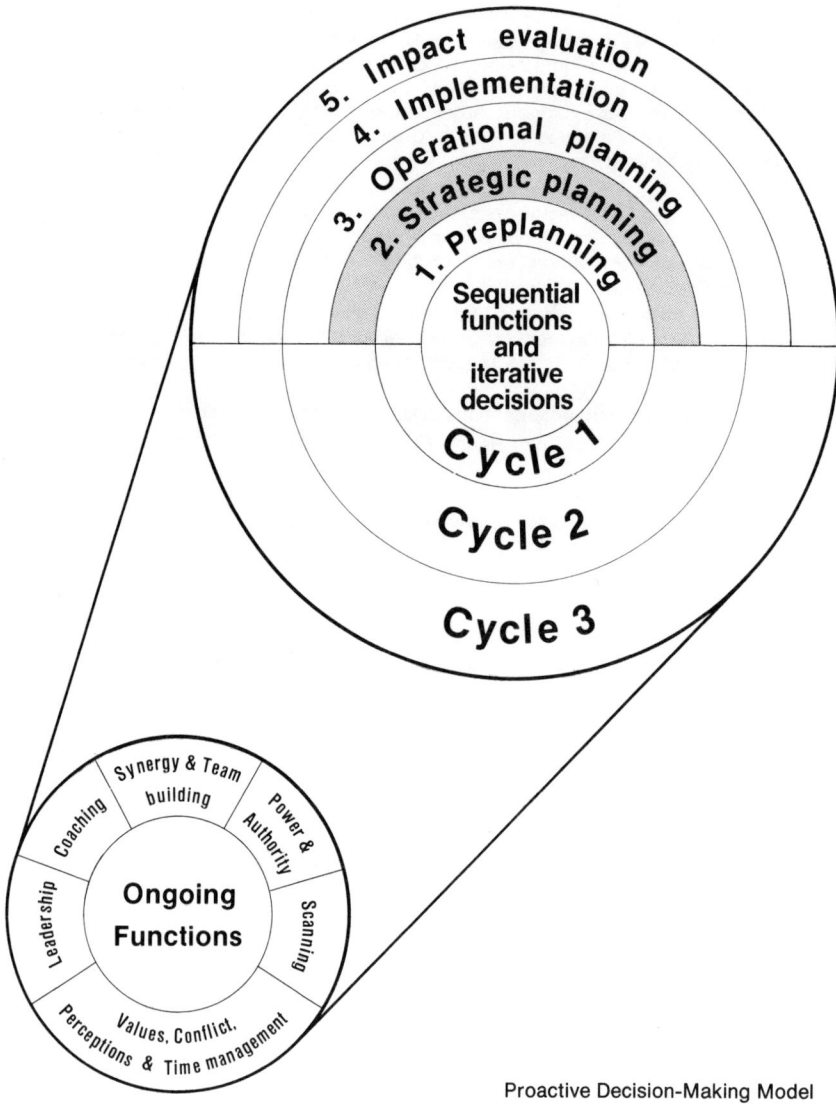

Proactive Decision-Making Model

Chapter thirteen

Strategic planning phase
Work definition instruments

13.1 Strategic planning instruments

From the preplanning phase, a strategic plan is drafted for each objective. Strategic planning is essentially a detailed plan to permit effective mobilization, coaching and allocation of the scarce resources of the organization. It formulates bottom-line targets with respect to market share, pricing strategies, distribution channels, quality and service, innovation and production, as well as the control systems and decision-making structures. The process is again iterative—each step is undertaken subject to the final review at the end of this phase. The documentation resulting from the strategic plan varies depending upon the organizational needs, although the following elements are extremely useful:

1. Work definition instruments
    a. Program charter
    b. Risk estimate
    c. Value analysis of the plan
    d. Evaluation and control scheme
    e. Interdependence grids
    f. Prework strategy
2. Organization design instruments
    g. Responsibility chart
    h. Authority structure
    i. Termination plan

Figure 13.1: The program charter

Decision elements	Critical success factors & performance indicators	Evaluation methods	Uncertainty, risks & assumptions	Indicators to verify risk, assumptions & legitimacy	Contingency plans
Mission-raison d'être:	Equity				
Objectives/goals:	Effectiveness				
Products/services:	Efficiency				
Resources & Processes:	Economy				

© Copyright, A.P. Martin, 1983   ISBN 0 86502 000 0

13.2 The charter

A charter (Figure 13.1) is prepared for each project, policy, operation and pilot experiment. The document formulates in a grid form the decision logic and boundaries. It is also sometimes called a *work plan,* a mandate, a program profile or a decision profile. Vertically, it specifies the overall mission to which this program is a precondition, the program objectives, the expected products or services in the form of outputs necessary and sufficient to meet the objectives, and the resources and work processes, including production and marketing strategies, capital equipment, materials, human resources, technology, information and veto powers.

Horizontally, the charter outlines several elements. These include the critical success factors and performance indicators, evaluation methodology, assumptions about risk and uncertainty, indicators to validate the assumptions and related contingency plans. The horizontal logic defines precisely each element in the vertical input-output-objective hypothesis chain as well as the means to monitor assumptions and the required contingency measures. A description of each element follows.

13.3 The critical success factors

The critical success factors (C.S.F.'s) determine the required degree of viability and legitimacy of each element in the vertical logic. "They are the areas subject to change but where the things must go right for the results to be achieved."[1]

The evaluation methodology outlines the plan for experiment design, data collection, analysis and monitoring each C.S.F. A short description of the evaluation scheme will be provided later. Six types of *performance indicators* specify the required targets for each C.S.F. (see illustrations in Figure 13.2 and 13.3).

13.3.1 Equity indicators

At the mission level they indicate the contribution of the objectives to the mission. To determine the degree of equity, the validity of the objectives should be tested. This is precisely the level where most quantification efforts have failed since the mission-objective linkage is usually either too complex or too ill-defined to be analysed by conventional statistical methods. As an alternative to precise quantification, peer reviews and fuzzy sets theory play a major role in this area where decisions are required under conditions of uncertainty and partial information.[2]

An exercise to measure the degree of contribution of a project or a policy to the corporate mission has been carried out by the U.S.

Figure 13.2: C.S.F. illustration—Business case

A Canadian manufacturer of bicycles and fitness equipment is interested in the Californian market. The critical success factors explored could be:

- **Equity**
  Would our organization be better served by capturing a share of the bicycle market in California or by penetrating the roller-skate market in Western Canada? Which option would provide more *equitable* returns to our shareholders? What is the importance of market share?

- **Effectiveness**
  Assuming the Californian option was selected, what pricing and volume targets should we pursue? The degree of achievement of these targets will be a measure of effectiveness (e.g. 85,000 bikes sold at $100 each). Effectiveness is usually better expressed in terms of market share. If the target is to capture 50% of a new and expanding market and the actual results are 45% share then, other things being equal, effectiveness is 90%. What should our pricing strategy be to attract customers and establish a barrier to competitors (e.g. unattractive sales margins)?

- **Efficiency**
  How to achieve our market share? Is acquisition better than expansion? Is it more efficient to produce bicycles in our domestic plant, open either a production or assembly plant in California or even subcontract and use our trademarks only? What is the opportunity cost of producing a bike? Which is the most efficient? Should we focus on production quality and styling (identity) or innovation?

- **Economy**
  How much should we pay for skilled and unskilled labor, supply materials, facilities, services and information compared to our competitors? How could we explain the difference (e.g. loyalty, quality, minimum wage constraints, union-management harmony, distance from market)?

- **Legitimacy**
  Would our shareholders *support* the project? How should it be *perceived* by our domestic union? What should our *reputation* be in California? How could we establish a clear *identity?* Should we be identified with the jet set bikers, the emulators or new fitness values consumers? Should the Californian venture be autonomous or highly controlled by the parent company headquarters? Who are the potential adversaries? What is their potency in the worst case? Who are the *potential allies* (Dun & Bradstreet, unions, McDonell Douglas, City Hall, the Canadian Trade Commission, suppliers, etc)? What are the dynamics of *power?*

- **Assumption indicators**
  What is the projected growth of the bicycle market? the competition strength? the roller-skating threats? population trends? consumer preferences? disposable income? inflation? supply costs? labor availability? tariffs and import quotas? capital cost allowances and tax incentives? plant security? fire protection? back up and insurance requirements? *surprise events* (oil embargo, etc)? What is the likelihood of each projection?

© Copyright, A.P. Martin, 1983   ISBN 0 86502 000 0

Strategic planning phase - Work definition instruments

Figure 13.3: C.S.F. illustration—Government case

New York State Police is interested in forming a new agency to deal with white collar crime.

- **Equity**
  Would the mission of the state be better served by fighting white collar crime or protecting citizens against violent crimes? Which of these needs is now below the threshold of acceptance? Should we focus simultaneously on both? Which level of protection would be *equitable* to citizens? How does it compare to other states? Which state is geopolitically comparable? How could we account for the difference?

- **Effectiveness**
  Assuming the state wishes to eradicate serious white collar crimes, what targets should be pursued? For instance, the target could be to improve the incidence of discovering and prosecuting E.F.T. (Electronic Fund Transfers) crimes. The degree of achievement of that target would be a measure of effectiveness.

- **Efficiency**
  Is it more efficient to build safer E.F.T. data bases, retrain data processing auditors, upgrade the competence of prosecution lawyers or focus on prevention and deterrence measures such as revised security clearance guidelines for recruiting computer staff? Should the state do it alone or combine its efforts with the federal and city law enforcement agencies, the U.S. Banking Institute or the telecommunications industry?

- **Economy**
  Is it more economical to build an internal nucleus of experts (e.g. criminologists, auditors, investigators, lawyers) or to buy these services in the market place? Are we getting more mileage from our equipment and facilities than the states of Connecticut, New Jersey, Massachusetts or Ohio? How could we explain the difference?

- **Legitimacy**
  Is this effort *perceived* to be in the domain of the state, the federal government or the banking industry? Do we have the *critical mass* to support us in this endeavor? How do we monitor its support? Should we use a pilot experiment and capitalize on its success or stage advocacy advertising to improve the legitimacy of our efforts? Should we establish a clear *identity* with respect to white collar crime prevention or *work underground*? What are the risks associated with covert and overt operations? How should legitimacy be monitored?

- **Assumption indicators**
  What projection can be made concerning the quality and magnitude of support from federal and state agencies? the level of cooperation from industry? the incidence of white collar crimes? the growth of the E.F.T. market? the state-of-the-art of telecommunications networks? new developments in the justice system? criminology? individual awareness? understanding of E.F.T. systems? behavior modification? banking practices? surprise events? What is their likelihood of occurring?

© Copyright, A.P. Martin, 1983

ISBN 0 86502 000 0

Department of Housing and Urban Development. To this end, a unit-free C.S.F. called the inequity index provided insights into the maldistribution of fire protection and municipal police service among geographical districts or groups of citizens. The same process can apply to crime protection, health promotion and new business development.[3]

13.3.2 Effectiveness indicators

At the objective level, the C.S.F.'s specify the conditions that establish that the objectives have been achieved. Effectiveness is therefore a comparison of the end of project or program status to a target. It considers the extent to which objectives have been achieved in terms of quality, quantity, timing, legitimacy, target population and other characteristics.

13.3.3 Efficiency indicators

Efficiency is a resource *allocation* indicator. It measures outputs by specifying the timing, the quantity, the quality and other characteristics necessary and sufficient for each product or service to meet objectives. Efficiency is the ratio of outputs to inputs compared to a standard. The standard should provide a sound basis for comparison of costs within a given range of quality, quantity, time and environment.

13.3.4 Economy indicators

Economy is a resource *mobilization* indicator. At the input level, it defines the quantity, quality and availability of resources and processes necessary for each output. Economy is the relationship between the opportunity cost of mobilizing resources incurred by the organization and a standard. The standard is usually the market place.

13.3.5 Legitimacy indicators

These are soft measures based on the stakeholders' perceptions of the organization *identity* and the right to change its *boundaries,* performance or mode of operation. They consider visibility, public support, credit rating, neighborhood acceptance and government vested interest in the organization, the program or the project.

13.3.6 Indicators to verify the assumptions

These indicators permit decision-makers to monitor the variables beyond their domain of control. The majority of management textbooks and public seminars are devoted to efficiency and effectiveness while experience has repeatedly shown that decision-makers ought to pay more attention to the Achilles' heels of corporate management: assumptions.

13.4 Assumptions

Assumptions are all conditions and events beyond the decision-maker's control but which must exist for the input-output-objective-mission chain (I.O.O.M.) to be achieved. The assumptions are of critical importance to management, perhaps even more than the I.O.O.M. chain. Indeed, these uncontrollable conditions can make the difference between success and failure of strategic planning. Several levels of assumptions should be identified as outlined below. Each statement should reflect the status of the assumption as it is developing today and as it may appear in the future.

In Proactive Decision-Making, assumption identification is a by-product of the processes previously described. Firstly, the on-going scanning function provides a permanent instrument for identifying the environmental assumptions. Secondly, the interface planning exercise describes the assumptions related to the stakeholders. Finally, the charter gives an additional opportunity to identify the assumptions at the input-output levels, related linkages and other element dependencies.

13.4.1 Assumptions about mission

The achievement of all objectives is necessary but not sufficient for the mission to be accomplished. Some assumptions at the mission level must exist:

$$\text{Mission}_{organization} = \text{Sum (Objectives)} + \text{Sum (Assumptions about organization environment \& boundaries)}$$

These environmental and organizational boundary assumptions include the power of corporate leadership, governmental stability, the health of the economy, community acceptance, changes in social needs, technology, tariff barriers, competitive threats, advocacy, organized hostility, regulatory constraints and interorganizational synergy or complementarity, natural and person-made disasters and the organization's ability to predict surprise events, monitor risk, build contingency plans and respond adequately.

13.4.2 Assumptions about objectives and outputs

Likewise, the production of outputs is necessary but not sufficient for a given policy, operation or project objective to be realized. Another level of axioms or assumptions should be clearly expressed. This set applies to the boundaries of either the project, policy, pilot experiment or program. It includes the impact of public visibility, external support, corporate stability, senior management attitude toward the project or program, the degree of interdependence among operations, projects, policies and pilot experiments (later discussed in section 10 of this chapter).

$$\text{Objectives}_{\text{project A}} = \text{Sum (Outputs)} + \text{Sum (Assumptions about project environment \& boundaries)}$$

13.4.3 Assumptions about resources and processes

Finally, the outputs require not only the integration of all inputs through management and production processes but the existence of another level of assumptions. These conditions outline the sources of uncertainty about resources. They include quality and availability of labor, inflation in the relative price level of critical resources, potential work stoppages, supply risks, technology hazards, weather uncertainty, availability of information and the impact of public awareness.

$$\text{Output}_a = \text{Integration(Inputs)} + \text{Sum (Assumptions about resource environment)}$$

13.5 Assumptions management

The probability of each assumption should be determined. Then, attempts and strategies to reduce risk should be explored. For the remaining risk, contingency plans and monitoring indicators should be identified and regularly evaluated. The mechanism to set contingency plans in motion should be explicit. Figure 13.4 illustrates this process.

13.6 Summary

The information generated so far in the *program charter* is a work plan to render the objectives operational. It makes explicit the contribution of each individual resource to the mission via the objectives. It provides the manager with a comprehensive mandate. It stipulates clearly what is expected and under what conditions. The following paragraphs outline the remaining elements of the program charter and include an analysis of risk and value, evaluation schemes and program interdependence.

Strategic planning phase - Work definition instruments

Strategic planning—Managing the unpredictable

1. Make explicit all **assumptions** and conditions beyond the control of the organization, the branch, the performers or the client. Include the assumptions about the stakeholders, the environment and the potential for surprise events. *Validate* the assumptions (semantics, genuine misperceptions, paradigm traps, hidden agendas, values).

2. Express the **probability** of each assumption and its fluctuations over the time horizon. Use the best/worst case criteria to express a range of probabilities. Consider the interdependence between assumptions and the possibility of converting the threat of an assumption into an opportunity. *Validate* the probability estimate using the shortest decision-making cycle.

3. Develop a **risk profile** over the time horizon with the help of people close to the best information sources. Risk consists of the potential adverse consequences of each assumption. Precision is desirable but not necessary.

4. Explore **strategies** to reduce risk to a manageable level. Consider the four options and adverse consequences. The options are: wait and see, compliance, active and proactive. Select the best combination of strategies over the time horizon. Match strengths with risks when feasible. Use the 5F classification as a planning aid to explore potential interventions by the family, the friends, the foreigners, the foes and the fools.

5. Draft the profile of **residual risk** and its likelihood over the time horizon.

6. Explore **contingency plans** to cope with residual risk and select the best combination of contingency options (wait and see, compliance, active, proactive).

7. Draft **operational plans** to monitor each assumption, a procedure to review its validity and to reassess both the strategies and residual risk. Outline the policy to set in motion the contingency plans. Develop a schedule and a budget, allocate resources and review costs and benefits.

8. Revise the plans until a satisficing solution is obtained. *Validate* the results by considering semantics, hidden agendas, genuine misperceptions, paradigm traps, values and subjective validity. Update the program charter.

Figure 13.4: The process of assumption management

13.7 Risk analysis

Each charter will be analysed to determine the range of risk and its likelihood. This section outlines sources of poor estimating practices and provides insights on how to improve the quality of risk estimating and also defines the process of risk analysis.

13.7.1 Sources of risk assessment deficit

In strategic planning, most decision-makers seem far too sure of themselves. They tend to think of probability values of either zero or one, while they ought to think in terms of every probability except zero or one. In recent years, experts have repeatedly underestimated investment risk by failing to adequately consider future unknowns.

The issue in strategic planning is not to guess the expected cost-benefits but rather to outline candidly the likelihood of each of a series of values. To this end, on-going practice should be combined with teamwork, rapid feedback, action-research, influential role models and a greater attention to lessons from the field regardless of whether such experience is good, bad or inconclusive. Practice requires professional development, coaching opportunities and grace periods for risk-taking while learning.

Although necessary, rapid feedback is, alas, wishful thinking in business decisions where the results take several years to arrive. Fortunately, a similar effect can be achieved inexpensively as outlined below.

The ability to forecast can be developed by practicing regularly in non-threatening milieux such as predicting the weather, the stock market, daily corporate sales and even sports scores. Instead of point estimates, the range of expected values should be predicted along with an explicit measure of the degree of confidence or probability in order to avoid the certainty trap. By comparing the actual results with the forecast, one gets an immediate feedback which is seldom available in decision-making.

Regular practice will not *ipso facto* result in a magic winning number, but may ultimately lead to a better grasp on how to set probabilities correctly. As an example, the remarkable performance of meteorologists gives an indication of the merit of rapid feedback[4].

13.7.2 Risk analysis process

The process of risk analysis includes two steps. It commences with external risk, i.e. a review of each assumption and an assessment of its likelihood over a range of potential values. For instance, an assumption about maintaining an open relationship with union leadership would lead to the following review questions:

Is it plausible? What are the stakes? Under the best case what benefits would be derived by the organization, the union, the employee and the labor leader? What would be the cost, risk, benefits and the likelihood of both the worst and the best cases? What side effects would result? What is the expected value? How close is it to the best or worst case? What is its likelihood? What contingency plans are required to shelter the organization from the worst case? What monitoring system would be used to report risk and trigger contingency plans?

Secondly, the likelihood of risk is used to revise the values of the performance indicators for the inputs, outputs and objectives. Sources of internal risk are identified to further discount these values and to finalize the range. Large variances may point to the need for additional critical success factors. Since the risk increases with the variance in estimates, the greater the risk, the more requirement for strict monitoring and contingencies.

To sum up, a risk profile will be developed for each resource, product, service, objective and assumption. Strategies should also be drafted to reduce risk to a manageable level. For the residual risk, status reporting and contingency plans are required.

13.8 Value analysis of the plan

Having analysed the risk elements, the next issue will be to estimate the strategic plan from multiple perspectives. Cost benefits include economic, technical and psychosocial forms. The process is an assessment of the best and worst scenarios of each program charter.

The best case expectation is used as a benchmark so that the relevant power group does not misjudge or underestimate a good idea. The worst scenario value is to help build contingencies against risk and uncertainty. Value for money projections are necessary but not sufficient. In addition, psychosocial costs and benefits should be explicit whenever relevant. Value analysis determines the capability for survival and the effectiveness of the strategic plan over three horizons:

1. The short term analysis is based on the ability to respond promptly to external threats.
2. The medium term focusses on the ability to manage perceptions and maintain a balance between issues and demands from customers, constituents, shareholders, change advocates, suppliers, technology, employees, unions, managers and other significant forces.

3. The long term is based on the ability to adapt to the pace of the single most predominant driving force (e.g. technology, owner, president, key scientists) and ultimately serve the public interest.

13.9 Evaluation scheme

The evaluation scheme includes experiment design, data collection, analysis, feedback and problem solving plans. The instruments for data collection include questionnaires, face to face interviews, telephone interviews, observations, and secondary data sources. A combination of these tools is often required, to capitalize on their strengths and overcome their respective weaknesses.

The evaluability criteria should be built into the decision-making process. The result is an evaluation scheme based both on the performance indicators and the indicators to monitor risk, uncertainty and legitimacy. Quantification is not absolutely necessary, particularly in aggregation where it may be subject to a severe data reduction loss.

The evaluation should emphasize positive instead of negative controls. Positive controls lead to productive energy and reinforcement. Furthermore, the process of control should aim at locating the data collection and interpretation points as close as possible to the information source(s) to minimize contamination through aggregation, management tiers and authority bias.

Reports containing descriptive data should be enhanced by allowing space for the opinion of performers or immediate supervision, whenever feasible. While seldom sought by executives, the opinion of key performers may lead to more informed decisions and minimize the risk of erroneous interpretation of the data.

13.10 Interdependence grids

Like the issues they address, projects, policies, operations and pilot experiments are also interdependent. Having defined the input/output requirements for each, it is now possible to display a network of interdependencies using two impact grids originally developed by George Bernstein at the U.S. Navy. These matrices are valuable for strategies and risk analysis and are often drafted during the preplanning phase as a result of the differentiation and integration step.

13.10.1 Cross relevance grids

This document (Figure 13.5) outlines in matrix form the positive and negative contribution of each project, policy, operation and pilot experiment to each objective of the organization. Objectives are grouped under two sets of columns: specific and common objectives. Specific objectives are directly related to the working mission of the organization in terms of service delivery, cost savings or revenue generation and corporate values. Common objectives are either shared with other organizations or imposed for the common good of the organization or the society in general, e.g. equal opportunity for minorities, personal growth, language education and preretirement programs, safety and security, compliance and legitimacy objectives.

13.10.2 Cross supporting grids

A cross supporting grid (Figure 13.6) indicates the type(s) and degree of support, both positive and negative, obtained by each project, policy, operation and pilot experiment from others. For instance, row A identifies the interdependence between policy A and other policies, operations, projects and pilot experiments. It shows the contribution A makes to others as well as the support it gets from them.

Support is in the form of input/output interdependence, economy of scale leverage, and impact contribution. The popularity of A could be due to a precedent established by B. The success of D could be at the expense of depriving E and G of a scarce resource! The assessment does not have to be absolutely perfect to be useful in strategic planning.

13.11 Prework strategy

The objective of this step is to explore the *means to mobilize energy*. Prework includes all conditions to unfreeze the present state and facilitate the transition toward the future. To determine whether prework is necessary, attention should be paid to multiple issue interdependencies, the level of dissatisfaction with the status quo and to the critical mass for change.

13.11.1 Readiness and the level of dissatisfaction with the present

For each objective, the level of dissatisfaction with the status quo is reassessed. Unless people are sufficiently dissatisfied with the present, the resistance to change is usually too high to undertake change without

Think Proactive: New insights into decision-making

Figure 13.5: Cross relevance grid

	Contribution										
	Specific objectives							Common objectives			
	Western market network	Export development	New product XYZ	Phase-out non profitable "W"	Economy of scale purchasing			Equal opportunity	Student employment	Corporate reputation	Decentralization of training
Policies											
Operations											
Projects											
Experiments											

Indicate whether the contribution is positive or negative, significant (high: H), low (L) or irrelevant (I).

Strategic planning phase - Work definition instruments

Figure 13.6: Cross-supporting grid

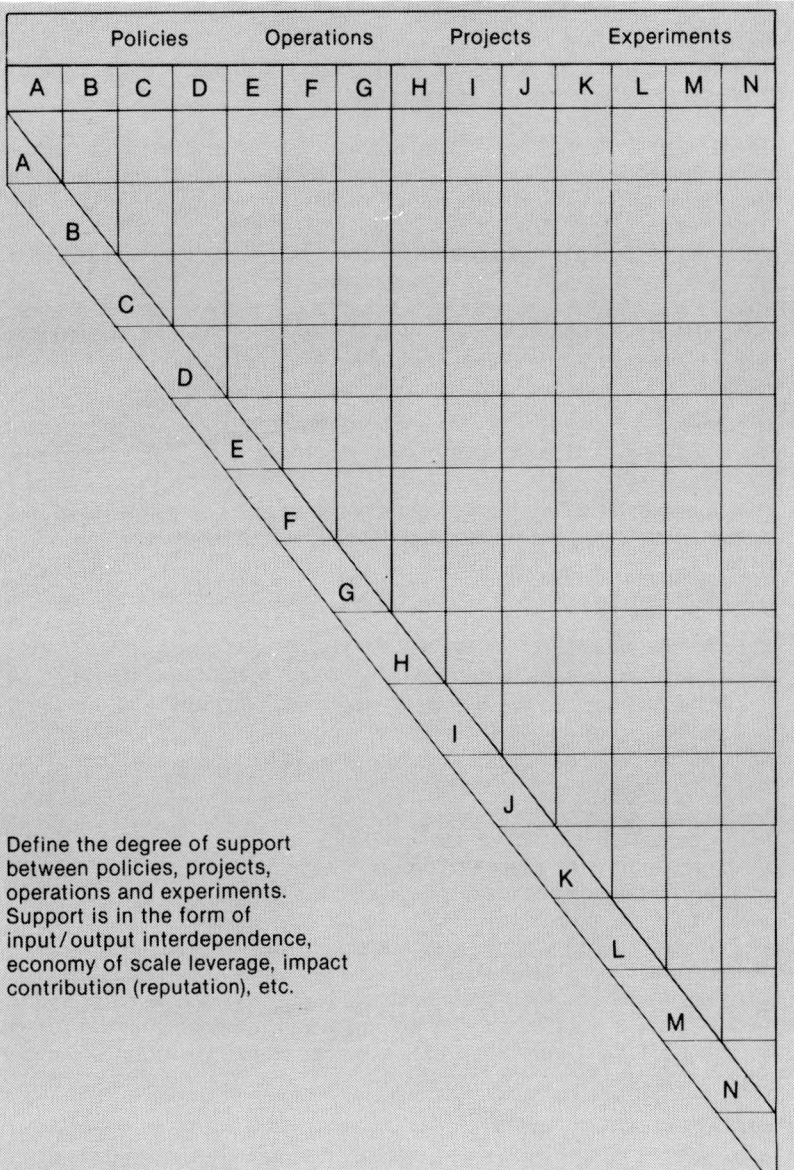

Define the degree of support between policies, projects, operations and experiments. Support is in the form of input/output interdependence, economy of scale leverage, impact contribution (reputation), etc.

severe adverse transition effects. To this end, alternatives are developed to identify what should be reinforced, ignored, created, treated, made further independent or interdependent, or even worsened to get results. The "what" refers to issues, coalitions, tasks, policies, systems, standards, conflicts, perceptions, rewards and values.

There is no universal correlation between job satisfaction and performance. Even when it exists, the results are short lived[5] and due to a Hawthorne or a macro Hawthorne effect like the early quality of work life (QWL) experiments. That is why prework strategies are not necessarily designed to increase satisfaction, an effort that is likely to be perceived as phony or manipulative. The alternative strategy is how to make it *work,* i.e. increase readiness and acceptance of the decision whether people like it or not. However, there is a personal level of satisfaction which is necessary to maintain harmony in work relations.

13.11.2 Critical mass commitment planning

Readiness is necessary but not sufficient to secure commitment. To this end, a *commitment plan* is required. It has five steps.

1. Identify the critical mass.
2. Indicate how to gain access to its members.
3. Outline thoroughly their respective roles.
4. Develop a strategy to get the commitment toward the change or, at least, to prevent the exercise of veto. The commitment can be open or tacit, active or laissez-faire.
5. Draft a contingency plan to deal with a premature abortion of the critical mass.

In this context, the *critical mass* is the nucleus of a constituency. It is the minimum number of people or groups whose commitment is necessary to unfreeze the present resistance, facilitate the readiness for change or prevent the exercise of veto. For instance, former Prime Minister Lester B. Pearson brought Messrs. Jean Marchand, Gérard Pelletier and Pierre Trudeau into the Liberal Party in order to win massive support from Quebec. These so-called three wise men were the critical mass in the mid-sixties. For the Liberals to overcome western alienation or the Tories to penetrate the Quebec fortress, a similar course of action could be explored today.

Recently, a foreign tire manufacturer was trying to defend its waste management record. Despite the series of TV ads produced by Madison Avenue, the pressure from special interest groups kept growing. During a Christmas party, a senior Vice-President was startled to discover the embryo of the critical mass for the change in the company's own backyard, namely the blue-collar workers.

These employees faced daily criticism from spouses, children and neighbors who were influenced by environmental protection movements. Like many corporations, the manufacturer underestimated the potency of the interpersonal and social networks of the employees.

Early the following year, prework strategies were developed to raise employee awareness. Through a comprehensive educational program, the personnel was brought up to date on the company waste management efforts and the powerful considerations that sustain the local pressure groups. The employees were also briefed about the unusual opportunities for influence and the corporate support available to this end. The orientation sessions led to a massive voluntary involvement of responsible employees. They conducted meetings, disseminated information and film strips through their own informal and powerful social networks in an effort to change community perceptions.

13.11.3 Forming a critical mass

In instances where the critical mass does not exist, the strategist should either stay put or work to create it. The author faced such a situation in the process of introducing an advanced data base technology for a major multinational corporation in 1971. The proposed software supplier was unfairly discounted by the client's controller who was responding to undue pressure from a powerful competing supplier. Repeated attempts by middle management to change the controller's perception failed.

Invited by the Operations Vice-President to explore alternative strategies, the author sought a critical mass for the change within and outside the conglomerate, but in vain. Yet several local companies had been evaluating data base offerings by trial and error. In order to exchange information among users, an informal Data Base Management Group was established. Monthly meetings were organized to share available experience. Within four months, a clear consensus among users emerged about the viability of the system discounted by the client.

During the fifth month, the controller was invited to attend a major conference where a panel of users and suppliers debated the state of the art of data base technology. He was impressed by the quality of the panel and the achievements made by a large chartered bank and other users of the discounted system. As a result, he reversed his previous decision even before the end of the conference. He promptly instructed middle management to go ahead with the change. He concluded that if a major bank was going that route despite its traditional conservative roots, his company ought to try it!

This illustration demonstrates how the critical mass, in this case a user's group, can be formed to counter undue pressure and achieve a power balance which will facilitate the change.

13.11.4 Change management framework

Having determined the level of dissatisfaction with the status quo and identified the critical mass, a *change management model* is developed to define *strategies, contingency plans,* concession options and *rewards/penalties* to broaden the existing pockets of internal and external support, build and maintain a constituency for sailing the program with the critical mass on board and leaving the irreducible opposition (if any) fragmented and anchored sufficiently far behind. The model outlines in a grid form the strategic change factors, their current status, and finally the desirable status in the present, the transition state and the future state (Figure 13.7).

In order to be effective, rewards to staff should first and foremost be related to work. Penalties serve as a deterrent. Both rewards and penalties are necessary. They should take into account knowledge, capability and the degree of effort or commitment. A review of the content of the charter is generally imperative at this point before allocating the specific role of each resource, the subject of the next chapter.

References and notes

1. John Rockhart: A New Approach to Defining the Chief Executive's Information Needs, CISR No. 37, May 78, MIT, Cambridge Mass.
2. L.A. Zadeh: US-Japan Seminar on Fuzzy Sets and their Applications, University of California, Berkeley, July 1974.
3. Jean Larvo: Measuring the Equity of Service Delivery Systems, US Department of Housing and Urban Development, Washington DC.
4. R.L. Winkler: Evaluation of Subjective Precipitation Probability Forecasts, American Meteorological Society, l968
5. Ralph Katz: Time and Work: Towards an Integrative Perspective, MIT-WP 1029-78, Cambridge, Mass.
   Project Performance and Job Longevity presented at the International Conference of Industrial Relations and Conflict Management, April 1980 (available from MIT, Sloan School of Management).

Strategic planning phase - Work definition instruments

Figure 13.7: Strategic model for management of change

Strategic change factors	Current status	Desired status		
		Present	Transition	Future

© Copyright, A.P. Martin, 1983   ISBN 0 86502 000 0

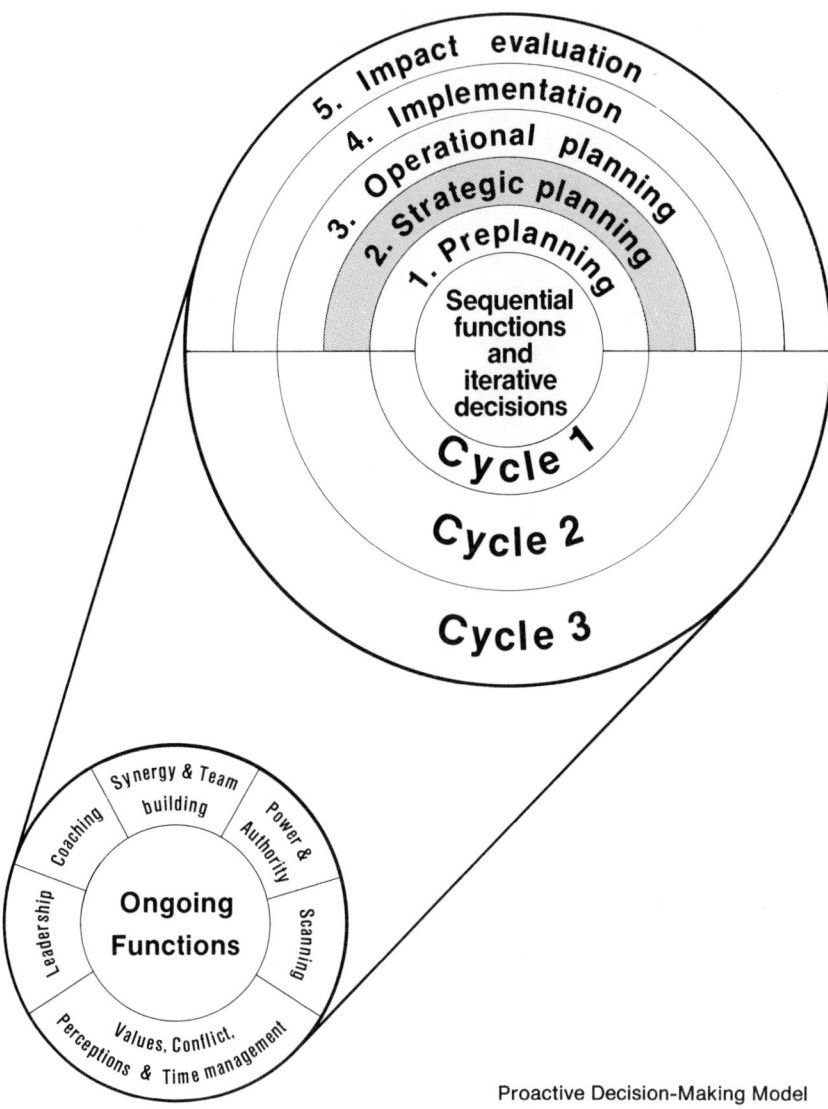

Proactive Decision-Making Model

Chapter fourteen

Strategic planning phase Organization design instruments

14.1 Responsibility chart

Once work and associated strategies are identified, the next task is to assign responsibility. The process used for this purpose dates back to the sixties.[1] However, the framework presented here is a by-product of more than twelve years' application by a host of clients.

A responsibility chart (Figures 14.1, 14.2 and 14.3) is basically a grid defining the specific role required by each actor in each decision or activity of the strategic plan. Originally the multiplicity of roles created redundancy, ambiguity and confusion. Since the technique was streamlined throughout the seventies, four roles (R, A, S, I) have been retained as necessary and sufficient to reflect the contribution of each participant.[2]

Responsibility charting is done in two stages. The roles are first differentiated to optimize interfaces at the work boundaries and achieve both equity and effectiveness. Then, an integration stage is necessary, to achieve economy of scale and efficiency where feasible before preparing the organization structure.

Figure 14.1: Responsibility Chart

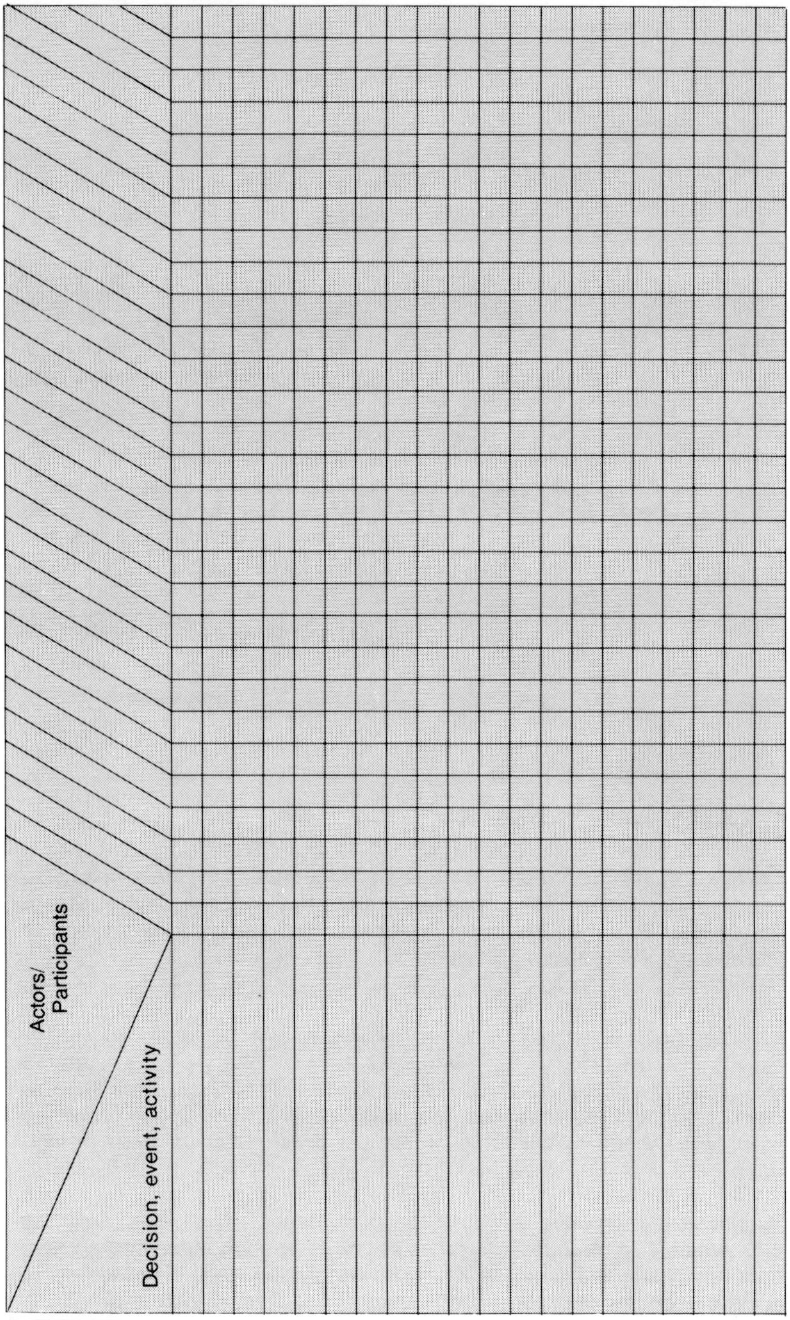

Actors/Participants

Decision, event, activity

R = Responsibility   A = Approval   S = Support   I = Information

© Copyright, A.P. Martin, 1983

ISBN 0 86502 000 0

Strategic planning phase - Organization design instruments

Figure 14.2: Basic responsibility chart for building a garage

Participants → Activities ↓	1 Project manager	2 Landlord	3 Tenant	4 Architect	5 Drafts-person	6 City hall	7 Estimator	8 Contractor	9 Suppliers	10 Neighbors	11 Taxation
1- Project Management	R	A	I	I	I	I	I	I	I	I	
2- Set objectives	A	I	I	R	S	A	S	I	I	I	
3- Design	I	I	I	R	S	A	S	I	I	I	
4- Write specifications	A	I	I	S	I	I	R	I	I	I	
5- Estimate cost	A	I	I	I	I	I	R	I	I	I	
6- Call for tender	A	I	I	S	I	I	R	I	I	I	
7- Negotiate a contract	A	I	I	I	I	I	R	A	I	I	
8- Order materials	I	I	I	I	I	I	S	R	S	I	
9- Mobilize resources	I	I	I	I	I	I	I	R	I	I	
10- Build	A	I	I	A	I	A	S	R	S	I	
11- Inspect	I	I	I	S	I	R	I	S	I	I	
12- Use	A	R	I	I	I	I	I	I	I	I	—

R: Responsible   A: Approve   S: Support   I: Must be informed

Figure 14.3: Master responsibility chart:
Planning the U.S. President's trip to London (United Kingdom)

	1	2	3	4	5	6	7	8	9	10	11	12	13	14	15
	Program manager	Director US-UK relations	US President	Secretary of State	White House	President's family	Secretary of Defence	Secretary of Commerce	British Foreign Office	US embassy–London	British embassy–Washington	Press	All US embassies around the world	President's Secret Service	Scotland Yard
1. Management & coordination															
2. Draft objectives of trip	R	–	A	I	–	S	A	–	S	–	–	–	–	–
3. Approve objectives of trip	I	A	R	S	I	I	I	A	I	S	I	I	I	I	I
4. Define topics of discussion	R	A	A	S	–	A	A	A	S	S	I	I	–	–
5. Define critical factors for success	R	I	A	A	–	I	A	–	S	–	–	–	–	–
6. Plan strategies	R	A	A	S	–	A	A	–	S	–	–	–	–	–
7. Set contingency plans - issues	R	I	I	A	–	I	A	–	S	–	–	–	–	–
8. Finalize agenda	R	A	A	A	–	A	A	A	S	S	I	I	–	–
9. Plan itinerary & schedule	I	I	I	A	I	I	I	R	A	I	I	I	I	I
10. Plan security — USA	I	I	–	S	I	–	–	S	S	S	–	–	R	I
11. Plan security — UK	I	I	–	S	I	–	–	S	S	S	–	–	A	R
12. Budget	R	–	I	S	–	–	–	–	S	–	–	–	S	–
Etc.															

© Copyright, A.P. Martin, 1983   ISBN 0 86502 000 0

14.2 Role differentiation

14.2.1 Responsibility role

'R' reflects responsibility. Each activity or decision within the strategic plan should have one and only one *responsible* individual (or group) to whom the R is assigned, R meaning the person sees that the job gets done. The recipient of R is usually sought among the first two categories of stakeholders (family and friends).

When multiple R's seem to be necessary, it is more likely that several decisions have been arbitrarily grouped into one. A review of the decision or activity is imperative to explore activity splitting or redefinition along geopolitical, functional boundaries or different budget ceilings. If multiple R's still exist, the decision to allocate the R should be elevated to the common boss (if any), or the R itself should be elevated and assigned to the common boss but only as a measure of last resort.

However, it is always preferable to locate the R as close as possible to the source(s) of information rather than based on the individual role in the hierarchy. This practice increases the velocity, the quality and the capacity of the decision-making system. Alternatively, the decision-maker can act differently if prepared to live with the consequences! Apart from relinquishing other opportunities, heart failures and pacemakers are unfortunately among the featured long term consequences.

Denying the local manager responsibility is precisely what former President Carter did during the aborted hostage rescue mission to Iran in early 1980. Actually, Jimmy Carter's centralized decision-making style almost made kamikaze pilots out of the best U.S. rescue team. By being personally responsible for the decision to call off the mission once underway, the President imposed on the rescue team hours of delay at critical moments where time was of the essence, thus increasing the risks and overtaxing local leadership endurance.[3] The rescue mission manager should have been directly responsible for the decision to withdraw.

14.2.2 Approval role

Individuals with an 'A' role must either *approve* or veto the decision. There should be only as many A's as necessary; the greater the number of vetos, the less likely the job gets done. Multiple A's are therefore early warning signals for potential delays. The number of A's should be limited to the minimum necessary and sufficient. Furthermore, efforts should be made to clearly define the boundaries of remaining A's to speed up the decision-making process.

For instance, instead of allocating an A for equipment acquisition to both the controller and the production manager, perhaps the production manager should be vested with an A for acquisitions of up to a certain dollar value and for equipment standards. The controller would be informed and could only veto the lease, buy or rent options for decisions exceeding that value, assuming equitable return on investment (R.O.I.).

By the same token, the marketing manager may want to approve all export decisions. A better arrangement may be to explore a differentiated approach where the manager's approval is necessary only for selected combinations of products, export destinations and order volume.

Likewise, the British Prime Minister may want to veto her trip agenda. The Foreign Office could negotiate a better deal with the P.M. She would keep her veto power over agendas for trips to the U.S. and the Common Market, be informed promptly about the agendas for the Commonwealth meetings, and find out about the agenda once en route for state funerals or courtesy trips to the remaining destinations!

When multiple A's exist, subscripting can be used to reflect the sequence in which approvals should be sought. The ordering process should take into account established protocols and strategies to secure both the approval and the commitment of the critical mass. Sometimes, it is easier to allocate the sequence of approvals using the process of elimination.

Where either hostility is expected or inappropriate competition is encouraged, the worst case is to group all A's in a single meeting. The likelihood of getting consensus is usually remote and much lower than with personalized meetings. Since a chain is only as strong as its weakest link, the process of getting consensus should be initiated by separate meetings starting with the individual most likely to agree with the proposal in order to get momentum and build a power base.

R and A can have legal implications. In the case of the U.S. President's trip, for instance, the Secret Police can delegate responsibility to the British counterpart, but not accountability. Dramatic scenarios can be helpful to point out the legal implications of each choice of roles. As an example, in the event of a surprise attack of the U.S. President in London, the U.S. Secret Service is fully accountable to Congress regardless of whether it has delegated responsibility to Scotland Yard or not. That explains the U.S. Secret Service's reluctance to delegate R even when the move can be justified by past experience.

For each A, assumptions should be made explicit with a risk profile, strategies to reduce the likelihood of a veto including the use of the 5F opportunities, and contingency plans if the veto cannot be overruled.

14.2.3 Support role

The third role is 'S' for *support*. Recipients of this role must invest time, resources and effort to help the event happen. By definition, support resources do not have veto power and should not be blamed de facto for delays in work progress particularly when faced with several vetos.

Support resources derive their power from knowledge, experience and uniqueness. It is important to design the reward system to ensure that all scarce resources are in a forced collaboration mode to prevent the emergence of *disguised vetoes*. Management should make special efforts to evaluate the contribution of each support resource according to merit and to provide constructive feedback about performance regularly, regardless of the expertise or the seniority level of the individual.

14.2.4 Information role

Finally, 'I' is assigned to groups or individuals who must be *informed* about the result of the decision or activity. There should be as many I's as necessary, keeping in mind that I's represent *hidden costs;* it takes time and energy to inform each. Virtually all management time is spent in writing memos, briefing people and attending meetings. Such costs are usually buried in overhead while product budgeting is usually limited to costing resources in the S role.

It is desirable to assess the strategic merit of informing some stakeholders earlier than necessary. The aim is to move them from the "foreigner" or "potential foe" category to "friends" or even "family" classes, though technically such action is not required.

Subscripting should be used to reflect the sequence of information dissemination particularly where a protocol is established. Sometimes information dissemination to interested parties (e.g. the press) must be subject to a short time embargo until a confirmation is received from key people to ensure they have indeed received the message. This fact can be specified by two forms of embargo.

The first is illustrated by $I_{6/5}$ which means that the recipient of that I will be the sixth in sequence and will not be informed unless a confirmation has been received from the fifth I. A variation of this could be $I_{6/5+3H}$ which means that the sixth I will be informed three hours after a confirmation has been received from the fifth I. This variation is used in diplomatic circles. The three hours can provide a valuable opportunity for an ambassador (I_5) to make new friends or tip allies among peers or key correspondents of the press establishment while "foreigners" and "foes" are still in the dark.

The second form of embargo is called the countdown embargo. For instance, I_{0-4H} may indicate that the press will get the U.S. President's agenda only four hours before his/her arrival. All zero subscripted I's require alternative contingency plans.

I's sometimes can be A's in disguise. This is often the case in win-lose situations where the recipient of information is a loser or a "foreigner" who has nothing to lose by acting as a disguised veto. All I's should be tested with respect to their potential for mischief. When in doubt, the informer should therefore make assumptions explicit, develop a risk profile and strategies to manage risk and explore contingency plans to avoid being caught off-guard by a disguised A.

14.2.5 Summary

Vertically, the responsibility chart reflects the multiple roles held by each person based on work requirements. Horizontally, all parties to an activity or decision can be seen both within and outside of the organization. It is worthwhile to indicate that veto powers are in many instances outside the organization's boundaries, thus out of the reach of the linear authority hierarchy structure. This trend should accelerate as we near the year 2000. That is why reorganization and corporate performance evaluation cannot be undertaken effectively without responsibility charting.

A recent retrospective analysis of several responsibility charts drafted with the author's assistance for clients in the early seventies revealed a significant increase in the number of external veto powers over the past ten years. This fact is corroborated by Stanford Research Institute studies indicating that four out of five major corporate decisions have shifted from the Board room to the government in the sense that some regulatory agency is involved.[4] By the same token, governments have suffered a net deficit in decision-making power over the past ten years, to the benefit of self-proclaimed advocacy groups! In such an environment, the need for responsibility charting is imperative, as it clearly indicates the degree of dependence on the outside world.

Finally, a last minute test to determine where each participant stands in the 5F classification can be enlightening and may lead to proactive ideas.

14.3 Role integration

So far, differentiation has been pursued expressly to assign specific roles and maximize effectiveness. As a result, nobody has a mandate over the whole process. In view of the diversity of roles for each person, it is necessary to integrate by adding liaison tasks to manage the activity linkage and provide overall leadership.

The process of integration starts with the addition of the necessary row(s) for coordination activities or decisions. Regardless of how many coordinators are required, for the time being only a single column is introduced for leadership.

Vertically, the role of the leader(s) is identified with respect to each activity and should be at least an I; that is, the leader should at least be informed of the progress and result of other activities. R is assigned when the leader is close to the source of information. In the opposite situation, the leader should delegate the R and retain an I if the individual holding the R is known to perform and deliver, or, if not, an A. The leader is responsible for coordination tasks and the role of the remaining actors is indicated horizontally where appropriate.

Subsequently, the leadership column is compared with the remaining columns to identify the actor most closely related to the leader's role. Then, the following questions are discussed:

1. What is the workload of the leadership column? Can it be fulfilled by a single resource or should a hierarchy be explored? How much staff support would be required to assist in administrative duties?
2. Should the activities be grouped into a single or a multiple center of responsibility and leadership?
3. Who should have overall leadership? That is, which player column is the closest to the sources of information and the most likely to pass the acceptance test of the veto powers and gain the respect of the authorities?
4. Does the current recipient of that position (i.e. player column) have the capability and the readiness to fulfill adequately the roles indicated in the leadership column? Would the additional tasks result in overload? Which assignment should, then, be reviewed, kept, postponed or delegated? How should the decisions be divided between the leader and the deputy(s)?
5. If the leadership should come from elsewhere, how would it be mobilized?
6. How should the conflicts within the existing structure be managed?

7. Should an information directorate or unit be created to take care of all I roles? What decision support systems should be designed to inform the recipients of I efficiently and at the right time?

These questions conclude the responsibility charting exercise and provide a foundation for drafting the organization chart, the next topic in the process.

A review of the prework strategy should take place after the responsibility charting exercise to update the strategic change factors by incorporating new elements to deal with veto powers and review the critical mass scenario.

14.4 Emerging applications of responsibility charting

Responsibility charting is proving to be useful not only to clarify participants' roles but also in time management, legal matters, new product launching, diversification opportunity analysis, diagnosis of strategic weaknesses and as a potent instrument for Management Information System design.

As a time management aid, users can see where their time goes. With the chart, they can explore alternatives to remove redundant A's and I's, combine residual I's, set new boundaries or strategically realign remaining A's, seek support where it is missing and delegate R's to trusted people who are closer to information sources.

Lawyers can use responsibility charting to overcome interpretation problems facing authors of bilateral loans and multilateral agreements, treaties, business contracts and arbitrators of cease-fires. Auditors and law enforcement investigators find it helpful to diagnose loopholes and reduce the risk of white collar crime. Some U.S. bankers require it as background documentation for capital project financing.

New product launching is the area where responsibility charting has the longest track record. It provides insights into the threats and opportunities to be dealt with at each step of the product development, testing, introduction and market penetration.

With respect to diversification, a corporate responsibility chart can flag S's, A's and R's held by outside suppliers as potential candidates for acquisitions, licensing, joint ventures or internally induced growth.

A corporate responsibility chart exercise can point to strategic weaknesses when essential A's and S's are beyond the organization's control, particularly when held by F3 (foreigners), F4 (foes) or F5 (fools) or even unstable friends and family members. A search for substitutes, back up options, acquisitions or linkage strategies should follow the exercise.

In designing Management Information Systems, analysts have found responsibility charting better than structured programming logic, particularly when top management is actively involved in the analytic process. At Du Pont, the author added to the chart the frequency with which each role should be fulfilled. For instance, S_{W1} and I_{M1} respectively meant that the support resource is required once per week and the information report is due on the monthly basis.

14.5 Authority structure

There is a fundamental difference between a responsibility chart and an organization chart. The former reflects the ordinary course of decision-making while the latter is a contingency structure to be considered when the normal working climate process is in a fallback mode. Building on the result of the responsibility chart, the authority structure is developed.

Organizational structures are either functional, product/program, matrix, collateral, mixed, or "non-organization" (Figure 14.4). Functional organizations are structured based on resources, know-how, technology and input requirements. Their origin dates back to the Catholic Church and the military. Program hierarchies are structured based on outputs, i.e. products or services. In modern times, Pierre Du Pont, Alfred Sloan and Konosuke Matsushita are credited with the introduction of the first product structures which were called *divisional* organizations. Both program and functional organizations espouse the unity of command principle.

Matrix structures are based on dual or multiple command systems. Collateral organizations such as task forces are parallel structures within the main structure. Mixed organizations combine elements of each. Considering the complexity of matrix structures and the misleading publicity surrounding its effectiveness, a separate paper has been devoted to this elusive structure.[5] A *"non-organization"* is a relatively new experimental forum to deal with transorganizational issues. The emphasis is on establishing a dialogue. Immediate results are not sought.

It is relatively easy to challenge the benefits of any corporate structure because of the lack of controlled conditions under which the process is carried out. By the same token, taken out of context, any structure stands on its own feet. The existing evaluation data about structural change are less clear-cut than is generally believed and the probable differences in performance between alternative structures are by no

Functional	The functional organization is input-based. Its boundaries are set to combine resources from the same discipline. Integration is predominant to achieve skills quality, economy of scale and efficiency.
Program	The program organization is output-based. Its boundaries are set by combining all resources involved in the design, production, marketing and delivery of a single product or a service. Differentiation buys prompt response and impact on the client. Program structures are sometimes also called divisional or product organizations.
Matrix	The matrix organization is a compromise between the above extremes. It is neither functional nor program. Resources have multiple memberships and may report to several functional and program managers concurrently. It is a differentiated-integrated approach.
Collateral	A collateral organization is a temporary structure to deal with a critical issue which cannot be addressed effectively under the regular structure without creating a conflict of interest or interfering with day-to-day throughput (performance).
Mixed	A mixed organization may use any combination of the above forms concurrently depending on work requirements.
Non-organization	A non-organization is a quasi-amorphous structure to permit sovereign and suspicious stakeholders to get together in a non-threatening and non-committing forum, which is generally closed to public scrutiny. The objective is to encourage a genuine dialogue. The idea was pioneered by the Danish Association for Industrial Training (DASIT) and was the featured "structure" at the North-South Summit in Cancun, Mexico. A non-organization may be the embryo of a future organization, but this is rarely the case.

Figure 14.4: Organization structures

means self-evident. A lot more thinking about the norms and standards to be attained in organizational design is required. While the following observations are far from universal, they represent a reasonable account of what has been learned from clients' experience.

Structures should be adopted by necessity rather than desire. As Drucker said, "Reorganization is surgery. One doesn't just cut"—unless the benefits are validated and the skills, systems, strategies and rewards are at par with the requirements of the new structure.

The responsibility chart is an essential instrument for exploring the usefulness of common as well as hybrid organization forms. An intensive interaction with a dynamic outside world may point to a program organization, decentralization or even to the need for acquisition or merger with suppliers or other external entities. Program and divisional structures tend to have the advantages of smaller companies, including strong consumer orientation, a product identity distinct from the parent organization (eg. Tide from Procter & Gamble), entrepreneurial and autonomous management. They require a dynamic central coordination network to head off inappropriate competition among divisions and promote synergistic collaboration.

On the other hand, the existence of expensive support resources with the potential for economy of scale through specialization or capital intensive expertise in a relatively stable market environment may lead to the consideration of either a functional organization (telephone companies and railways) or a job shop organization (e.g. Peat Marwick or P.S. Ross & Co.). The common services such as accounting, banking, procurement, personnel, production engineering, data processing and research tend to be organized functionally. Such practice is only legitimate when there are strategic reasons for it.

Likewise, a collateral organization (e.g. task force) could be selected for a series of crunch activities requiring high visibility or for work totally unrelated to, if not in conflict with, the existing organization chart (good for day-to-day decisions). Task forces are sometimes called intelligence squads. They have a clear mandate to diagnose an issue and a clear authority to "intrude" in the day-to-day operations with all the power of top management.

The issue of single versus dual leadership is usually raised in task forces dealing with conflicting issues of a complex magnitude and national, international or union management scope. Royal commissions debating bicultural issues are usually led by two co-chairpersons, one representing each ethnic group. Quality of work life experiments are also jointly managed by co-presidents from union and management.

Some task forces are no-win interventions created to deal with an unpopular issue for which the best strategy is to keep the organization out of jail. Alfred Kahn's U.S. Prices and Wages Commission and Jean-Luc Pepin's Anti Inflation Board are such examples. If the task force leader is considered an asset to the organization, it is imperative to save the leader's credibility before terminating the task force. This is usually done by gracefully retiring or nominating the task force head to a better position elsewhere and replacing her/him by a low profile caretaker who is explicitly mandated to bring the task force to an end. In this context, Trudeau made Pepin a hero, while Carter failed to save Kahn and inadvertently almost made him a kamikaze pilot.

Before finalizing the authority base, in either case, several additional factors should be taken into account, namely:

1. **Risks of decentralization versus centralization**

    Sometimes neither extreme is desirable. A novel experiment is currently underway both to free the Manitoba health care system from the bureaucracy of Mr. Sterling Lyon's government centralization and to avoid the tyranny of total decentralization of hospital management. Managed by the Manitoba Health Organization, the project explores the feasibility of creating health district boards to extend resource allocation for health services beyond the narrow concerns of individual hospitals.

    Two demonstration sites are already in operation. The boards consist of a small nucleus of representatives from the provincial government, the health care and social service agencies and have the active participation of community leaders. The structural change is expected to increase the flexibility of the system so that it can be more responsive to changing local needs and minimize the duplication of existing services. It is also worthwhile to indicate that taxpayers will not bear the cost of running the two demonstration projects. The Kellogg Foundation of Michigan is sponsoring the program for three years.

2. **Number of levels between the productive base and the ultimate authority**

    In order to increase the decision and information processing capability, consultants tend to advise clients to minimize the number of levels between the Chief Executive Officer and the rank-and-file members. However, this leads to the so-called flat organization, in which some achievers do not *perceive* the potential for gradual growth and career development. These organizations tend to retain deadwood.

3. **The span of control at each level**
   The subordinate/boss ratio varies depending upon:
   a. degree of complexity and uncertainty of tasks (Figure 14.5)
   b. magnitude of discretionary work and power to set job priorities and select jobs
   c. boss' capability and experience
   d. homogeneity of skills
   e. past history of span of control appropriateness
   f. risk of sabotage, obstruction or hostility
   g. geographic dispersion and size of local work units
   h. availability of professional support to share the boss' workload and slack resources, particularly among senior management, to handle unanticipated problems.

4. **The need for stability and continuity**
   It is essential to assess continually the desirable ratio of new job holders to veterans in order to maintain stability and adequate service delivery.

It is becoming progressively clearer that a single structure may not be adequate throughout the life cycle of a program or a megaproject (one billion dollar plus range category). For example, the Trans Alaska Pipeline went through three major reorganizations (Figure 14.6) ranging from a totally centralized organization at the early design stages to a decentralized matrix during the multibillion major construction phases to a recentralized structure when 90% completion was reached to speed up project termination—the subject of the next section. The largest project ever to be undertaken by private industry (at the time) was completed almost to the day of the scheduled deadline. It also was within the budget forecasted in the design stage.

14.6 Abortion, succession and termination planning

Projects, operations and programs continuously fall into the *unfinished business trap,* a process which drains energy. The Pareto syndrome usually affects the last part of an undertaking with maldistributions such as 20% of the end results requiring 80% of the total effort or even worse with the termination deficit becoming permanent (e.g. completion of the Montreal Olympics billion dollar stadium).

While the academic and consulting world have devoted more than a fair share of attention to the issues of planning and control, they have tended to neglect *closure and withdrawal.* Effective termination of programs requires complex institutional, psychosocial and technical strategies. The technical aspects are usually well managed, building on content and task

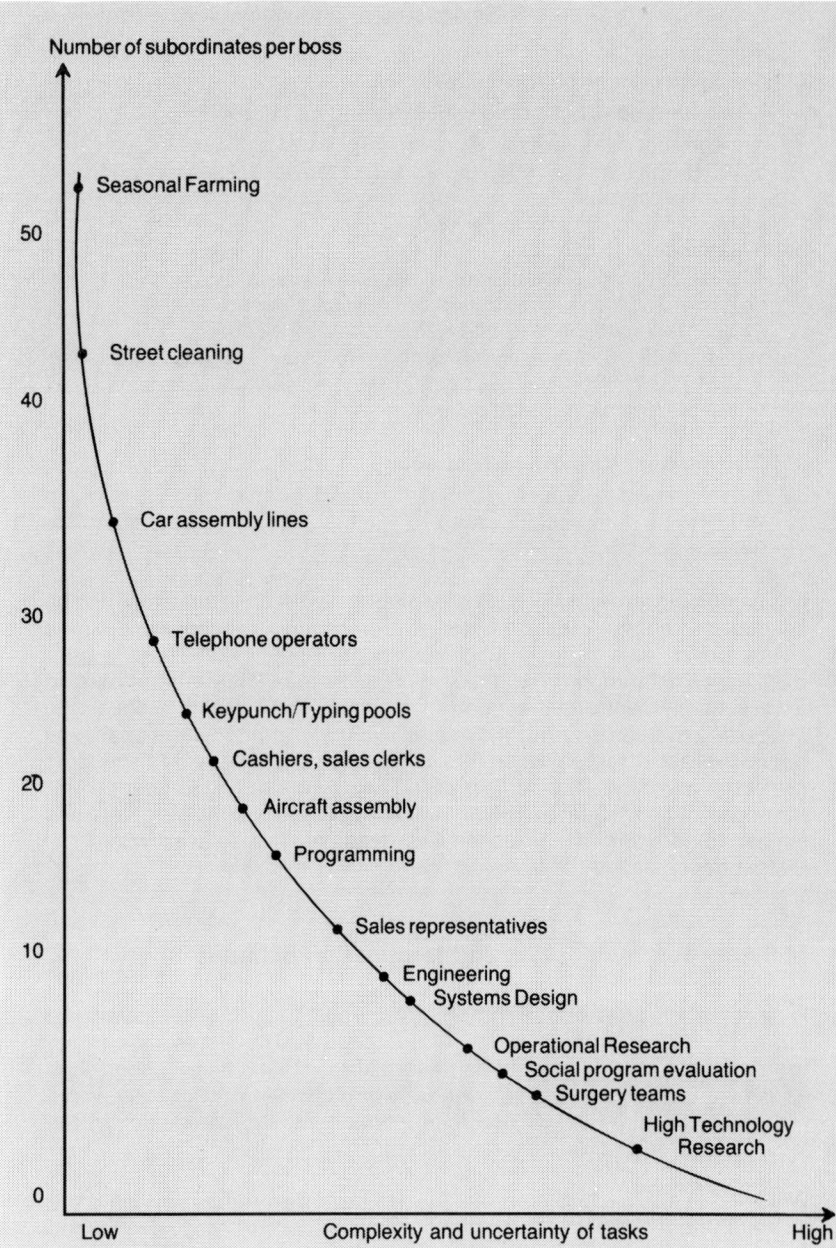

Figure 14.5: How task complexity affects subordinate/boss ratio

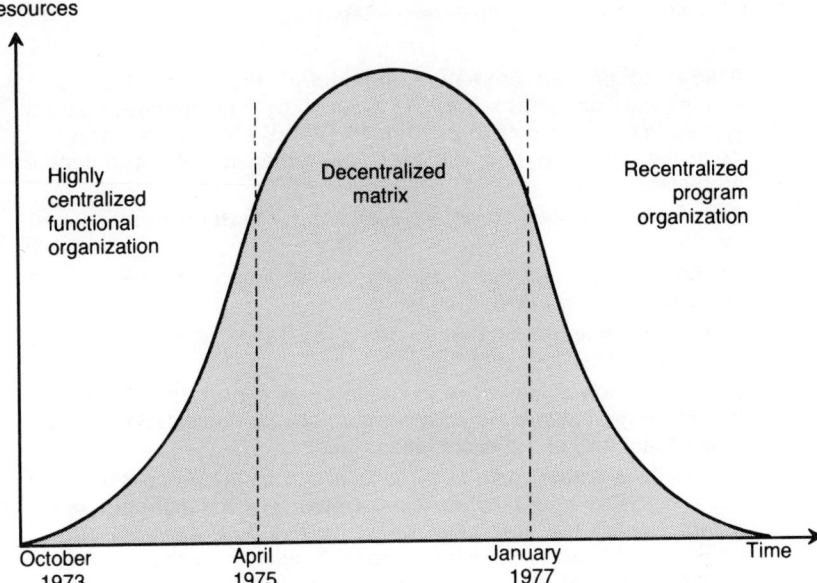

Figure 14.6: Trans-Alaska pipeline — organizational changes

expertise of the performers. As for the psychology of healthy termination, it requires not only skills and efforts, but ingenuity and power. The purpose is to either abort or disconnect a program wisely at the right time prior to obsolescence with little, if any, adverse consequences for the performers and all stakeholders. In the western hemisphere, the termination planning methods of Esso Resources (eg. Cold Lake project) and the International Group Skanska Cement of Sweden are commendable and clearly at par with the Japanese counterparts.

Termination planning is basically a *succession* plan with contingency options. It includes specific strategies for addressing the following:

1. Readiness to face surprise events (deaths, accidents, market gluts, embargoes, wars, skyrocketing interest rates, etc.)
2. The risk of task dependence on scarce resources and related possessive ambitions emerging from the inherent power derived from task knowledge
3. Individual competence deficit
4. Individual commitment deficit
5. Job security plan to facilitate transition to other assignments at an appropriate time

6. Policies to prevent premature departures. Premature departures and succession delays may be caused by the employee social system (e.g. spouse, children status). That is why it is important to draft the interface plan of each performer to detect potential problems.
7. Early warning system to detect delays, poor performance and cost overruns
8. Reward, bonus and non-monetary reinforcement mechanisms to energize a healthy termination behavior
9. Penalty scheme to act as a strong deterrent against voluntary extension of task life cycle
10. Communication of intentions to employees (i.e. no surprises). Where the termination plan is either absent or not communicated to people, a significant loss of achievers takes place.
11. Optionally, a "ritual" plan to symbolically close the process. It could pay tribute to the terminated social system (e.g. a minute of silence) before turning the final page on it. To this end, Esso Resources Company of Exxon requested Herbert Shepard to write a wake for the "funerals" of the aborted giant Cold Lake project which was gracefully aborted far before Shell et al pulled out of the ill-fated counterpart (Al Sands) in Western Canada.
12. A restart and recovery plan in the case of abortions

14.7 Conclusion

This section completes the strategic planning phase. Iterations at this point are more desirable than a premature transition to operational planning. The purpose is to review the logic and information elements building the linkage from mission to issues, from objectives to policies, projects and programs, from products and services to strategies, from pre-work to succession and termination planning. Upon completion of the exercise, the next phase, operational planning, can be undertaken.

References and notes

1. Robert Melcher: Roles and Relationships: Clarifying the Manager's Job, Personnel, May-June 1967.
2. Richard Beckhard & Reuben T. Harris: Managing Organization Transitions in a Complex Environment, Addison Wesley, 1978.

3. The data sources include Time Magazine (Volume 115, No. 18, page 19) and several issues of Le Monde and Washington Post, early May 1980. The author takes full responsibility for the interpretation outlined in this article.
4. S.R.I.: Options for the Eighties, paper delivered by the Stanford Research Institute at the 1979 convention of the American Society for Association Executives, St. Louis, Missouri.
5. A.P. Martin: Shifting Gears to Matrix, Top Management Beware! paper delivered at the Joint North American Operations Research Conference in May 1981, sponsored by CORS, TIMS and ORSA, published in the Project Management Quarterly, March 1981; also available from The Professional Development Institute, Box 1181, Station B, Ottawa K1P 5R2 Canada.

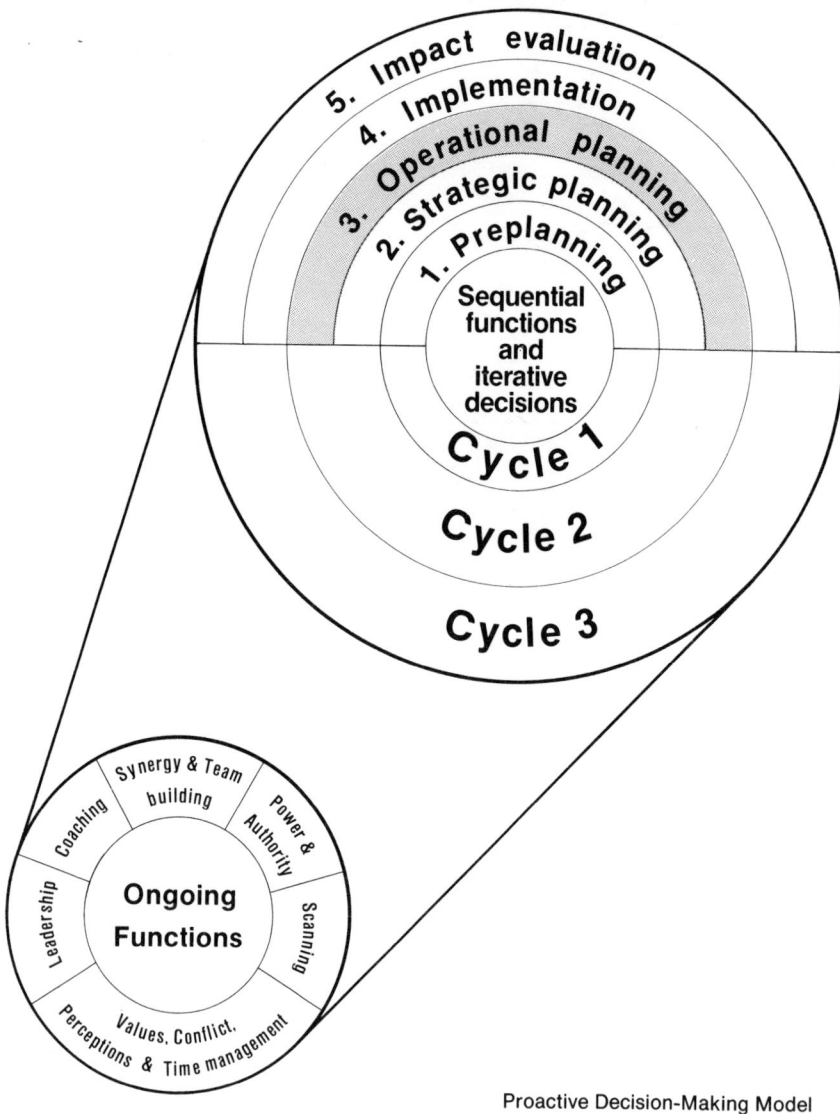

Proactive Decision-Making Model

Chapter fifteen

Operational planning

To complete the planning phase, a schedule, a resource allocation plan, a budget and a management information system (MIS) for feedback and progress control are developed prior to implementation. A newly developed framework has integrated scheduling with budgeting, resource allocation and earned value. The Global Method was designed to permit a phased-planning approach and continuous modification to the plan with the least paperwork and clerical support. It combines the advantages of PERT and CPM networks without being taxed by some of their chronic weaknesses. A more comprehensive coverage of these topics can be found in an upcoming publication by the author.[1] This is also the area where planning literature and instruments abound. For the purpose of this book, it is worthwhile to summarize the characteristics of good operational planning.

15.1 Scheduling

The schedule should be accessible not only to the performers but to all management tiers to permit prompt and comprehensive decision-making. It should be compatible with optimum team size estimating. The activity interfaces, duration, slacks and status should be displayed graphically rather than digitally to enhance communications and be promptly updated with the least managerial and clerical effort.

15.2 Resource allocation and budgeting

The resources required for each activity are allocated and levelled across projects, programs, operations and pilot experiments based on optimization heuristics. Emphasis should be on strategic resources as indicated in the pre-planning chapter. A budget is drafted translating the strategic plan into commitment and cash flow projections. A financing plan terminates the budgeting process assuming no iteration is required.

15.3 Management Information System (MIS)

Proactive Management considers information a decision-support resource to be developed, disseminated, used and safeguarded with cost/benefit in mind. To this end, a good MIS should provide a ready access to reliable, factual, pertinent and useful information, taking into account the opportunity cost of the decision-maker's limited time. The importance of assigning experienced professionals to MIS design and implementation even in the absence of automation options cannot be underestimated. The definition of information needs and reporting requirements should be conducted jointly by executives and technical experts. Otherwise the surrender of management responsibility would inevitably lead to adverse consequences.

15.4 Conclusion

Operational planning completes the planning process. Before deciding to move to the implementation phase, it is imperative to review the assumptions and all available information and to secure the strong commitment of the critical mass and the readiness of a broad constituency, at least in principle. The opportunity cost of a premature transition to implementation should be weighed against further planning effort. The introduction of a pilot experiment or phased implementation should be always kept in mind.

References and notes

1. A.P. Martin: Breakthroughs in Project Management: The Global Method, The Professional Development Institute, PDI Press, 1984.

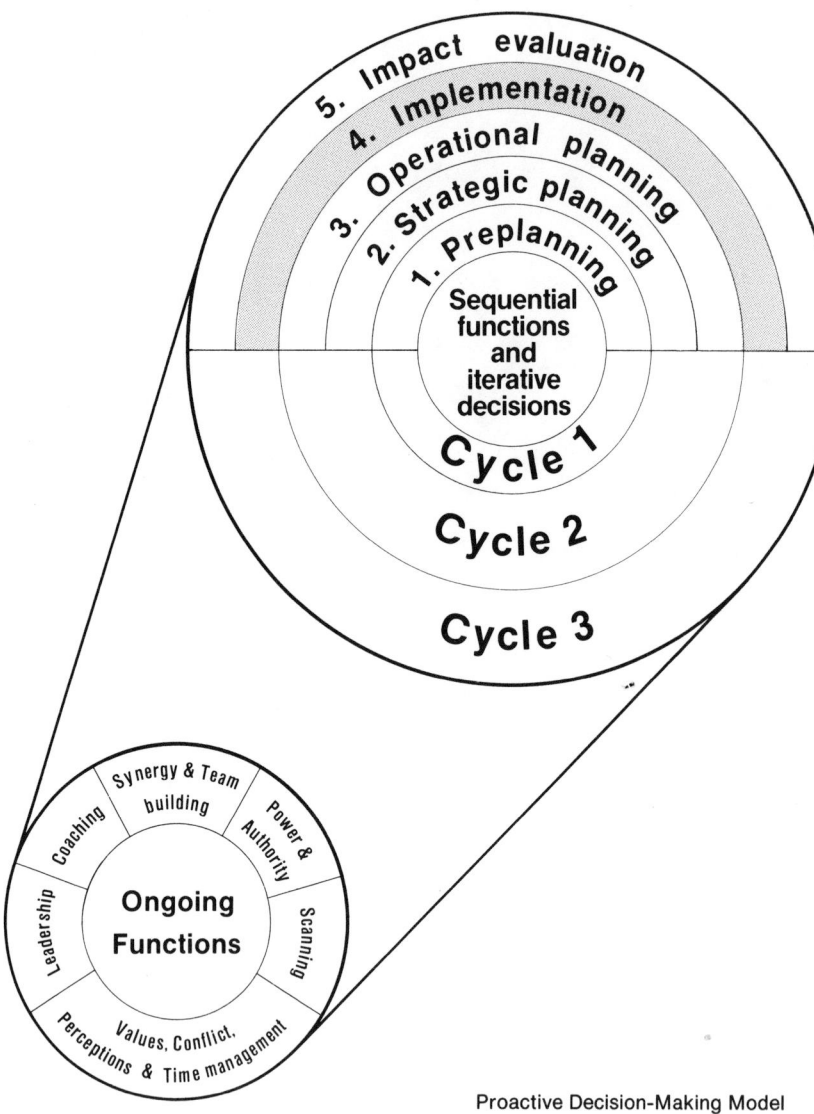

Proactive Decision-Making Model

Chapter sixteen

Implementation

So far, no money has been spent in productive effort. Only planning costs have been incurred. The plan is integrated, approved and ready for implementation. Soon the honeymoon will be over. The real issue will be: "Who is going to do the dishes?" A plan, no matter how great, will soon be useless unless it is kept up to date.

Implementation is action and resolution. It includes pre-work, negotiations, contracting, procurement, resource mobilization, work, issue tracking or progress evaluation, conflict management, replanning and termination management or abortion if required. Rapid feedback is the basis for the on-going formative evaluation. It attempts to assess progress while the process is going on.

A detailed coverage of the implementation phase is outside the scope of this book. Apart from the evaluation information to be covered in the next chapter, all the other topics were discussed in the planning sections. Indeed, implementation control is a series of mini replanning sessions. The following case illustrates how the proactive framework can be used to *implement and operationalize* a major policy change in a complex setting. It includes progress evaluation, conflict management and replanning decisions.

16.1 Implementation case

A Fortune 1000 corporation decided to take a proactive approach to equal opportunity legislation. The responsibility of EOM-EOW (Equal Opportunity for Minorities and Women) was assigned to the President's assistant, a young lawyer and an outspoken change advocate. An educational intervention was prescribed. Audio-visual training sessions were selected. The President acting as a role model was filmed promoting equality between employees. He sent personal letters to solicit the active cooperation of each manager and front line supervisor.

Despite the President's sincerity and the change advocate's struggle, the change was cosmetic and efforts remained in vain. Concerned about the lack of progress, the President called an experienced consultant who made the following diagnosis.

The change advocate had a high readiness for change but a low capability to make it happen. Despite the President's clout, he was *perceived* in a staff role as a biased issue champion! The President was too remote from the day-to-day action. Despite his candid and active efforts, his role was symbolic. The personal letters reminded the staff of the President's Christmas and New Year messages. They were doomed to the waste basket!

Every supervisor reported to the Executive Vice-President through a hierarchy which based all rewards on the actual performance in manufacturing and marketing. The importance of the EOM-EOW was neither reflected in the management information system nor in the criteria for reward and punishment.

Moreover, the Executive V.P. was perceived as the real power by the supervisors. His attitude seemed anti-black and anti-women! The regular functional hierarchy did not have the mechanism for planning and controlling the EOM-EOW change, but was adequate for the bread and butter activities of the corporation.

Following the diagnosis, the consultant suggested an eight-step plan of action.

1. Retain the regular structure "as is" since it is an *asset* to the organization's productivity.
2. Use the Executive Vice-President as a *role model* to capitalize on his power and natural leadership abilities.
3. Create a *collateral organization structure* namely an Equal Opportunity *Task Force*. Two members will form it. The Executive V.P. will act as chairperson and *coach* while retaining his regular job. The young lawyer will be the secretary of the task force.
4. Set the *objectives* for individual departments based on the compliance legislation requirements as the worst-case criteria.
5. Set promotion *standards* to control the quality of the scheme's beneficiaries and prevent cosmetic appointments. The young lawyer or his representative would sit as a full member of the promotion boards and approve candidacies on non-objection basis.

Implementation

6. Implement a simple *information system* to control progress. Each division continues to gather data about productivity. In addition, it adds a single page annex stipulating EOW objectives, achievements, reasons for not meeting objectives (if applicable), contingency plans and action for the next period.

    A copy of the annex is forwarded to the task force secretary while the regular productivity report keeps flowing up the hierarchy as before. The young lawyer aggregates the annex reports, records the exceptions and informs the task force chairperson, regional vice-presidents and the President about variations from objectives.

7. Set a *reward/penalty scheme* affecting the task force chairperson's pay and the front line management bonus. Where the pay scheme is not subject to change, senior management is instructed to report each individual's contribution to the EOW project on the staff evaluation forms semi-annually. Considering the perceived importance of performance review for each manager's promotability, this subtle move had a significant impact and resulted in immediate behavior modification.

8. Establish a mechanism to *maintain the change* process in place beyond the point of no return and prevent a reverse to a pre-change condition.

Within a few months, the organization was on target making real progress. The new plan was unlike the earlier intervention which concentrated solely on attitude change. The proactive option proposed behavior modification through clear objectives, a differentiated structure, information systems and rewards/penalties. Whether the Executive V.P.'s attitude was for or against women was irrelevant, he had to behave in a way which was conducive to the fulfillment of organizational goals. A behavior modification intervention requires less energy than attitude changes (Figure 16.1).

Front line supervisors also received a disconfirmation message by witnessing the change in the Executive V.P.'s behavior. By chairing the task force he became a far more appropriate *role model* to the organization than the President because his influence was direct and real. The change advocate acted in a support role channeling his expertise via the Executive V.P. who was the power base. He also benefited immensely from the coaching abilities of the chairperson and derived knowledge and referral power from the experience.

In short, the systematic approach for managing the change under the collateral organization achieved results in a relatively short period of time and with less resistance to change than the previous intervention. However, once the change had taken place through behavior modification, it became important to consolidate it beyond the point of no return.

Think Proactive: New insights into decision-making

With enough blacks and women in the executive suite, *ipso facto attitudinal* changes took place over a three year period (Figure 16.2).

16.2 Summary

Successful implementation of policies, projects, operations and pilot experiments requires a complex set of strategies, tasks and decisions. By focusing on preplanning and strategic planning, the Proactive Management model helps corporate and political leaders to identify the issues and assess the consequences of alternative decisions before implementation. The illustration provided a real-life case in which the elements of the framework were selectively used to manage the implementation process successfully.

The next chapter examines the technical and behavioral issues related to impact evaluation.

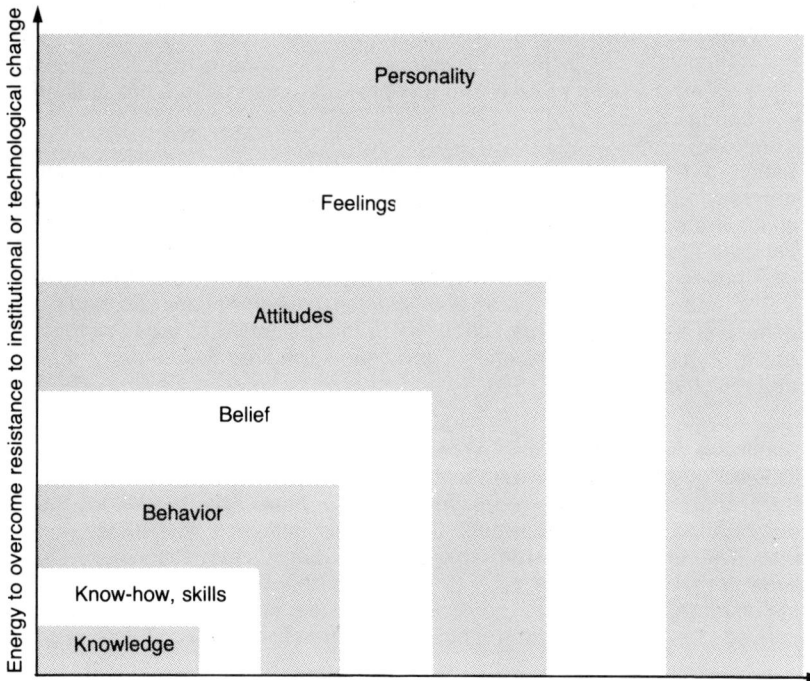

Figure 16.1: Expected time and resistance to institutional or technological change for different levels of intervention

N.B.: An embryonic version of the above model can be found in P. Hersey and K.H. Blanchard: Management or Organizational Behavior, Prentice-Hall, 1972 p. 160.

212

Implementation

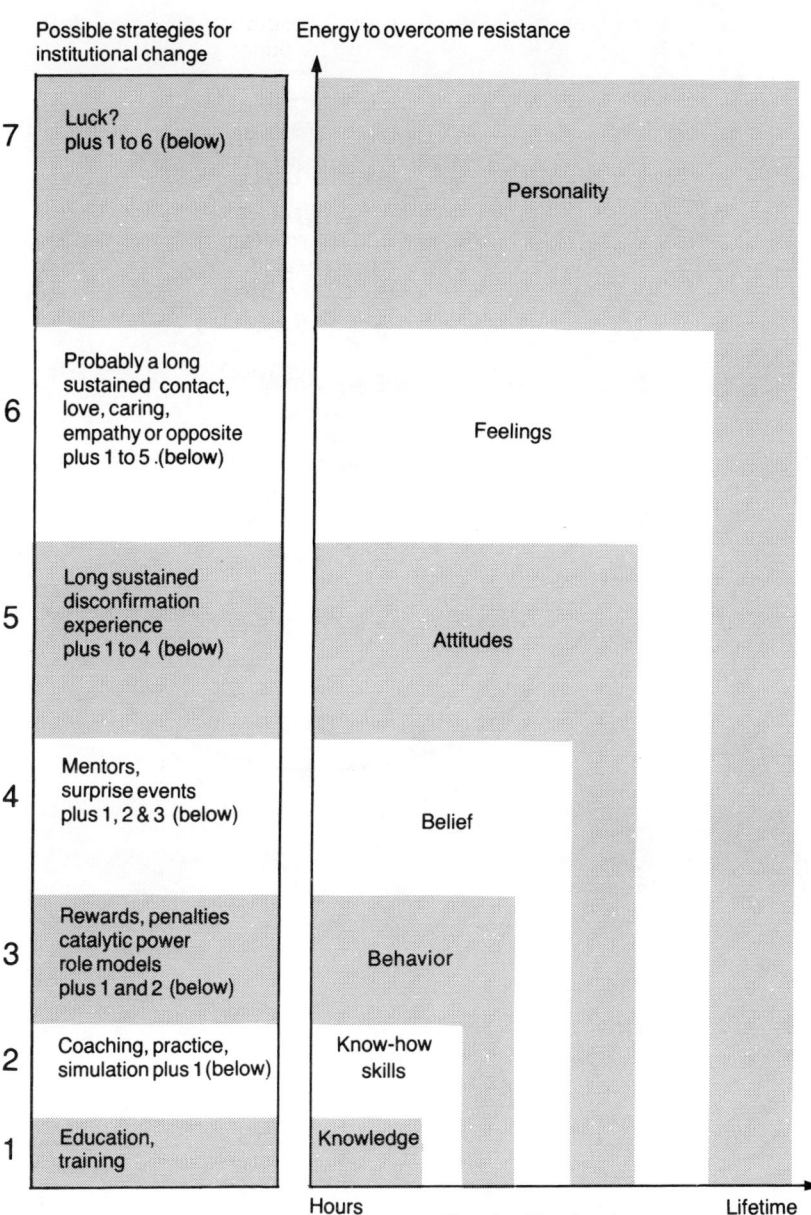

Figure 16.2: Alternative interventions for change and related time/effort

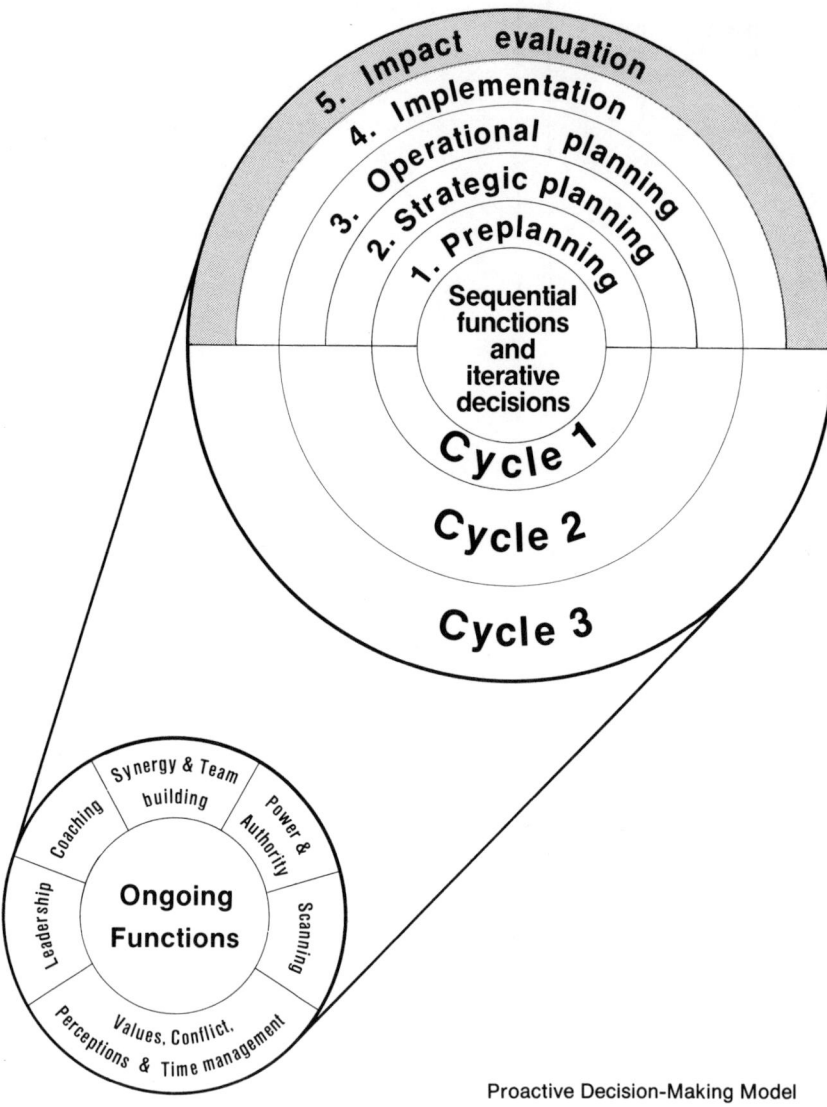

Proactive Decision-Making Model

Chapter seventeen

Impact and process evaluation

17.1 Evaluation wisdom

Evaluation completes the Proactive Decision-Making process. It includes experimental design, data collection, data analysis and feedback. None of these activities is neutral. Quite the contrary, each can generate enough dysfunctional energy to write off accrued gains. Generally, managers and professional staff either equate evaluation with justification or adopt a dysfunctional attitude by responding to perceived threats and negative findings.

That is why evaluation must be carefully planned and managed with behavioral consequences in mind. This is rarely done even among decision-makers in international organizations. Evaluators should have the "insight to know what can (or cannot) be changed and the wisdom to appreciate the difference." They should accept the fact that sometimes evaluation findings are error prone and of limited value particularly in dealing with rare events. Rather than disseminate or use knowledge of dubious character, the evaluator should accept failure and conscientiously avoid mischief, as MIT's Professor Arnold Barnett said. The stakeholders should be candid and prepared to consider inconclusive evaluations as inevitable in some situations.

17.2 Strategic and behavioral issues in evaluation

The data collection process generates expectations with either negative or positive energy. The direction of energy is based on:

1. the respondent's perception of the data collector's competence, motivation, integrity, trustworthiness, power and appearance;
2. the perception of management credibility, past experience in using the data, the capability, the potency of the reward punishment power, and the readiness to use it;
3. the perceived validity and reliability of the data collection medium and format such as a questionnaire, telephone enquiry, interview, observation (direct or remote, blind, covert or overt), etc.;
4. the perceived relevance of the data collection content and the clarity of the questions;
5. the respondent's capability, competence, integrity, stakes, cultural tendencies and the range of available responses;
6. the location of data collection particularly when interviewing a sensitive clientele (e.g. ex-inmates, ex-patients, mental health or infectious disease clinic patients, battered women, rape victims, motel/hotel patrons, informants, drug addicts);
7. surprise events bias: the respondent's awareness of surprise events related to the issue being surveyed may lead to misperceptions and overreaction, particularly if the issue is institutional change;
8. the timing of data collection: as an illustration, airlines interview short-haul passengers after security clearance in the departure lounge and long-haul travellers in flight. Client satisfaction interviews before check-in or after landing have almost always failed due to respondent perception of time.

Feedback and reporting are not unobtrusive either. They can be at least equally significant in energy generation. Reporting should be planned to avoid several types of errors. Among the commonly committed errors, it is useful to mention three kinds:

Type 1   Provide information people are not ready to hear, no matter how loud or how often it is expressed.

Type 2   Withhold information people would have been prepared to hear, assuming they are not.

Type 3   Measure something no one cares about.

The important factors in feedback management are timing, relevance, format, perceived validity of data, responsibility, appropriate membership, perceived ownership of the data, power, perceived rewards/punishments and tolerance for errors while learning. Furthermore, the time lapse between data collection and feedback can either reinforce or adversely change the direction of the positive energy created during the collection stage.

17.3 Evaluation timing

Introducing evaluation into an ongoing program is difficult, to say the least. It is therefore imperative to build the evaluative information system into the product, service, policy or program design as early as possible. That is why the evaluation methodology was discussed during the strategic planning phase. The objective was twofold: firstly, to build a sound experiment, collect prior data and build control groups where necessary and, secondly, to sharpen the implementor's mandate and energize work behavior.

17.4 Data validity

As indicated in the pre-planning chapter, both subjective and objective validity tests should be passed. Criteria should be established for the usefulness, validity and relevance of data. With respect to the threats to validity, it is worthwhile always to remember that physicians rarely trust the thermometer. A measure indicating either an exceptionally high or a low temperature is invariably revalidated. Indeed, the thermometer trap is almost an epidemic problem in automated information systems. Decision-makers tend either to rely overly on MIS reports, taking validity for granted, or to discard the content altogether; neither approach is appropriate.

More recently, a veteran Air Canada pilot was asked about altitude validation on the L1011 jumbo jet. He pointed to three different altimeters and then said, "These servo-, baro- and radio altimeters are among the best and most reliable instruments in civil aviation today but frankly I still have to look out the window sometimes just to make sure we are safe." If pilots require several readings to validate something as concrete as altitude, the elusive instruments to measure soft institutional change need to be validated and acted upon with even greater caution.

17.5 Summative evaluation

In addition to the on-going formative process evaluation, Proactive Decision-Making includes provision for a yearly summative evaluation and a complete sunset review to determine overall impact and decide about either continuing, aborting or terminating existing policies, operations, projects and pilot experiments. Acquisition, integration or disposal of assets and other resources is explicity studied.

Prior to formulating recommendations, it is important to question the role of luck in performance changes. For example, a decrease in crime rate coming after a record year may be due to chance variation alone or it could be a great accomplishment. Governing politicians naturally prefer to credit such decreases to their actions. Summative evaluators should be alert to the luck phenomenon. That is why the idiosyncrasies of the problem should be crucial and should dominate the evaluation issue. There are instances where conflicting findings can be drawn from the same pattern of data. Neither view is right or wrong because we do not have clear evidence to discard either.

17.6 Process evaluation

The process evaluation follows two steps. The *formal step* uses the instruments developed during the strategic planning phase, including the termination planning and succession scheme. This evaluation can be directly linked to reward/punishment expectations. It should not present people with *faits accomplis,* which leave little room for recipient intervention and for searching out new directions.

The *informal step* uses synectics, synergy and databased feedback to generate useful information in the absence of coercive-competitive threats and punishment fears. It is most useful when the feedback is given in descriptive terms. It aims primarily at directly benefiting the participating staff. No one else becomes privy to the informal feedback findings unless a clear unanimity to this effect exists. The informal feedback is perhaps the most crucial in collecting information for related developments, new opportunities and future improvements. It is a valuable instrument for learning from the mistakes of others because the data that surface are the most sensitive. They are not available to management otherwise.

It is interesting to note that the informal step was originally introduced by the Pentagon during the Vietnam war and has been carried out ever since with remarkable results. American Express Travellers Cheques Division has also experimented with it in New York, Brighton and Singapore. In the public sector, a correctional institution assessed the possibility of granting guards time off to this end.

17.7 Metaevaluation

Finally a metaevaluation[1], namely an evaluation of the evaluation process itself, is conducted for the benefit of the evaluator(s), among others. Metaevaluations not only help evaluators to get client feedback about how they have done, they often challenge the evaluator's claim to objectivity, recognizing the fact that biases can come up in all kinds of ways. The case of a large Australian voluntary organization is illuminating.

The core mission of the Brotherhood of St. Lawrence is to research, disseminate information and educate Australians about the structural roots of poverty. The objective of its Material Aid Program was to collect used clothes from donors for distribution to welfare recipients at no cost. An original evaluation recommended that Material Aid be disbanded. The program's old fashioned "charity" orientation was contrasted with the innovative mission of the organization.

The president mandated a metaevaluation prior to abolishing Material Aid. In contrast with the previous assessment, the metaevaluation paid attention to unanticipated effects which were absolutely unnoticed in the program evaluation context. The Material Aid Program was actually an extremely important cover for the Agency. It legitimized the Brotherhood's existence as a religious charitable organization. Legitimacy permitted the Agency to engage in innovations without provoking controversy. Moreover, people identified with the Material Aid Program through the personal give away, which resulted in large legacies, a high profile and community presence. These in turn provided political protection and assured resources. The original evaluation was indeed extremely narrow in scope. The metaevaluation was proactive and seemed more useful to policy-makers.

References and notes

1. Metaevaluation: Meta: from Greek meaning "after", "beyond" and often denoting change. Current Evaluation Research literature does not confine the term metaevaluation to its original meaning as defined in this document.

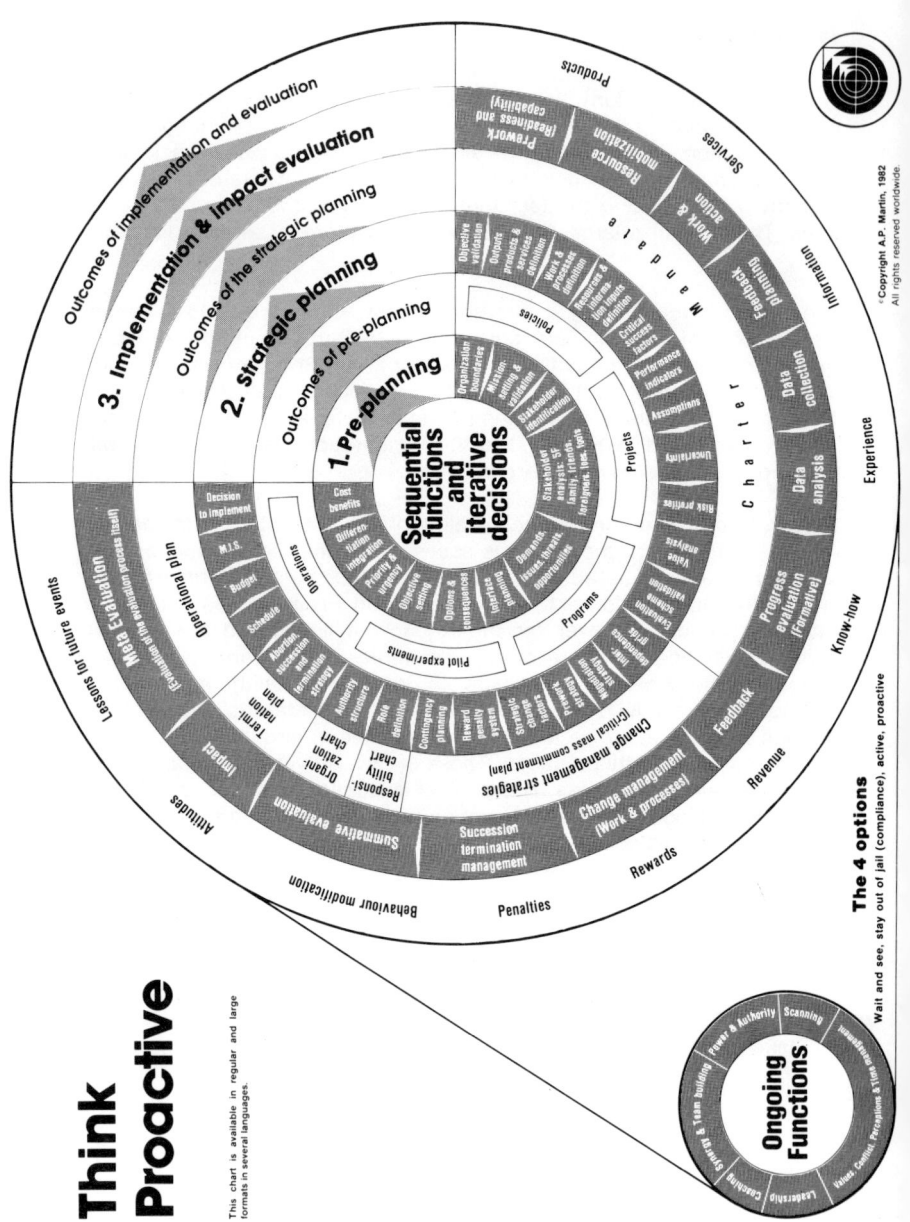

Chapter eighteen

Concluding remarks

Proactive Decision-Making is a further point of departure from orthodox management methods which have, far too frequently, led corporate and political leaders to make fragile and short-lived right or wrong decisions. It is a comprehensive framework to improve the quality and value of decision-making in a dynamic world.

The increasing turbulence in the environment will indeed continue to challenge corporate stability. "Cheer up, it can only get worse!" said Ed Schein in talking about the subject. As management attention shifts increasingly toward external issues, the conscious application of Proactive Decision-Making offers a capability for *internalizing environmental uncertainty and ambiguity* so as to provide adequate response and *uncover new opportunities.*

The quest for effective decision-making knows neither disciplinary nor national boundaries. Examples provided in this book have ranged from private to public sectors, from Australia and Japan to Brazil, Europe and North America. While the issues and the problems are becoming world-wide, the solutions are far from obvious and are still being sought largely by trial and error. Proactive Decision-Making builds on the heritage of available methods that have been used and have been shown to work. It is only as good as the people it serves. It is not the kind of thing that can be applied cookbook fashion because each organization presents a separate set of problems and opportunities. Its application should be compatible with the practitioner's own *personal* leadership style.

It provides a framework to draft a hypothesis, account for each relevant kind of behavior, formulate a diagnosis, design specific interventions taking into account issue interdependence, test prior to implementation, control progress, evaluate impact from multiple perspectives and manage the succession and termination process adequately.

Proactive Decision-Making is *easier said than done*. It can rarely be undertaken with a shoestring budget in terms of management time and dedication. It is not cheap and requires from the practitioner a constant effort to look at the evidence of success or failure much more carefully than is usually done now. It does not provide simple answers to complex problems. It implies the rejection of easy compromises. Compromises are all very well in classical management theory but they do not work in practice unless socioeconomic costs and benefits are kept in mind.

Allies are needed to build the critical mass for change. The reader planning to make a whole organization proactive should *go slow*. The mere mention of a new management method is enough to create alarm, confusion and hostility. Names are issue tags. The reader could go quite far just by selectively applying the process without ever naming it. The opposition would have a hard time fighting a no-name issue. Actually the no-name bar in Sausalito (just across Golden Gate Bridge from San Francisco) is among the coziest and friendliest pubs on the West Coast!

Unlike political ideologies, Proactive Decision-Making has no natural constituency. Consequently, as a final caveat, Proactive Decision-Making will only survive if it keeps adapting to the needs of organizational, geopolitical, institutional and social change.

Index

ARPANET, 121
AT&T, 118, 120
Abacus, 144
Abortion, 23, 199
Absenteeism, 50
Acquisition, 197, 218
Action research, 51, 127
Activair, 97
Active stance, 31
Admiral, 144
Advocacy advertizing, 65
Africa, 61
Agee, Bill, 21, 44
Agence France Presse, 121
Agenda, 84, 108, 111
Agriculture, 61
Air Canada, 144, 217
Air Florida, 144
Airvelop, 144
Al Sands, 202
Alcan, 35
Ali, Mohammed, 61
Allies, see Family
Allstate Insurance, 117
Amdahl, 31
American, see United States
American Express, 21, 218
Anonymity, 66
Anti Inflation Board, 198
Approval role, 189
Arab University, 118
Arbitration, 76, 90
Associated Press, 121
Assumption identification, 171
Assumption indicators, 168, 169
Assumptions, 166, 171, 173
Atlanta, 101
Atlantic Richfield Co., 118, 119
Attitudes, 44
Australia, 219, 221
Authentic leadership, 41, 42, 108
Authority, 20, 70, 76
Authority structure, 195
Autonomy, 71

BOSS, 121
Bank of America, 118
Barnett, Arnold, 215
Batelle, 125
Baysian decision theory, 127
Behavior modification, 69
Behavioral issues, 216
Beirut, 118
Bélanger, Michel, 60
Bell, 31
Bendix, 21, 44
Bennis, Warren, 74
Bernstein, George, 176
Blanchard, K.H., 212
Blind resource, 23, 216
Boe, Archie, 117
Bombardier, 146
Boundaries, 85, 147, 170
Boundaries of perception, 81
Braniff, 144
Brazil, 35, 221
Brighton, 218
Britain, 65
British Columbia, 65
British Petroleum, 35
British Prime Minister, 190
Broadbent, Ed, 65
Brookings, The, 61
Brotherhood of St. Lawrence, 219
Budgeting, 205
Bundy, McGovern, 143
Bureautics, 124
Business contracts, 194
Business Outlook, 130
Business Round Table, The, 61
Business Week, 127

CP Air, 144
CPM, 205
CWG Inc., 159
Cabinet Agenda, 137
California, 96, 124
Cambridge Reports Inc., 125
Canada, 65, 71, 98, 124, 125, 136

Canadian Broadcasting Corporation, 121
Canadian Constitution, 63
Canadian Establishment, The, 57
Canadian government, 63
Canadian Imperial Bank of Commerce, The, 35
Canadian Parliament, 109
Canadian Press, 121
Cancun, 196
Capability, 23
    see also Power, Resources
Carroll, Daniel, 145
Carter, Jimmy, 58, 61, 63, 96, 119, 189, 198
Catalytic-charismatic power, 60, 75, 76
Catholic Church, 61, 195
Cease-fires, 194
Census Bureau, 121
Center for Future Research, 125
Chambers of Commerce, 124
Change, 64, 84
Change management, 182
Chariots of Fire, 54
Charlebois, Robert, 33
Charter (mandate), 167
China, 57, 75
Choices, 36, 79
    see also Options
Cincom Systems, 31, 60
City Wood Grains Inc., 159
Cleveland, Harlan, 36
Client-centered objectives, 154
Coaching, 20, 43, 54, 127, 210, 211
Code of conduct, *see* Ethics
Coercive-competitive power, 58, 59, 76
Cognitive interventions, 53
Cold Lake, 201, 202
Collaboration, 50, 70, 197
Collaborative-synergistic power, 59, 76
Collateral organizations, 195
Collier Books, 128
Columbia Books, 124
Columbia University, 87
Comfort level, 153
Commitment, 21, 22
Commitment plan, 180
Common Market and EEC, 125, 190
Common objectives, 177
Commonwealth, 190
Communication, 83
Compatibility, 42
Compatibility tests (FIRO-B, SDI), 90

Compliance option, 30
Concession strategies, 44, 65, 182
Conference Board, The, 124, 125
Conflict, 79
    boundaries, 80
    diagnosis, 80, 81, 87, 92
    management, 85, 90, 209
    source, 80, 85, 87
Congress, 58, 63, 118, 124, 190
Connecticut, 124
Consensus, 51, 76, 190
Constructive influence, 22
Contingency plans, 52, 63, 166, 173, 182, 192
Control, 69
Control Data, 31
Coordination, 193
Council on Foreign Relations, The, 61
Countdown embargo, 192
Covert, 23, 32, 216
Critical mass, 22, 52, 66, 97, 180, 194, 206
Critical success factors, 166, 167
    illustrations, 168, 169
Cronkite, Walter, 61
Cross over point, 73
Cross relevance grids, 177
Cross supporting grids, 177
Cross-impact analysis, 130
Cunningham, Mary, 22, 44
Cushioning, 52

DASIT, 196
DC 10, 17
Danish Association for Industrial Training, *see* DASIT
Data Base Management Group, 181
Data collection, 216
Data General Corporation, 60
Data reduction, 69
Databased feedback, 218
Davis, Bill, 65
De Decastro, Edson, 60
Deadlock issues, 53
Decentralization, 197
Decision points, 23
Decision support system, 130, 194
Decision-making power, 192
Decision-making cycle, 23
De-escalation, 86
Degrees of freedom, 54
Deily, Myron B., 100

Delphi, 90
Denver City, 125
Department of Commerce, 121
Department of Defence, 146
Department of External Affairs, 121
Department of Finance, 121
Department of Housing and Urban Development, 170
Dependence, 71, 73
Desmarais, Paul, 33, 61
D'Estaing, Valéry Giscard, 96
Detective Columbo, 156
Detroit, 124
Differentiation, 35
Differentiation and integration step, 157
Differing, 42
Digital Equipment Corporation, 31
Directing, 43
Disneyland, see Walt Disney
Disneyworld, see Walt Disney
Disposal of assets, 218
Dissatisfaction, 22, 63, 151
Distributive leadership, 51
Diversification, 194
Divisional organizations, 195
Dome, 144
Dopers Formula, 64
Drapeau, Jean, 101
Drucker, Peter, 54, 103, 197
Du Pont, 19, 195
Du Pont, Pierre, 195
Dubé, Bernard, 108
Dun & Bradstreet, 124, 156
Dutch TNO, 125
Dyad, 85

EEC, see Common Market
E.P.C.O.T., 96
Early adopters, 32, 124
Economy indicators, 166, 168, 169, 170
Economy of scale, 185, 196
Education, 79
Effective leaders, 42
Effective leadership, 67
Effectiveness indicators, 166, 168, 169, 170, 185
Efficiency indicators, 166, 168, 169, 170, 185, 196
Egypt, 33
Empathic rehearsal, 156
Empathy, 42
Empowering, 65, 66, 67
Equal Opportunity, 209
Equity indicators, 166, 167, 168, 169, 185
Escalation, 86
Esso, see Exxon
Esso Resources, see Exxon
Ethical dilemmas, 22
Ethics, 22
Etiological intervention, 85
Europe, 221
European common market, 125
Evaluability Assessment (EA), 18
Evaluation, 135, 211
Evaluation methodology, 166, 167
Evaluation scheme, 176
Exploratory planning, 117
Exxon, 51, 201, 202

Family (F_1) and allies, 23, 63, 81, 128, 147, 153, 160, 173, 189, 191, 192, 195, 222
Fayol, Henri, 41
Federal government, 72
Feedback, 216
Fill-in work, 109
Fishery Treaty, 63
5F's, 63, 128, 147, 150, 160, 173, 191, 192
Flat organization, 198
Flooding, 91
Florida, 96
Foes (F_4), 23, 63, 81, 128, 147, 153, 162, 173, 192, 195
Fools (F_5), 23, 63, 81, 128, 147, 153, 173, 195
Ford Foundation, The, 61, 143
Force-field analysis, 151
Forecast, 174
Foreign Office, 190
Foreigners (F_3), 23, 63, 81, 128, 147, 153, 160, 173, 191, 192, 195
Foreman, Carol, 61
Fortune, 44, 70, 127, 209
4C's, 153
France, 66
Frazee, Rowlie, 60
Frazer Institute of Vancouver, The, 125
French International Association of Futuribles, 125
Friends (F_2), 23, 63, 72, 81, 128, 147, 153, 160, 161, 173, 189, 191, 192, 195
Fuller, R. Buckminster, 49, 100
Functional organization, 195
Future Wheels, 128

Gagnon, P.M., 32
Galbraith, John Kenneth, 59, 60
Gale Research Co., 124
Gallup, 124, 125
Gatekeeping, 145
Gdansk, 61
General Dynamics, 19
General Electric, 158
General Mills, 146
Germany, 66
Gestalt, 69, 90
Ghandi, Indira, 34
Ghandi, Mahatma, 60
Global Method, 205
Godfather, 53
Golden Gate Bridge, 222
Gordon, William J.J., 128
Gould Inc., 145
Great Britain, 63
Griffiths, Edgar, 21
Group-maintenance skills, 51
Gyllenhammar, Pehr, 33

Harris, Louis, 125
Harvard, 61
Harvard Business Review, 127
Hawthorne, 91
Hersey, P., 212
Hidden agendas, 156
Hidden costs, 191
Hierarchy, 76
Hitch hiking strategy, 32, 35
Honeymoon power, 66
Honeywell, 31
Host jurisdiction, 153
Hostility, 53
Houston, 97
Houston Intercontinental Airport, 98
Howe, C.D., 61
C.D. Howe Institute, 125
Hudson Institute, The, 125
Humanization of work, 33

IBM, 30, 31, 60, 128, 158, 161
Iacocca, Lee, 43
Images of the Future, 124
Imaging, 90
Impact evaluation, 215
Imperative work, 109
Implementation, 135, 209

Inactive stance, 29
Inappropriate competition, 50, 58, 70, 190
Incremental strength, 32
Incrementation, 41
India, 60
Individual compensation, 24
Industrial Outlook, 121
Inequities, 22
Influencing, 21, 22
Informal feedback, 51, 218
Information role, 191
Integration, 161
Intelligence-gathering, 41, 117
Interdependence, 75
Interdependence grids, 176
Interface planning, 130, 146, 160, 171
Interim strategy, 30
International Institute for Applied Systems Analysis, 125
Internorth, 119, 137
Interpersonal skills, 42
Interview, 216
Intimacy, 43
Intimate systems, 24
Iran, 17, 119, 189
Issue Briefs, 130
Issue champion, 210
Issue management, 17
Issues, 17, 150
Iterative decisions, 40

Jackson, Maynard, 101
Japan, 71, 75, 124, 160, 201, 221
Jerusalem, 33
Job satisfaction, 180
S.C. Johnson & Son, 118

KWIC, 128
Kahn, Alfred, 198
Kalmar, 33
Katz, Ralph, 24
Kellogg Foundation, 198
Kennedy, John F., 60
Kinetics, 42
Kissinger, Henry, 33, 61
Knowledge, 66

L1011, 217
Laissez-faire, 76

Index

Laker, 144
Law of diminishing returns, 59
Law of positive returns, 57
Laxemburg (Austria), 125
Leadership, 193
Leadership is distributed, 49
Lebanese government, 118
Legal, 194
Legitimacy, 166, 168, 169, 170
Liberal Party, 180
Life of Our Times, A, 59
Linkage strategies, 195
Little, Arthur D., 125
Local government, 72
Lombardi, Vincent, 54
London, 190
L'Orient le Jour, 118
Los Angeles, 99, 118
Lyon, Sterling, 198

MIT, 24, 61, 215
MIT Endicott House, 100
MIT Systems Dynamics Group, 125
MacNamara, Bob, 33, 60
Madison Avenue, 180
Magazine scanning, 121
Management by Objectives (MBO), 18
Management Information System (MIS), 194, 206
Management styles, 76
Manitoba Health Organization, 198
Marchand, Jean, 180
Maslow, Abraham, 69
Massey Ferguson, 144
Matrix, 62, 91, 195, 199
Matrix structures, 195
Matsushita, Konosuke, 32, 61, 195
McColough, 146
McCormack, E.J., 19
McFarland, James, 146
McGregor, Douglas, 69
McHale, John, 121
Meeting management, 104
Merger, 197
Merit, 70
Metaevaluation, 219
Mexico, 124, 196
Michigan, 124, 198
Milan, 124
Minority governments, 158

Mission, 87, 171
Mission-setting, 141
Mixed organizations, 195
Modeling, 130
Monsanto, 119, 124, 130
Montreal, 101, 125, 199
Morphological forecasting, 130
Morse, Bradford, 60
Moscow Olympics, 61
Mouton, Jane, 58
Multiattribute utility, 90
Multilateral agreements, 194

National Training Labs, 52
Netherlands, The, 124
New Democratic Party, 65
New product launching, 194
New York, 128, 218
New York State Police, 169
New York Telephone, 128
New York Times, The, 61, 121, 127, 142
Newman, Peter, 57
Nies, Tom, 60
Non-option, 34
Non-organization, 195
North America, 61, 72, 75, 83, 221
North American airline, 97
North-South Summit, 196

OECD, 125
OPEC, 60
Objective validity, 160
Objectives, 141, 171, 177
Objective-setting, 154
Observation, 216
Observation grid, 82
Ochs, Adolph S., 142
Ochs-Sulzberger, 142
Oklahoma, 119
Olympics, 32, 199
Ombudsman, 90
On-going functions, 38, 40, 41
Oncken, Bill, 103
Ontario, 65
Open votes, 76
Operational planning, 135, 205
Operations, 158
Opinion Research Corporation, The, 125
Opportunities, 150

227

Options, 29
　active stance, 31
　compliance, 30
　inactive stance, 29
　non-option, 34
　proactive, 31, 152, 173, 211
　stay out of jail, 30
　wait and see, 29
Organization, 119
Organization chart, 194
Organization design, 185
Organization development, 19
Organization structures, 196
Overt, 23, 216

PERT, 205
Paradigms, 100
Paradigm shifts, 127
Pareto trap, 23, 199
Paris, 80, 124
Parity, 31
Parrot, Jean-Claude, 34
Pearls, Frederick, 69
Pearson, Lester B., 60, 96, 180
Peat Marwick, 197
Pelletier, Gérard, 180
Penalties, 182
Pennsylvania Department of Agriculture, 144
Pentagon, 218
Pépin, Jean-Luc, 198
Perceived validity, 97
Perception disconfirmation, 97
Perception management, 95
Perception testing, 158
Performance indicators, 166
Performance review, 211
Personal conflict, 80
Pilot experiment, 97, 158
Pitfield, Michael, 61
Planning Executives Institute, 119
Planning skills, 44
Poisson distribution, 99
Polak, Fred, 124
Poland, 61
Policies, 157, 173, 202, 209
Polish government, 61
Pollock, Kenneth, 87
Population, 81
Positive controls, 176

Positive energy, 216
Positive reinforcement, *see* Reinforcement
Positive sum game, 59
Post Office, 31
Potential foe, 191
　see also Foes
Power, 20, 24, 57, 71, 75
Power Corporation, 33
Precursor jurisdictions, 124
Preplanning, 117, 135, 141
Press, 65
Prework strategy, 177, 181, 194
Prince, George, 128
Priority, 112, 154
Priority myopia, 53
Proactive Decision-Making, 21, 97, 103, 124, 145, 171, 221
Proactive Decision-Making Model, 40, 160
Proactive intervention, 161
Proactive Management, *see* Proactive Decision-Making
Proactive Management functions, 38
Proactive Management philosophy, 21
Proactive Model, 40, 160
Proactive option, 31, 152, 173, 211
Proactive Passport, 104, 111
Proactive strategy, 34
Process evaluation, 215, 218
Process skills, 51
Procter & Gamble, 159, 197
Productive conflict, 79
Professional Development Institute, The, 31
Program, 159
Program charter, 166
Progress evaluation, 209
Project financing, 194
Projects, 158
Promotion standards, 210
Provinces, 72
Public approbation, 45
Publicity, 162
Published mission, 143
Puerto Vallarta, 59

Quality of work life, 197
Quebec, 34, 63, 180
Quebec Construction Board (OCQ), 108
Questionnaire, 216

Index

RCA, 21
Rand Corporation, The, 125
Rapid feedback, 209
Reagan, Ronald, 58, 118
Referral power, 211
Reinforcement, 20, 70, 86, 90, 176, 202
Remembrance Day, 144
Reorganization, 192, 199
Replanning decisions, 209
Reporters, 72
Republican National Bank of Texas, 100
Residual risk, 173
Resistance, 84
Resources
    allocation of, 23, 170, 205
    blind, 23, 216
    conventional, 23
    mobilization of, 170
    scarce, 75, 158, 201
    slack, 52, 109, 199
    strategic, 23, 151, 161, 206
    support, 191
    untapped, 34
Resonance, 54
Responsibility, 45
Responsibility chart, 185
Responsibility role, 189
Restart and recovery, 202
Reuters, 121
Reward cooperation, 90
Reward system, 87
Rewards, 63, 70, 182, 202, 218
Rich, Patrick, 35
Rickover, Admiral, 108
Rio de Janeiro, 59
Risk analysis, 174
Risk management, 159
Risks, 166, 173
Rockefeller Associates, 19
Rogers, Carl, 69
Role, 87
    approval, 189
    information, 191
    responsibility, 189
    support, 191
Role integration, 193
Role model, 210
Rome, 146
Roper Organization, The, 125
P.S. Ross & Co., 197
Royal Bank of Canada, 35

SBA, 156
Sadat, Anwar, 33
San Fernando Valley, 99
San Francisco, 222
Sausalito, 222
Scan, 120
Scandinavian Employers Research Councils, 125
Scanning, 41, 44, 117, 153, 162, 171
    news, 121
    resources, 119
    sources, 120
    tips, 127
Scenario techniques, 130
Scenarios for the future, 151
Scheduling, 205
Schein, Ed, 51, 221
Schlessinger, Arthur, 61
Scotland Yard, 190
Screening techniques, 128
Sears Roebuck & Co., 117
Secret ballots, 76
Secret Police, 190
Security, 74
Self-awareness, 44
Sensitivity training, 52
Sequential iterative functions, 38, 40, 135
Shah, 119
Shell, 202
Shepard, Herbert, 51, 54, 58, 202
Silicon Valley, 124
Simmons, W.W., 119
Singapore, 218
Skanska Cement, 201
Ski-doo, 146
Skill, 43
Skills quality, 196
Skinner, B.F., 69
Skovde, 33
Slack time, 109
Sloan, Alfred, 195
Smoothing, 90
Socializing, 43
Sociotechnical costs and rewards, 66
Source, 121
Sources of demands, 150
Sources of power, 65
Southern California, 59
Span of control, 90, 199
Special surveys, 125
Stakeholders, 32, 63, 147, 150, 171, 189
Stakes, 84

Stanford Research Institute, The, 125, 192
States, 72
Statistical Abstract, 121
Stay out of jail option, 30
Strategy, 29, 35, 152, 153, 158, 173, 180, 182, 192, 199, 201, 212
    concession, 44, 65, 182
    contingency, 52, 63, 166, 173, 182, 192
    covert, 23, 32, 216
    hitch hiking, 32, 35
    interim, 30
    linkage, 195
    overt, 23, 216
    proactive, 34
    temporary, 30
    to deal with foes, 153
Strategic plan, 137, 175, 185
Strategic planning, 117, 119, 130, 135, 147, 165, 171, 173, 174, 177, 185, 217, 218
Strategic weaknesses, 194
Strengths, 43
Stress, 50
Stroup, Margaret, 124
Structure, 87
Subjective validity, 156, 160
Succession, 23, 199
Sunset review, 218
Support, 23
Support role, 191
Supporting, 42
Surprise events, 17, 66, 84, 100, 152, 160, 171, 216
Survey research, 117, 124
Survey Research Center, 125
Sweden, 30, 33, 124, 146, 201
Swedish Department of Agriculture and Food, 146
Switzerland, 30
Symptomatic intervention, 85, 86
Syndicated studies, 124
Synectics, 128, 218
Synergy, 49, 66, 218
Systems and Procedures, 158

TRW, 51
Task forces, 195, 210
Task skills, 51
Taylor, Frederick, 41
Team, 21
Team-building, 50, 51
Teamwork, 52
Telefunken, 144
Teleglobe, 137
Telephone enquiry, 216
Telidon, 121
Temporary strategy, 30
Termination, 23, 199
Terrorism, 33
Texas Department of Education, 144
Think Proactive, 42
Three Mile Island, 17
Tide, 197
Time, 83
Time embargo, 191
Time Magazine, 127
Time management, 103, 194
Tories, 180
Tracking studies, 125
Trade directories, 124
Training, 54
Trans Alaska Pipeline, 199
Transactional analysis, 90
Treasury Board, 121
Treaties, 194
Trilateral Commission, The, 61
Tris, 118
Trudeau, Pierre, 180, 198
Tung, Mao Tse, 60
Turnover, 50
Tylenol, 17

US Bankruptcy Law, 119
US Navy, 108, 176
US President, 63
US Prices and Wages Commission, 198
US Secret Service, 190
USDA Graduate School of Management, 144
Ultimatum, 76
Unaninimity, 76
Uncertainty, 166
Understand people, 43
United Auto Workers, 74
United Nations, 60, 72, 74
United Press International, 121
United States, 97, 118, 121, 124, 125, 136, 189, 190
Unity of purpose, 51
University of Cincinnati, The, 74
University of Michigan, The, 125
University of Southern California, The, 125
Urgency, 112, 154

Index

Validate the objectives, 50
Validation, 22, 154, 173
Validation process, 156
Validity, 22, 216, 217
   objective, 160
   subjective, 156, 160
Value analysis, 175
Values, 22, 79, 100
Vancouver, 59
Veto, 189
Vietnam, 80, 218
Volvo, 33

Wait and see option, 29
Waldheim, Kurt, 96
Wall Street Journal, The, 127
Walt Disney, 96
Walters, Barbara, 61
Wang, 31
Washington, 124, 156
Wells, Dr. Kenneth, 60, 61

West Coast, 222
Western Canada, 202
Western Europe, 125
White collar crime, 194
White Motors, 144
Win-win, 50, 59, 67
Withdrawal, 76
Working mission, 142, 143
World Bank, 33, 60
World Food Conference/Congress, 60, 146

Xerox, 32, 146, 159

Yankelovich, 125
Yellow Pages, 118

Zaire, 61
Zen, 90
Zero-sum game, 58

About the author

A.P. Martin is the Chief Executive Officer of the Professional Development Institute. He has been the strategist behind the consistent profitability and steady growth of the Institute for nearly a decade. He is known for creating *The Global Method* to manage capital and soft projects and the *Proactive Passport*—a novel diary combining an agenda, a work plan (do list) and a time log, all in pocket size. In Canada and the United States, his papers on the merits of matrix management, strategic planning, international standards for capital projects and on the need for program evaluation have been featured in professional journals and international conferences.

Mr. Martin is the recipient of awards from a General Dynamics subsidiary in the sixties for his innovative engineering work. He has developed business scanning and strategic planning systems for engineering companies, micro-electronics firms and manufacturers of construction materials. In broadcasting, he has participated in the development of policies to ensure a fair coverage of political parties during election periods and to evaluate the content and quality of the nation-wide election night television programs. He has also evaluated government performance in food inspection, purchasing, grain handling, law enforcement and airport security controls.

The Professional Development Institute regularly organizes seminars given by Mr. Martin, including a five-day World Seminar titled *The Complete Project Management Cycle,* a four day workshop titled *Proactive Decision-Making and Problem Solving* and a three day seminar *Breakthroughs in Planning and Evaluation Methods.* His recent clients include the Swedish Employers Federation, Teleglobe, Skanska Cement of Stockholm, the University of Sherbrooke, several Canadian manufacturers and engineering firms as well as the Dutch Ministry of Finance, the Governments of Canada, Alberta, British Columbia, Quebec and Ontario and AFIPS (the American Federation of Information Processing Societies). A citizen of Canada, Mr. Martin is fluent in several languages.